Robustness Optimization for IoT Topology

Tie Qiu • Ning Chen • Songwei Zhang

Robustness Optimization for IoT Topology

 Springer

Tie Qiu 🆔
College of Intelligence and Computing
Tianjin University
Tianjin, China

Ning Chen 🆔
College of Intelligence and Computing
Tianjin University
Tianjin, China

Songwei Zhang
College of Intelligence and Computing
Tianjin University
Tianjin, China

ISBN 978-981-16-9611-4   ISBN 978-981-16-9609-1   (eBook)
https://doi.org/10.1007/978-981-16-9609-1

This Springer imprint is published by the registered company Springer Nature Singapore Pte Ltd.
The registered company address is: 152 Beach Road, #21-01/04 Gateway East, Singapore 189721,
Singapore

Preface

The Internet of Things (IoT) is an interdisciplinary subject that integrates computer networks, electronic communications, and sensor technologies. It deploys a large number of wireless sensing devices in a certain area (could be air, space, ground or underground, and ocean) and interconnects through wireless or wired technology. IoT has undergone transformative development in the twenty-first century, especially in the fields of smart cities, industrial production, and environmental monitoring. As the network scale increases, the probability of node malfunctions, network attacks, and local network failures will increase. If local failures cannot be effectively controlled, it is easy to cause cascading collapse effects, which will lead to a decline in the quality of service (QoS) of the entire network. Therefore, it is greatly significant to study the topology robustness for large-scale IoT.

The IoT is a huge and complex network system. In recent years, researchers and engineers have paid attention to the robustness of IoT topology. Since 2013, SmartIoT laboratory (the team of the book authors) has started to research on robustness of IoT topology. We explored and designed some novel algorithms and solutions based on the types of IoT node failures, the methods of network attacks, and the impact of local adjustments on the global network. This book focuses on the IoT topology robustness, the main work is as follows:

- **Robustness Optimization Based on Self-Organization:** By analyzing the principle of the self-organizing network of IoT topology, using the scale-free and small-world property of the complex network, self-organizing methods of network topology nodes are designed to improve the robustness of the network.
- **Robustness Optimization Based on Evolution:** Introducing the viewpoint of evolution, combining genetic algorithms with multiple populations, ant colony algorithms, and particle swarm algorithms, we designed heuristic topology robustness optimization strategies to guide the evolution of network topology in a more robust direction.
- **Robustness Optimization Based on Machine Learning:** Introducing the viewpoint of artificial intelligence, combining reinforcement learning, neural network, and designing anti-failure schemes for IoT topology, so that the IoT nodes

can automatically reconnect and dynamically change by themselves, and the topology can be more robust from topology data set learning.

Aiming to improve the robustness of the IoT topology, the research theme of this book is "**Self-Organizing-Based Scheme** $\rightarrow$ **Evolution-Based Scheme** $\rightarrow$ **Machine Learning-Based Scheme**." For each point, we proposed a series of algorithms or solutions, and did a lot of simulations and experiments. We look forward to in-depth exchanges with readers and continuous revision and optimization.

In the process of writing this book, we have received strong support from the members of the SmartIoT Lab, including Diansong Luo, Aoyang Zhao, Yushuang Zhang, Jie Liu, Zilong Lu, Bolun Li, Heyuan Wang, Qianzhen Sun, Jiancheng Chi, and Zhao. International scholars Prof. Dapeng Oliver Wu, Prof. Mohammed Atiquzzaman, and Dr. Weisheng Si et al. gave us many comments and useful suggestions.

Furthermore, this work was partially supported by the National Natural Science Foundation of China (Grant No. 61374154 and 61672131) and the Joint Funds of the National Natural Science Foundation of China (No. U2001204).

Finally, we really appreciate all who attended idea or scheme discussion and organizations that provided fund and platform supports.

Tianjin, China   Tie Qiu
                                                                                         Ning Chen
                                                                                    Songwei Zhang
November 2021

Contents

Acronyms

5G	Fifth Generation cellular networks
6G	Sixth Generation cellular networks
AMDR	An adaptive data reduction method
AREA	Adaptive Robustness Evolution Algorithm
AS	Autonomous System
AUVs	Autonomous Underwater Vehicles
B6G	Beyond Sixth Generation cellular networks
BA	Scale-free model proposed by Barabsi and Albert
BiLSTM	Bidirectional Long and Short-Term Memory network
BiRNN	Bidirectional Recurrent Neural Network
BN	Backbone Nodes
BP	Back Propagation
CC	Clustering Coefficient
CESP	Coefficient Exchange Synchronization Protocol
DASM	Directed Angulation toward the Sink node Model
DDLP	Deep deterministic policy reinforcement learning network model
DDPG	Deep Deterministic Policy Gradient
DFS	Depth First Search
DoS	Denial of Service
EABA	Energy-Aware scale-free topology model based on the BA model
EB	Edge Betweenness
ECN	Energy-aware Common Neighbor scheme
EE	Electrical Engineering
EGP	Effective Gene Positions
EI	Edge Intelligence
ELDCN	Energy-aware Low potential-Degree Common Neighbor scheme
eMBB	Enhanced mobile broad-band
ER	Random model proposed by Erdos and Renyi
EROS	Efficient robust networking strategy for scale-free IoT
FID	First Importance Degree
FNDT	First Node Died Time

GA	Genetic Algorithm
GDU	Gene Distribution Uniformity
GE	Global time Error
GMSW	Greedy Model with Small World
GPA	Groupwise Pair selection Algorithm
GPCR	Gene Position Coverage Ratio
GPS	Global Positioning System
GRU	Gated Recurrent Unit model
HBA	High Betweenness Adaptive
HBI	High Betweenness Initial
HBL	High Betweenness Largest
HC	Hill Climbing algorithm
HCA	High Closeness Adaptive
HCBI	High Current-flow Betweenness Initial
HCBL	High Current-flow Betweenness Largest
HCCI	High Current-flow Closeness Initial
HCCL	High Current-flow Closeness Largest
HCI	High Closeness Initial
HCL	High Closeness Largest
HDA	High Degree Adaptive
HDI	High Degree Initial
HDL	High Degree Largest
HFCM	Hybrid Fuzzy C-Means clustering algorithm
IC	Influence Coefficient
IIoT	Industrial Internet of Things
IoT	Internet of Things
k-MVC-impact	Robustness metric based on maximal vertex coverage
LB	Load Balancing
LC	Largest Component
LDA	Linear Discriminant Analysis
LE	Local time Error
LID	Local Importance Degree
LIDT	Local Importance Degree Threshold
LM-GAS	Load-balanced Multi-Gateway Aware long link addition Strategy
LSTM	Long and Short-Term Memory network
LSWTC	Local Small-World Topology Control algorithm
Mesh	Grid network based on IoT wireless link model
mMTC	Massive machine-type communication
MPGA	Multi-Population Genetic Algorithm
MSE	Mean Square Error method
MTTFT	Mend-Tolerance Tit-for-Tat
MVC	Maximal vertex coverage
NAW	Neighbor Avoiding Walk
NN	Neural Network
NS2	Network Simulator version 2

NSGA-II	Non-dominated Sorting Genetic Algorithm II
NTP	Network Time synchronization Protocol
NW	Small world model proposed by Newman and Watts
ODASM	On-line Directed Angulation toward the Sink node Model
P2P	Peer to Peer
PBS	Pairwise Broadcast Synchronization protocol
PCA	Principal Component Analysis
PCS	Power Control algorithm based on the Small-world theory
PD	Population Diversity
PG	Power Grid Network
PN	Passive Nodes
PT	Pulling Timer
PTNS	Public Transit Networks
QoS	Quality of Service
RAM	Random Addition Model
RB	Replay Buffer
RBS	Reference Broadcasts Synchronization
RMA	Reality Mining Algorithm based on k-means
RNN	Recurrent Neural Network model
ROCKS	Robustness optimization algorithm based on multi-population co-evolution
ROEL	Robustness Optimization based on Evolution Learning
ROSE	Robustness Strategy for Scale-Free Wireless Sensor Networks
RRP	Receiver-to-Receiver Protocol
RSN	Regular Sensor Node
RSSI	Received Signal Strength Indicator
R-Sync	Robust time Synchronization scheme for industrial internet of things
SA	Simulated Annealing algorithm
SAPS	Shortcut Addition strategy based on the Particle Swarm algorithm
SID	Second Importance Degree
SIGMM	Spammer Identification scheme based on Gaussian Mixture Model
SRP	Sender-to-Receiver Protocol
SSN	Super Sensor Node
ST	Sync Timer
SWEE	Small World Energy-Efficient mechanism
TCN	Temporal Convolutional Neural network model
TDMA	Time Division Multiple Access
TDOA	Time Difference Of Arrival
TOA	Time Of Arrival
TOSG	Topology Optimization Scheme with Global small world for industrial heterogeneous internet of things
TPSN	Time synchronization Protocol based on Spanning tree Network
UIoT	Underwater Internet of Things

UN	Undefined Nodes
URLLC	Ultra Reliable Low Latency Communication
VANET	Vehicular Ad-Hoc Network
WS	Small world model proposed by Watts and Strogatz
WSNs	Wireless Sensor Networks

Chapter 1
Introduction

This chapter mainly describes the research of Internet of Things (IoT) topology and the motivation of building robust topology. It helps to identify the breakthrough in topology optimization through analyzing the characteristics of the IoT topology. In addition, this chapter also compares different attack strategies for network topology, which provides a targeted optimization direction for topology robustness.

1.1 Background and Motivation

IoT integrates computing capability, communication function, and control capability to form a large-scale complex network system [1]. This network can conduct real-time monitoring and data collection of objects or environment through the densely deployed sensor devices and smart terminals in the perception layer. Then routers and gateways in the network layer aggregate and transmit the collected sensing data, and finally realize intelligent connection and interaction among people, objects, and the environment [2]. The IoT is a large and complex system formed by the interconnection of many intelligent terminals with unique tags, such as various sensors [3], intelligent components [4], hand-held mobile terminals in the real world [5] and smart industrial systems, etc. These smart devices transmit data to destinations with communication tags through the IoT, which can provide accurate location information. For example, the IoT has achieved important applications in smart cities, intelligent transportation, smart oceans, smart ports, battlefield safety, disaster assistance, environmental monitoring, smart medical care, crashed industries, and homeland security.

The development of 5G communication and artificial intelligence technology has injected new impetus into the IoT [6]. The devices connected to the IoT are increasing exponentially, and the connections among devices have become more complicated [7]. To plan the connection between many devices, the researchers

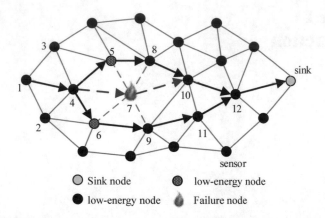

Fig. 1.1 Node cascading failure in the perception layer of the IoT

abstract the connection between devices into a topology structure and use the correlation method of graph theory to optimize the links in the topology. Because sensor nodes in the IoT have small energy, limited processing, storage, and communication capabilities, and are usually deployed in harsh environments, some nodes often fail due to their own energy exhaustion, hardware failure, software error, or intentional attacks by the enemy. The failed node will increase the load of its neighbor nodes, and consume energy quickly [8], which will cause a successive failure and the paralysis of the entire network.

In Fig. 1.1, when the data flow from node 1 to $sink$ is $1 \to 4 \to 7 \to 10 \to 12 \to sink$, node 7 suddenly fails. The forwarding path is changed to $1 \to 4 \to 5 \to 8 \to 10 \to 12 \to sink$ or $1 \to 4 \to 6 \to 9 \to 11 \to 12 \to sink$, which increases the loads of nodes 5 and 6. When the energy of nodes 5 and 6 is exhausted, the load on their neighbors will increase. The entire network nodes have a cascading failure, which eventually leads to the collapse of the entire network [9, 10]. Therefore, it is important to optimize the connection relationship between devices to improve the robustness of the network. Network can maintain a certain degree of stability when the network is under various attacks [11, 12]. However, building a robust topology in the large-scale IoT is still a challenge.

1.2   Characteristics of IoT Topology

The topology is originally extended from geometry, and the IoT topology refers to the network shape formed by the connection relationship among networked devices. The connectivity of the topology is the prerequisite for ensuring the communication among devices in the network. With the rapid increase of connected devices and the diversity of application fields, the IoT has become a complex and massive system. Through the analysis of the potential properties and complexity in the IoT system, it can optimize the structure of the system. Complex network theory can describe complex systems in different fields through the form of networks. Different types of networks contain two entities: nodes and connections. In different complex systems, nodes can represent entities with different meanings, such as transformers in the power grid and neurons in the brain. Connection represents the interaction between two entities, such as familiarity in interpersonal relationships.

From the perspective of graph theory, any network topology in real life can be regarded as a graph. The graph here is commonly represented by $G(V, E)$ in academic circles, where V contains all communication individuals in the network, while E stores the relationship between any two communication individuals in the network. Network topology is the fundamental factor affecting network performance, such as network data transmission delay, energy consumption of various nodes and the life cycle of the entire network. At the same time, network topology is also the design basis of various network protocols, such as various routing protocols and communication protocols.

According to the complex network theory, the actual network topology can be divided into four types of models. The regular and random models are the simplest network structures. The nodes in the network are deployed in a regular structure, and each node has an equal number of neighbors. The networks with regular topological structures include global coupling networks, nearest neighbor coupling networks and so on. A random network is one in which nodes are connected in a random way rather than in accordance with certain rules. Different networks can be evolved based on different self-organizing connection principles, such as Zigbee networks between sensor nodes, and Erdos-Renyi (ER) random graph [13]. Figure 1.2 shows a grid regular graph and an ER random graph respectively. But not all topologies are regular graphs or random graphs. Through the analysis of many actual network characteristics, Watts and Strogatz [14] revealed the small-world characteristics of

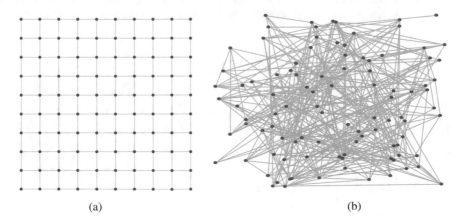

(a)   (b)

Fig. 1.2 Two artificial network topologies. (**a**) Grid regular graph. (**b**) ER random graph

the network, while Barabsi and Albert [15] discovered the scale-free characteristics
of the network.

1.2.1   Small-World Model in IoT Topology

Small-world model belongs to the complex network theory [16]. At that time,
mathematician Euler created graph theory to study the problem of Seven Bridges.
Then, scientists often use graph theory to abstract complex problems in real life,
such as ER random graph theory created by Erdos and Reny [13]. The small-world
model combines the advantages of regular and random models, and has the smaller
shortest path and larger clustering coefficient. The network degree distribution is
like Poisson distribution. This feature exists in many networks in real life, which
has certain research significance.

WS small-world model [14] starts from a regular graph and re-links each edge
of the network according to a certain random probability p, but no repeated edge
is allowed between any nodes, nor can it be connected to itself. In this way, the
transition from a regular graph to a small-world graph to a random graph can
be controlled by adjusting the parameter p. Figure 1.3 is an example of WS
small-world model, and Fig. 1.3a is a fully regular diagram. With the increase of
probability p, some edges are randomly selected from Fig. 1.3a for reconnection,
and the graph gradually becomes the small-world model shown in Fig. 1.3b. When
the probability $p = 1$, as shown in Fig. 1.3c, all edges are randomly reconnected,
and the network is a random graph.

The WS small world model has an obvious problem, that is, it destroys the
connectivity of the entire network topology. Therefore, Watts and Newman [17]
proposed another method of constructing the small-world network, which is called
NW model. This model no longer re-links edges, but adds new edges to the network
topology, which is also called Random Addition small-world Model (RAM). The

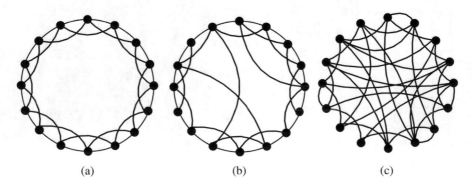

         (a)   (b)   (c)

Fig. 1.3 WS small-world network. (**a**) Regular graph. (**b**) Small-world graph. (**c**) Random graph

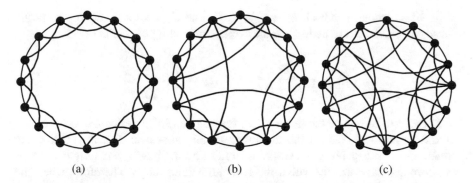

Fig. 1.4 NW small-world network. (**a**) Regular graph. (**b**) Small-world graph. (**c**) Random graph

new edge is added between any two nodes with a probability p. Similarly, no duplicate edges are allowed between any nodes, nor can they be connected to themselves, and the parameter p can be used to control the evolution of the small-world graph. Figure 1.4 shows an example of the NW small-world model. When $p = 0$, no edges are added in Fig. 1.4a, and the network is still the same as the initial regular graph. As the probability p increases, after randomly adding some edges, Fig. 1.4b shows the same small-world characteristics. When $p = 1$, as shown in Fig. 1.4c, all nodes have undergone randomization and edge addition. Currently, the network is a random graph. Compared Fig. 1.3 with Fig. 1.4, the NW small world has not destroyed the original network structure and connectivity.

Topologies with small-world feature show smaller average path length and larger clustering coefficient. The number of edges between i and j is defined as the path length of these two vertices. The shortest path length between two nodes is the minimum number of hops between them. Considering all vertices in the network, the average shortest path length (L) reflects the overall ability of the network to forward data, and the calculation method is shown in Eq. (1.1). N is the total number of network nodes, and d_{ij} indicates the minimum number of hops between two nodes, where $i \neq j$.

$$L = \frac{2}{N(N+1)} \sum_{i \geq j} d_{ij} \qquad (1.1)$$

The clustering coefficient is an indicator that describes the node clusters. Suppose node i has m neighbor nodes, and the maximum number of edges among node i and these m neighbors is n. In fact, there are p edges among node i and these m neighbor nodes. The clustering coefficient of the node i is p/n, and the average clustering coefficient of the network can be obtained. In Eq. (1.2), E_i represents the number of edges that exist between node i and neighbor nodes. k_i is the number of nodes within the communication range of node i, and the maximum number of edges between these nodes is $k_i(k_i - 1)/2$. C_i and C_{avg} respectively represent the clustering coefficient of node i and the average clustering coefficient.

$$C_i = \frac{E_i}{k_i(k_i - 1)/2}, \quad C_{avg} = \frac{1}{N} * \sum_{i=1}^{N} C_i \qquad (1.2)$$

In order to introduce the small-world feature into IoT topology, it is necessary to add some long links to the topology, namely shortcuts. But in the IoT, the communication capability of sensors is limited by the power, and only two nodes can communicate directly within the communication range. Therefore, when the shortcuts are added to the network, it needs to increase the communication range of the nodes. But the long-wired cable or the base station will increase the cost and cannot be used in many environments. With the development of the IoT technology, multiple transmit power modules are equipped on sensor nodes, which can make nodes realize remote communication. However, long-distance communication will consume more energy of the node. Therefore, the endpoint of the shortcut needs to be equipped with a device with a larger communication range and more initial energy, which is called a super node. Building a small-world model in the IoT topology is mainly carried out by constructing shortcuts between super nodes.

1.2.2 Scale-Free Model in IoT Topology

Another important model in complex networks is scale-free model, in which nodes with high degree only account for a small proportion part of all nodes. For example, the world wide web, airport transportation networks, and metabolic networks all have obvious scale-free features, and the degree of nodes presents a power-law distribution. The scale-free topology is not fixed, it is formed by gradually increasing the size of network. Newly added nodes preferentially connect to important nodes in the network. For example, when a person joined a social circle, he or she is more likely to associate with the people in the circle who have the most friends. Accordingly, people who have more friends are more likely to continue to make more friends. In order to explain this phenomenon, Barabsi and Albert proposed the BA model [15], and they summarized the two basic principles of the scale-free topology.

- Growth: The scale of the topology is continuously growing, and nodes are continuously added to the topology.
- Preferential connection: Newly joined node tends to establish a connection with important nodes. This means that the more edges a node has, the greater the probability it has to add new connections.

Barabsi and Albert found that the two characteristics of growth and preferential connection can make the degree of nodes in the topology present a power-law

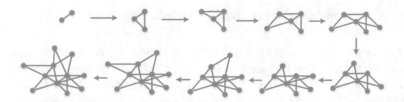

Fig. 1.5 The evolution process of BA scale-free network

distribution [18]. Suppose that the initial network contains m_0 nodes, then at most one node joins the network in each round, and new node must establish m ($m \le m_0$) connections. By calculating the degree d_i of the node i in the topology, the selected probability $P_s(i)$ of the node can be obtained.

$$P_s(i) = \frac{d_i}{\sum_{j=1}^{n} d_j} \tag{1.3}$$

In Eq. (1.3), n is the total number of nodes within the communication range of node i. The new node preferentially selects the node with the larger P_s value to connect. Figure 1.5 shows the evolution process of BA network when $m = m_0 = 2$. In the initial topology, there are only two nodes, and a connection is established between two nodes. All nodes will select appropriate targets to establish connections and join the topology in the way of preferential connections. Therefore, the scale of the network continues to expand, and the connections between nodes become gradually complex. Finally, the degree of nodes in the network presents the characteristics of power-law distribution.

In the practical deployment environment of the IoT, the communication range of nodes is limited, and a central node with many neighbors accelerates its own energy consumption. Due to the above limitations, the traditional BA model based on the global preferential connection strategy is no longer applicable. The scale-free IoT topology model needs to follow the two principles.

- Select a node from the communication range to connect preferentially. In traditional scale-free networks, any two nodes can be directly connected, regardless of distance constraints. However, in the IoT, two distant sensor nodes can only transmit information through multi-hop connection.
- Limit the degree of node to prevent excessive load. If the degree of a node is very large, it will forward more data and consume more energy. Since the energy of nodes in the IoT is limited, more energy consumption will cause the network to collapse prematurely.

This chapter constructs a scale-free model for the IoT topology based on the above two principles. The robustness optimization of the IoT topology is mainly carried out according to the characteristics of small-world network and scale-free network.

1.3   Attack Strategies Against Network Topology

In order to better analyze the stability of the IoT topology after optimization, this section introduces more fine-grained attack methods and explores more effective attack strategy for the IoT topology. Common attacks against network topology are mainly divided into two types. Random attacks are mainly manifested as hardware failures or energy exhaustion of nodes, which can be simulated by generating random sequences as the attack sequence. Malicious attacks mainly destroy the most important nodes in the network and quickly paralyze the whole network. This section focuses on more harmful malicious attacks.

1.3.1 Existing Attack Strategies

Infrastructure networks such as power grids are vital to people's daily lives. They are attractive targets for cyber-attacks because they usually do not take security as the main concern in the initial deployment and have a greater impact after damage. In addition, due to the large scale of the network, it is very difficult to repair the entire network. For example, the power grid of Venezuelan was attacked by a cyber-attack, which causes a large-scale power outage across the country and serious economic and personnel losses. Therefore, in recent years, cyber-attacks against infrastructure networks have become very frequent and serious [19]. We consider those attacks that destroy the infrastructure network topology by deleting the most important nodes and the adjacent links [20]. By studying the process of this attacks, we can obtain effective measures against such cyber-attacks.

The key point of the above-mentioned network attacks is how to measure the importance of nodes in the network, and centrality is an effective indicator to reflect the importance of nodes. Different centralities reflect the characteristics of the network from many aspects. Except for the commonly used attacks based on degree centrality, betweenness and closeness centralities [21] have also been applied to network attacks, and there are two existing attack strategies.

- Initial strategy: The centrality of each node in the initial topology is calculated. The attack order of each node is determined according to the centrality. In each round attack, nodes are selected to remove in a fixed order.
- Adaptive strategy: After each round of attack, the centralities of the remaining nodes are recalculated. Then the node with the largest centrality is selected as the target in the next round of attacks.

Therefore, this section can obtain two sets of attack methods according to the above three centralities and two strategies. According to the existing naming format [22], the attacks under the initial strategy are respectively called High Degree Initial (HDI), High Betweenness Initial (HBI) and High Closeness Initial (HCI). The attacks under the adaptive strategy are High Degree Adaptive (HDA), High

Betweenness Adaptive (HBA) and High Closeness Adaptive (HCA). Research shows that the adaptive attack strategy is better than initial attack strategy in attack effect. The attack effect here is presented by the robustness indicator R [23]. In order to explore a more effective attack strategy, this section proposes a Largest Component (LC) strategy [24]. Under this strategy, the attack methods based on different centrality measures are not only superior to adaptive attack strategy in the R value, but also involve less calculation in the average case. Through many experiments on different types of network topologies, the effectiveness of the LC strategy can be verified.

1.3.2 Different Centralities and Network Topologies

The following describes the concept, calculation methods and computational complexity of five centralities. These five centralities include degree, betweenness, closeness, current-flow betweenness [22], and current-flow closeness centralities [22]. The total number of sensor nodes is represented by n, and m is the number of edges in the network. Suppose that the topology is an undirected connected graph. The above centrality is explained below:

(1) Degree centrality: It is equal to the normalized value of the degree of a node divided by $(n - 1)$. Obviously, the time complexity of calculating the degree centrality of all nodes is $O(m)$.

(2) Betweenness centrality: It reflects the occurrence frequency of a node on all shortest paths between node pairs. The Betweenness centrality $C_B(v)$ of node v is calculated as follows.

$$C_B(v) = \frac{1}{(n-1)(n-2)} \sum_{i,j \in V} \frac{\tau(i, j|v)}{\tau(i, j)} (i \neq v \neq j) \qquad (1.4)$$

In Eq. (1.4), i and j are different nodes except v in the network. $\tau(i, j)$ represents the total number of paths for data transmission between the two nodes, and $\tau(i, j|v)$ is the number of these shortest paths containing node v. $1/(n - 1)(n - 2)$ is the normalized factor. The time complexity of calculating the betweenness centrality of all nodes is $O(nm)$.

(3) Closeness centrality: It indicates the distance between a node and other network nodes. Specifically, the closeness centrality $C_C(v)$ is inversely proportional to the distance traveled by the node v to other $n - 1$ nodes. The $d(v, i)$ is the shortest path length from node v to i, and the time complexity of calculating the closeness centrality of all nodes is $O(nm)$.

$$C_C(v) = \frac{n-1}{\sum_{i \in V} d(v, i)} (i \neq v) \qquad (1.5)$$

(4) Current-flow betweenness centrality: Different from the previous three central-
    ities that transmit data through the shortest path, the current-flow betweenness
    centrality $C_{CB}(v)$ imitates the flow mode of current in the circuit, and the data
    is transmitted along all paths instead of only along the shortest path. In order to
    determine the $C_{CB}(v)$ of node v, a unit current is added between the two nodes
    except v, which considers the proportion of the unit current passing through
    node v, the specific calculation method is as follows:

$$C_{CB}(v) = \frac{1}{(n-1)(n-2)} \sum_{i,j \in V} I_{i,j}(v)(i \neq v \neq j) \tag{1.6}$$

In Eq. (1.6), $I_{i,j}(v)$ is the current flow through node v after applying a unit
current between nodes i and j. $(n-1)(n-2)$ indicates the normalized factor.
The time complexity of calculating the current-flow betweenness centrality of
all nodes is $O(n^3 + nm \log n)$ [22].

(5) Current-flow closeness centrality: In current-flow network, the potential dif-
    ference between nodes v and i can be regarded as the distance between two
    nodes. Therefore, the current-flow closeness centrality $C_{CC}(v)$ of node v is the
    reciprocal of the average potential difference between node v and other $n-1$
    nodes.

$$C_{CC}(v) = \frac{n-1}{\sum_{i \in V} PD(v,i)}(i \neq v) \tag{1.7}$$

$PD(v,i)$ represents the potential difference between nodes v and i, which
is also equal to the effective resistance between nodes v and i, and the time
complexity of calculating the C_{CC} is $O(n^3)$ [22].

In order to verify the effectiveness and universality of malicious attack methods
composed of different centralities, four traditional artificial network topologies and
two existing network topologies in the real world are used as attack targets. The four
kinds of artificial networks are ER model, WS model, BA model, and grid network
based on IoT wireless link model (Mesh). The first three networks are classical
models existing in complex network theory. In order to unify these networks,
the number of nodes in the first three networks is set as 100. The last network
is a wireless link model based on sensor communication proposed by Zuniga
[25], which has been cited for more than a thousand times. The model includes
many characteristics of low power wireless links, such as transition regions, radio
irregularity, and antenna orientation. Mesh topology has 400 nodes, and the average
degree of nodes is 7. The following describes two real-world network topologies.

Figure 1.6a shows the Power Grid Network topology (PG) [26], where nodes and
edges represent generators and high-voltage transmission lines, respectively. This
topology includes 217 nodes and 320 edges. Figure 1.6b is the Autonomous System
topology (AS) in the internet backbone collected by the Routing View Project at the
University of Oregon [27], which includes 103 nodes and 243 edges.

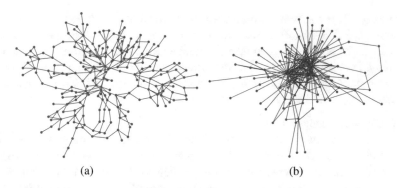

Fig. 1.6 Two network topologies in the real world. (**a**) PG, n=217, m=320. (**b**) AS, n=103, m=243

1.3.3   Attack Strategy of Largest Component

This section describes the operation steps of the LC strategy and analyzes the time complexity in the worst case and average case. Like the idea of R indicator introduced above, LC strategy is also proposed based on the idea that the largest connected component is crucial to the connectivity of the network. The network can be decomposed faster by destroying this structure. The process of LC strategy is described as follows:

- Search all the connected components in the current network and select the largest connected component according to the number of nodes.
- Calculate the centrality of each node in the largest component (any of the five centralities)
- Remove the node with the largest centrality and disconnect all connections with this node.
- If there are nodes in the network, go back to the first step.

As mentioned above, LC strategy can construct the attack methods based on the five centralities. As the current-flow betweenness and current-flow closeness centralities are based on the way the current flows in the circuit for data transmission, it is necessary to ensure that the current network is a connected graph. The initial strategy only calculates the centrality of nodes once, and the initial network is connected, so it can form new attack methods HCBI and HCCI with the above two centralities. In the adaptive strategy, when some nodes are removed, the whole network is no longer connected, and the two centralities can no longer be calculated. In the LC strategy, each attack only computes the centrality of nodes in the largest connected component, so all the five centralities are applicable to LC strategy. In order to unify naming, HDL, HBL, HCL, HCBL and HCCL are used in this section to represent attack methods formed under LC strategy with different centralities.

The time complexity of LC strategy is analyzed below. Since the LC strategy involves the calculation of centrality measures, its complexity depends on the complexity of the centrality chosen. In order to make the complexity analysis more universal, $O(C)$ is uniformly used to represent the complexity of the centrality of all nodes in the network. C can take different expressions according to the selected centrality. For example, if the betweenness centrality is selected, then $C = nm$. If current-flow closeness centrality is chosen, then $C = n^3$. Two scenarios are discussed: worst case and average case.

(1) Complexity analysis in worst case

According to the description of the LC strategy, it contains a loop of n iterations. In each iteration, the following four main steps are performed: calculate the connected component, which is $O(n + m)$; find the largest component, which is $O(n)$; calculate the centralities of all nodes in the largest component, which is $O(C)$; select the node with the largest centrality, which is $O(n)$. Therefore, the overall time complexity of LC strategy can be calculated.

$$O(n(n + m + n + C + n)) = O(n(3n + m + C))$$

$$= O(3n^2 + nm + nC) = O(nC) \qquad (1.8)$$

Since the number of edges m is between $[n - 1, n(n - 1)/2]$, the value of C is at least m, so nC is the dominant term in the above equation. For any centrality whose complexity is $O(C)$, the worst-case complexity of LC strategy is $O(nC)$. Similarly, the worst-case complexity of adaptive strategy is also $O(nC)$. Therefore, in the worst case, LC strategy does not reduce computational complexity. But on average, the LC strategy is less complex than the adaptive strategy because it only calculates the centrality of those nodes in the largest component.

(2) Complexity analysis in average case

Because it is very difficult to do a rigorous complexity analysis in general case, only a rough analysis is given here, and it works in most cases. To make the analysis easy to understand, betweenness centrality is used as an example. A similar analysis can be performed for other centralities. For betweenness centrality, the computational complexity is $O(nm)$. To further simplify the analysis, m and n are assumed to have a linear relationship, which is true for most network topologies in the real world. Thus, the complexity of betweenness centrality is $O(n^2)$.

In the adaptive strategy, the betweenness centrality of the remaining $N - i$ nodes is calculated in each round, where i is the number of attack rounds. By summing up the calculation results of these n rounds of attacks, the average complexity of the adaptive strategy can be obtained as $O(n^3)$.

$$n^2 + (n - 1)^2 + (n - 2)^2 + \cdots + 1^2 = \frac{1}{6}n(n + 1)(2n + 1) \qquad (1.9)$$

On the other hand, under the LC strategy, the betweenness centrality is calculated only for the nodes in the largest connected component. After each round of attack, the number of nodes in the largest component is expected to be halved. Therefore, when the calculation results of n rounds are added, the complexity of LC strategy is shown in Eq. (1.10), where $r = \log_2 n$.

$$n^2 + (\frac{n}{2^1})^2 + (\frac{n}{2^2})^2 + \cdots + (\frac{n}{2^r})^2 = (\frac{1 - (\frac{1}{2})^{2(r+1)}}{1 - (\frac{1}{2})^2}) * n^2 \approx \frac{4}{3}n^2 \quad (1.10)$$

Therefore, the average complexity of LC strategy based on betweenness centrality is $O(n^2)$, which is $O(n)$ factors lower than adaptive strategy. Note that this improvement of the $O(n)$ factor applies to any centrality whose complexity satisfies $O(C) \geq O(n^2)$. However, for degree centrality, since its complexity is only $O(m)$, this $O(n)$ factor improvement does not hold true. The following verifies the effectiveness of LC attack strategy from two aspects of robustness and running time.

Firstly, the attack effects of adaptive and LC strategies are compared on four artificial networks and two real networks. The selected centralities are betweenness and closeness. If the R value of a method is small, it indicates that the attack effect of this method is good. As can be seen from Table 1.1, the R values of HBL and HCL are smaller than HBA and HCA, respectively. In other words, the attack effect of LC strategy is better than adaptive strategy. This conclusion also applies to attack methods based on other centralities.

In order to verify the time complexity of LC strategy is lower than adaptive strategy, the attack methods based on the betweenness, and closeness centralities are selected to compare the running time of the two strategies. The reason is that degree centrality is relatively unimproved, and the other two current-flow centralities are not suitable for adaptive strategy. For fairness in time measurement, each attack runs as a process on a CPU. The BA network topology was selected as the attack target, and the running time of different attack methods was observed by changing the number of nodes in the network.

As shown in Table 1.2, as the number of nodes increases, the running time of each attack method increases. Under the same number of nodes, the running time based on LC strategy is shorter than adaptive strategy, which is consistent with the complexity analysis in average case. In conclusion, the malicious attack method

Table 1.1 The attack effect of Adaptive and LC strategies (R value)

Networks	HBA	HCA	HBL	HCL
BA	0.1294	0.1306	0.1242	0.1303
ER	0.2945	0.3142	0.2875	0.3115
WS	0.1510	0.1731	0.1400	0.1623
Mesh	0.1690	0.2316	0.1645	0.2279
PG	0.0674	0.0719	0.0630	0.0652
AS	0.0882	0.0880	0.0841	0.0859

Table 1.2 The running time of Adaptive and LC strategies on BA network (Seconds)

Nodes	HBA	HCA	HBL	HCL
1000	250	208	146	132
1200	554	390	265	218
1400	939	607	418	328
1600	1391	926	702	531
1800	2113	1459	1022	787
2000	2825	2153	1547	1143

based on LC strategy is superior to the existing attack strategy. In the subsequent chapters, malicious attacks on the network topology are carried out by LC strategy.

1.4 Book Organization

This book provides in-depth studies on the theories, solutions, and applications of the robustness optimization of the IoT topology. It also provides the relevant theoretical frameworks and the latest empirical research results for the robustness optimization of IoT topology. The research on topology robustness begins with the self-organization of network, and gradually moves to genetic evolution. The introduction of ant colony and particle swarm algorithm explores the method of topology robustness optimization from the perspective of swarm intelligence. The application of neural network and reinforcement learning endows the node with self-learning ability to realize intelligent networking. This book will present a complete topology robustness research framework for students, practitioners, industry professionals and researchers.

The organization of this book is as follows. Chapter 1 describes the background of the robust topology optimization problem and the characteristics of the IoT topology, and introduces related attack strategies. Chapter 2 presents the metrics of robustness and the related work of topology optimization. Chapters 3–8 show the optimization schemes of robust topology from the aspects of self-organization, evolution, swarm intelligence, multi-objective cooperation, self-learning, and node intelligence. Finally, in Chap. 9 the book discusses the future research directions.

This book helps readers to construct a robustness optimization framework from self-organizing to intelligent networking. Through the combination between theory and practice, readers can more clearly understand the construction process of robust topology. At the same time, it also provides a system maintenance direction from the network architecture layer for related researchers who are involved in cyber-attacks and security work.

References

1. Chettri, L., & Bera, R. (2019). A comprehensive survey on Internet of Things (IoT) toward 5g wireless systems. *IEEE Internet of Things Journal, 7*(1):16–32.
2. Ge, M., Bangui, H., & Buhnova, B. (2018). Big data for internet of things: A survey. *Future Generation Computer Systems, 87*:601–614.
3. Chen, Y., Chiotellis, N., Chuo, L.-X., Pfeiffer, C., Shi, Y., Dreslinski, R. G., Grbic, A., Mudge, T., Wentzloff, D. D., Blaauw, D., et al. (2016). Energy-autonomous wireless communication for millimeter-scale Internet-of-Things sensor nodes. *IEEE Journal on Selected Areas in Communications, 34*(12):3962–3977.
4. Ahn, J. H., & Lee, T.-J. (2017). Allys: All you can send for energy harvesting networks. *IEEE Transactions on Mobile Computing, 17*(4), 775–788.
5. Ng, I. C. L., & Wakenshaw, S. Y. L. (2017). The internet-of-things: Review and research directions. *International Journal of Research in Marketing, 34*(1):3–21.
6. Hu, C., Bao, W., & Wang, D. (2018). Iot communication sharing: Scenarios, algorithms and implementation. In *IEEE INFOCOM 2018-IEEE Conference on Computer Communications* (pp. 1556–1564). New York: IEEE.
7. Qiu, J., Tian, Z., Du, C., Zuo, Q., Su, S., & Fang, B. (2020). A survey on access control in the age of internet of things. *IEEE Internet of Things Journal, 7*(6), 4682–4696.
8. Qiu, T., Luo, D., Xia, F., Deonauth, N., Si, W., & Tolba, A. (2016). A greedy model with small world for improving the robustness of heterogeneous internet of things. *Computer Networks, 101*:127–143.
9. Buldyrev, S. V., Parshani, R., Paul, G., Stanley, H. E., & Havlin, S. (2010). Catastrophic cascade of failures in interdependent networks. *Nature, 464*(7291):1025.
10. Yan, J., He, H., & Sun, Y. (2014). Integrated security analysis on cascading failure in complex networks. *IEEE Transactions on Information Forensics and Security, 9*(3):451–463.
11. Savla, K., Como, G., & Dahleh, M. A. (2014). Robust network routing under cascading failures. *IEEE Transactions on Network Science and Engineering, 1*(1):53–66.
12. Chen, P.-Y., Cheng, S.-M., & Chen, K.-C. (2014). Information fusion to defend intentional attack in internet of things. *IEEE Internet of Things Journal, 1*(4):337–348.
13. Erdos, P., Rényi, A., et al. (1960). On the evolution of random graphs. *Publications of the Mathematical Institute of the Hungarian Academy of Sciences, 5*(1):17–60.
14. Watts, D. J., & Strogatz, S. H. (1998). Collective dynamics of small-worldnetworks. *Nature, 393*(6684):440–442.
15. Barabási, A.-L., & Albert, R. (1999). Emergence of scaling in random networks. *science, 286*(5439):509–512.
16. da Fontoura Costa, L., Oliveira, O. N. Jr., Travieso, G., Rodrigues, F. A., Boas, P. R. V., Antiqueira, L., Viana, M. P., & Rocha, L. E. C. (2011). Analyzing and modeling real-world phenomena with complex networks: A survey of applications. *Advances in Physics, 60*(3):329–412.
17. Newman, M. E. J., & Watts, D. J. (1999). Renormalization group analysis of the small-world network model. *Physics Letters A, 263*(4–6), 341–346.
18. Barabási, A.-L., Albert, R., & Jeong, H. (1999). Mean-field theory for scale-free random networks. *Physica A: Statistical Mechanics and its Applications, 272*(1–2):173–187.
19. Paté-Cornell, M.-E., Kuypers, M., Smith, M., & Keller, P. (2018). Cyber risk management for critical infrastructure: a risk analysis model and three case studies. *Risk Analysis, 38*(2), 226–241.
20. Zhang, H., Fata, E., & Sundaram, S. (2015). A notion of robustness in complex networks. *IEEE Transactions on Control of Network Systems, 2*(3), 310–320.
21. Liu, J., Zhou, M., Wang, S., & Liu, P. (2017). A comparative study of network robustness measures. *Frontiers of Computer Science, 11*(4), 568–584.
22. Brandes, U., & Fleischer, D. (2005). Centrality measures based on current flow. In *Annual Symposium on Theoretical Aspects of Computer Science* (pp. 533–544). New York: Springer.

23. Schneider, C. M., Moreira, A. A., Andrade, J. S., Havlin, S., & Herrmannm H. J. (2011). Mitigation of malicious attacks on networks. *Proceedings of the National Academy of Sciences, 108*(10), 3838–3841.
24. Zhang, S., Si, W., Qiu, T., & Cao, Q. (2020). Toward more effective centrality-based attacks on network topologies. In *ICC 2020-2020 IEEE International Conference on Communications (ICC)* (pp. 1–6). New York: IEEE.
25. Zuniga, M., & Krishnamachari, B. (2004). Analyzing the transitional region in low power wireless links. In *2004 First Annual IEEE Communications Society Conference on Sensor and Ad Hoc Communications and Networks, 2004. IEEE SECON 2004* (pp. 517–526). New York: IEEE.
26. Zhou, Q., & Bialek, J. W. (2005). Approximate model of european interconnected system as a benchmark system to study effects of cross-border trades. *IEEE Transactions on Power Systems, 20*(2):782–788.
27. Leskovec, J., & Krevl, A. (2014). *Snap datasets: Stanford large network dataset collection.*

Chapter 2
Preliminaries of Robustness Optimization

In this chapter, we first introduce nine metrics measuring network topology robustness, and then present several advanced topology optimization algorithms based on small world and scale-free network models. Before optimizing network topology, we should know the definition of robustness and what is important for network topology. Nevertheless, robustness optimization algorithms are essential for IoT applications to provide robust communication supports. This chapter outlines the preliminaries of related works about the robustness optimization for IoT applications, which is better for readers to easily understand the content of the book.

2.1 Metrics of Topology Robustness

2.1.1 Algebraic Connectivity and Natural Connectivity

In the 1980s, researchers began working on robustness metric to represent the network's performance. Bauer [1] and Harary [2] used super connectivity and conditional connectivity to measure the network's connectivity under external attacks, respectively. However, the metrics based on graph connectivity can only partially reflect the robustness of the network structure. Moreover, considering computational complexity, the metrics for general graphs need nondeterministic polynomial-time, which causes complex applications in complex network theory.

Furthermore, the second smallest eigenvalue of the Laplacian matrix (i.e., algebraic connectivity) [3] can measure the topology robustness. The magnitude of the algebraic connectivity can perform the connection for networks. The larger the algebraic connectivity is, the more robustness and connectivity is for networks. Jamakovic et al. [4] used algebraic connectivity as a measure of robustness and analysed the different robustness characteristics of three artificial networks under random attacks. However, the algebraic connectivity is not sensitive to monitoring

© The Author(s), under exclusive license to Springer Nature Singapore Pte Ltd. 2022   17
T. Qiu et al., *Robustness Optimization for IoT Topology*,
https://doi.org/10.1007/978-981-16-9609-1_2

and measuring critical failures in complex network structures. Therefore, Wu et al. [5] introduced natural connectivity that measures the redundancy of alternative routes. The formula of natural connectivity is shown in Table 2.1. As edges of the network are added or removed, the natural connectivity changes monotonically and smoothly. Thus, it can reflect small structure changes in the network and is acceptable to both large-scale and small-scale networks.

2.1.2   Metric R and Cumulative k-MVC-Impact

In 2000, Albert [14] et al. simulated another metric of structural robustness within the context of complex networks that emerged from the random graph theory. This statistical measure is called the critical removal fraction of vertices (edges). This metric can only be calculated through simulations. The complexity of the calculation is determined by the calculation of network features [5], including network diameter, the largest component, average path length, etc. The critical removal fraction can be obtained by analysis [15–18] for some special networks. However, in 2011, Schneider et al. [6] showed that the critical removal fraction ignores situations in which the network suffers big damage without completely collapsing. Therefore, they propose a unique robustness metric, R, which considers the size of the largest component during all possible malicious attacks. The specific formula is shown in Table 2.1. Since the metric R only considers attacks against nodes, Zeng and Liu [19] extended it to the attacks against edges and verified that it could achieve good performance.

In 2014, Li and Yu et al. [7] proposed another similar robustness metric cumulative k-MVC-impact based on maximal vertex coverage (MVC) from an attacker's point of view. And they developed a near-optimal randomized greedy algorithm using the FM sketch for computing the metric on the general network. The time and space complexity of the proposed algorithm are $O(kn + m)$, and $O(n + m)$ respectively, where n represents the number of nodes and m represents the number of edges. This metric can intuitively and naturally reflect the structural robustness of complex networks [7]. Its formula is shown in Table 2.1.

2.1.3   Temporal Robustness and Metrics Based on Betweenness

In 2011, Mishkovski et al. [8] proposed a metric to measure the network vulnerability, which is represented by the normalized average edge betweenness and its relative difference when a certain number of nodes and/or edges in the network are removed. The specific formula of the normalized average edge betweenness is shown in Table 2.1. If its value is close to 0, it means that the network is more robust. When the value is close to 1, the network is more vulnerable. They conducted network vulnerability assessments on four artificial networks and eight

Table 2.1 The nine kinds of robustness metrics of network topology

Metric	Formula	Symbols	Description
Natural connectivity [5]	$S = \sum_{i=1}^{N} e^{\lambda_i}$	S	Weighted sum of closed walks of all lengths.
		N	The number of vertices in the network.
		e	Natural constant.
	$\bar{\lambda} = \ln(S/N) = \ln\left[\frac{1}{N}\sum_{j=1}^{N} e^{\lambda_j}\right]$	λ_j	The j_{th} largest eigenvalue of the adjacency matrix of a simple undirected graph G.
		$\bar{\lambda}$	Natural connectivity.
R [6]	$R = \frac{1}{N}\sum_{Q=1}^{N} s(Q)$	R	The robustness measure.
		N	The number of nodes in the network.
		$s(Q)$	The fraction of nodes in the largest connected cluster after removing Q nodes.
Cumulative k-MVC-impact [7]	$\sigma_k = 1 - F^*(S)/m$	σ_k	k-MVC-impact.
		$\bar{\sigma}_n$	Cumulative k-MVC-impact.
	$\bar{\sigma}_n = \left(\sum_{k=1}^{n}\sigma_k\right)/n$	S	A set of nodes.
		$F^*(S)$	The max number of edges that are removed after deleting k nodes in S.
		m	The number of edges in the network.
Normalized average edge betweenness [8]	$b_{nor} = \frac{b(G)-b_{com}}{b_{path}-b_{com}}$	$b(G)$	Average edge betweenness of the simple undirected graph G.
		b_{nor}	Normalized average edge betweenness.
		b_{com}	Average edge betweenness of a complete graph.
		b_{path}	Average edge betweenness of a path graph.
Network criticality [9]	$\tau = \sum_s \sum_d \tau_{sd}$	τ	Network criticality.
		τ_{sd}	The resistance distance between two nodes s and d.
	$= \sum_s \sum_d \left(l_{ss}^+ + l_{dd}^+ - 2l_{sd}^+\right)$	l_{ij}^+	The entry of row i and column j in Moore-Penrose inverse of Laplacian Matrix L of graph.

(continued)

Table 2.1 (continued)

Metric	Formula	Symbols	Description
Temporal robustness [10]	$E(t_1, t_2) = \frac{1}{N(N-1)} \sum_{i,j} \frac{1}{d_{i,j}(t_1,t_2)}$	$E(t_1, t_2)$	The temporal global efficiency of a given temporal graph G.
		N	The number of nodes in the graph G.
		$d_{i,j}(t_1, t_2)$	The smallest length among all the temporal paths between node i and j in the time window $[t_1; t_2]$.
	$R_G(D) = 1 - \frac{\Delta E(G,D)}{E_G} = \frac{E_{G_D}}{E_G}$	$R_G(D)$	The temporal robustness of the temporal graph G against the damage D.
		$\Delta E(G, D)$	The loss in efficiency caused by the damage D on the temporal graph G as $\Delta E(G, D) = E_G - E_D$.
R_{CF} [11]	$R_{n,i} = -\sum_{i=1}^{L} \alpha_i p_i \log p_i$	$R_{n,i}$	The electrical nodal robustness of a node i.
		α_i	The network tolerance parameter of a line i.
	$\delta_i = \frac{p_i}{\sum_{j=1}^{N} p_j}$	p_i	Normalized flow values of line i on the out-going links.
		δ_i	Electrical node significance of an arbitrary node i.
	$R_{CF} = \sum_{i=1}^{N} R_{n,i} \delta_i$	R_{CF}	The network robustness with respect to cascading failures in power grids.
Effective graph resistance [12]	$R_G = \sum_{i=1}^{N} \sum_{j=i+1}^{N} R_{ij}$	R_{ij}	The effective resistance R_{ij} between any pair of node i and j.
	$R_{ij} = Q_{ii}^+ - 2Q_{ij}^+ + Q_{jj}^+$	Q^+	The Moore-Penrose pseudo-inverse of the Laplacian matrix Q of a power grid.
		R_G	The effective graph resistance R_G of a power grid.
Electrical betweenness centrality [13]	$C_B^E(i) = \sum_{s \neq v \neq t \in V} \frac{P_{st}(i)}{P_{st}}$	$C_B^E(i)$	Electrical betweenness centrality of node i.
		$P_{st}(i)$	The electric power that flows in the line linking node s to t needs node i to transmit power between them.
		V	A set of nodes in the power grid.

real-world networks. They found that the Watts-Strogatz (WS) model of small-world networks and biological networks (human brain networks) are the most robust networks among all networks studied in their work. Another metric based on the betweenness is the network criticality, proposed by Tizghadam et al. [9] in 2009. The network criticality determines a critical value for each link to form a weighted undirected graph, which shows the importance of each link to the network topology and traffic demand changes. This metric focuses on the impact of network properties on network structure, such as the impact of load and bandwidth allocation on robustness, and thus more applicable to communication networks. However, for time-varying networks such as mobile communication networks, static robustness metrics may over-estimate the network robustness [10]. Therefore, Scellato et al. [10] presented a robustness metric based on temporal graphs in 2013, called temporal robustness. Its formula is shown in Table 2.1. It is represented by the loss of communication efficiency after the network is attacked. And they tested it in a real opportunistic vehicle system of about 500 taxicabs. The results highlight that this metric can avoid over-estimating the robustness of a fragile network.

2.1.4 Three Robustness Metrics of Power Grids

Another typical complex network is the power grid, which is a system of structural interdependencies between components. In the power grids, the failures from the small localized region will propagate through the entire network, which can cause cascading failures. Therefore, when measuring the robustness of the power grids, the structural aspects needs to be considered, such as number of buses, the density of transmission lines, and interconnection of components. In 2013, Yakup et al. [11] proposed an entropy-based robustness metric R_{CF}, as shown in Table 2.1. The metric R_{CF} relies on two main concepts: electrical nodal robustness $R_{n,i}$ and electrical node significance δ_i. The product of these two values indicates the individual contribution of each node to network robustness. Therefore, this metric can be used to compare the robustness of different size grids under the cascade failures caused by malicious attacks. A year later, Yakup et al. [12] proposed a new robustness metric to improve the graph resistance against cascading failure, which considers power flow allocation according to Kirchhoff laws. Experimental verification on IEEE bus power systems and synthetic power systems shows that the effective graph resistance accurately reflect the grid robustness.

In 2015, Cuadra et al. [13] reviewed the related work of robustness in power grids using complex network theory. They discussed two types of robustness metrics of the power grids, i.e., solely calculating one topology feature, such as mean path length, clustering coefficient, etc. Another is a hybrid metrics consisting of electrical betweenness, net-ability, etc. They showed that the electrical betweenees centrality [13] is the most useful measure for quantifying the criticality of nodes in the power grids. Its formula is shown in Table 2.1.

Real-world networks have different topological properties in different application scenarios. We summarize the aforementioned robustness metrics and give reasonable suggestions. The natural connectivity has good performance on simple, undirected graphs, and Wu et al. [20] gave its calculation methods in regular ring lattices, random graphs, and random scale-free networks. The robustness metric R is applicable to most complex network models [6]. And Schneider et al. [6] used it as a robustness metric to design a cost-effective method for European power systems and the Internet to reduce the risk of malicious attacks. Similarly, the metric R can be used as a robustness measure in scale-free networks such as IoT [21], air transport networks [22], and energy networks [23]. When MVC strategies attack the network, the cumulative k-MVC-impact is more suitable for measuring the network robustness. Li and Yu et al. [7] used it to verify that the P2P networks and the cooperative author networks are very robust under MVC attacks, but the online social networks and the email communication networks are very vulnerable. Mishkovski et al. [8] analyzed the calculation methods of the normalized average edge betweenness for the four synthetic networks: Erdős-Rényi (ER) random networks, geometric random networks, Watts-Strogatz (WS) model of small-world networks and Barabási-Albert (BA) model of scale-free networks. And they applied it to measure the robustness of eight real-world networks. Both network criticality and temporal robustness are robustness metrics of communication networks. Temporal robustness focuses on the network structure's time-varying characteristics and has achieved good experimental performance for mobile communication networks. When it comes to measuring the robustness of power grids, the metric R_{CF} and the effective graph resistance can be used as a metric.

2.2 Related Work

2.2.1 Robustness Optimization Based on Small World Model

The small-world model combines the characteristics of a regular network and a random network, with a relatively short average path length and high clustering coefficient [24]. Many real-world networks such as collaborative networks and online social networks have proven to be small-world models. Watts and Strogatz first proposed the Small World Model in 1998, also known as the WS Small World Model, which is a commonly used modeling strategy [25]. In 2007, Jamakovic et al. [4] showed that the WS small-world model is extremely robust to random failures of nodes and links. The work of Kasthurirathna et al. [20] in 2013 showed that the robustness of small-world model is positively correlated with homogeneity, modularity, clustering coefficient, and average path length. This implies that designers can use some strategies to improve the robustness of small-world networks under persistent malicious attacks. For the first time, Helmy et al. [26] introduced

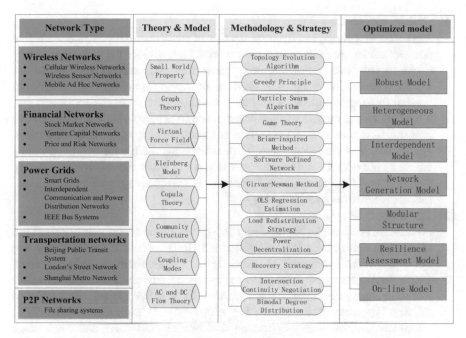

Fig. 2.1 Theories and strategies of robustness optimization for network topology based on Small World Model

the concept of small-world model into wireless networks. Adding some logically remote links may represent physical connections between random nodes to build shortcuts in the wireless networks. At present, the research on building a robust network structure using a small world model is not limited to wireless networks, but has applications in financial networks, power grids, transportation networks, and P2P networks. As shown in Fig. 2.1, this paper investigates the literatures of the past 10 years and summarizes the theoretical basis and modeling strategies for robust modeling of the five networks using the small-world model.

2.2.1.1   Wireless Networks

The scale and scope of wireless networks have expanded with the increasing number of users and more and more communication infrastructures deployed in cities. The rapid development of mobile applications, and the increase in dynamic high-speed information flows, have made the network require a more reliable self-organizing topology. Traditional network systems are represented by a regular Euclidean lattice structure, but this structure does not satisfy the self-organizing characteristics required by wireless networks.

(1) *Cellular wireless networks*

Dixit et al. [27] explored the application of small-world model and scale-free network model in cellular wireless networks. They divided the self-organization problems into two stages: topology generation and network routing. In the topology generation phase, they used the proposed improved BA algorithm to generate a topology model with small-world properties. In the routing phase, a load balancing routing method is proposed to achieve efficient utilization of network resources and to generate a cellular network with better robustness against failure of the base station. Their work is instructive for building reliable wireless networks. On this basis, researchers can study the relationship among the number of fixed relay nodes, the degree of connectivity, node coverage, and the robustness of network topology.

(2) *Mobile Ad Hoc networks*

In 2010, Brust et al. [28] conducted a topology control study on another kind of wireless network, backbone-assisted Ad Hoc network. In this network, the device is arbitrarily connected to other devices within their transmission range, and dedicated device can connect to the backbone network. Such networks have a short average path length, but are particularly sensitive to random attacks and failures. Therefore, they proposed a topology control algorithm called LSWTC, which can simultaneously optimize the clustering coefficient and the average path length by using local information. This algorithm enables dynamically changing, mobile, and unpredictable wireless networks to maintain small-world characteristics to improve network robustness against random attacks and failures.

In an Ad Hoc network, insufficient communication range or energy exhaustion may cause the absence of some relay nodes and links, further breaking network connectivity. On the other hand, nodes in the network may refuse cooperation due to objective faults or individual selfishness, thus hindering normal communication in the network. Therefore, Tan et al. [29] proposed a model called Repeated Game in Small World Network. In this model, an Ad Hoc network with small-world characteristics is first constructed by forming "communication shortcuts" between multiple wireless nodes. Then use MTTFT strategy (Mend-Tolerance Tit-for-Tat) as the rule of repeated game among neighbor nodes in the small world. This model not only utilizes the high clustering coefficient property of the small world model to improve the network's tolerance to faults, but also utilizes the MTTFT strategy to reasonably punish the selfish behavior of nodes. This approach has profound implications for designing an efficient and robust Ad Hoc network.

(3) *Wireless sensor networks*

Heterogeneous wireless sensor networks are based on a large number of low-end sensors and a small number of powerful high-end sensors. Using the small-world model to simulate its network structure, we can design a flexible network that is robust to node failures. Hawick et al. focus on the relationship between network coverage, fault tolerance, and sensor network lifetime [30]. And they showed that adding a small number of random links between sensor nodes can not only shorten the average path length, but also reduce the number of isolated clusters, which greatly improves the network coverage and lifetime. Guidoni et al. [31] designed a heterogeneous WSN model called on-line directed angulation toward the sink node model (ODASM). The ODASM is a distributed solution based on the real-time deployment information of sensor nodes and communication modes of WSNs. The network latency of the generated model is not significantly affected under random attacks and a few malicious attacks. In heterogeneous WSNs, in order to reduce energy consumption, as the distance between nodes increases, the probability of establishing shortcuts between them becomes smaller. Therefore, the idea of creating shortcuts using distance-related distributions and node locations is applicable to WSNs. Guidoni et al. [32] used their proposed modeling strategy to optimize the Kleinberg model with long-tailed distribution in the placement of shortcuts. This work is very useful for WSN applications that require low data communication delays such as fire detection.

Liu et al. [33] first proposed a heterogeneous WSNs model based on small world and scale-free concepts. Their work is achieved by applying preferential attachment mechanisms in heterogeneous WSNs, and a topology evolution algorithm is designed. They show that this method can significantly improve energy efficiency and enhance the robustness of the network to random node failure. Huang et al. [34] designed a WSNs topology optimization model with both small world effect and scale-free property by using software-defined network architecture. This model can contribute to extending the lifetime of WSNs with energy efficiency and improving the robustness of WSNs with structure invulnerability. The brain network has modular and small-world properties, thus it has high communication efficiency and robust connection in both local and global regions. Inspired by the brain network properties, Toyonaga et al. [35] constructed a hierarchical modular model of WSNs with high robustness under random attacks and malicious attacks. This model uses the concept of virtualization to make it possible for heterogeneous devices from different vendors to form robust large-scale WSNs. RONS is an important and challenging problem in the Internet of Things (IoT), which contains a variety of heterogeneous networks [36]. Qiu et al. [37] constructed a heterogeneous WSN using a greedy model with small-world properties. This model uses two greedy criteria to distinguish the local importance of different network nodes. And they design an algorithm that transforms a network to possess small-world properties by adding shortcuts between certain nodes according to their local importance. This method only needs to add a small number of shortcuts in the network to enhance the robustness and reduce the network latency.

2.2.1.2 Financial Networks

In practical applications, the stock market will generate huge amounts of data sets. By associating some attributes of the data sets with the vertices and edges of the network, we can build a network that can reflect market behaviors. Huang et al. [38] used the threshold method to model Chinese stock correlation network, and show that it follows a power-law network model. Therefore, the network is robust to random failures, but presents a vulnerability to malicious attacks. The research of robustness optimization on such networks is of great significance for portfolio investment and risk management.

Based on the 300 component stocks of Shanghai and Shenzhen, Li et al. [39] used tail correlation coefficient to build a network model of Chinese stock market. This model shares the small-world and scale-free characteristics, and the hub nodes of this model are mainly concentrated in the financial, manufacturing and construction industries, which shows that the financial, manufacturing and construction industries occupy an important position in Chinese economy. And they conducted robustness analysis of the Chinese stock market and achieved the same results with the work of Huang et al. [38]. With the development of globalization, the spillover effects of price fluctuations among international financial markets will also affect the stability of the stock market. Zhang et al. [40] simultaneously considered the similarity features of the stock price series and the high-risk features of the stock market, and innovatively constructed a multi-scale curve network and a risk network of the stock market. Based on this, they compared existing stock price network and analyzed the stability of the three networks. The multi-scale networks and risk networks have the characteristics of small-world model and scale-free networks, and the risk network has the best robustness, which provides a reference for the analysis of the short-term risks and stability of the Chinese stock market.

In the Chinese stock market, the partnership between venture capital firms constitutes a complex financial network. Jin et al. [41] established a Chinese venture capital network based on the Chinese GEM and SME board data. They used the Girvan-Newman method to analyze the network and found that it has a small-world property and a community structure, and is robust under both random attacks and malicious attacks. Their experimental results also show that there is no dominant venture capital firm as the center of the venture capital networks in China. Moreover, venture capital firms are mostly in developed regions, and more willing to cooperate with other venture capital firms from different developed regions.

2.2.1.3 Power Grid

In recent years, the reliability of power grids has attracted more and more attention, due to the frequent occurrence of large-scale blackouts and its catastrophic damage [42]. Cascading failure is one of the main causes of large-scale blackouts, which is the collective dynamic result of local faults propagating to the global network. Stability of power supply requires that the network structure of power grids is robust to failures. The complex network theory is often used to analyze the power grid structure. And it is found that the actual power grids have small-world properties and is robust of random failures, but it becomes very vulnerable to malicious attacks on critical nodes.

Ding et al. [43] studied the fault tolerance of power grids for different modes of failures, indicating that the vulnerability of the small-world power grids to cascading failures is closely related to the topological properties as well as the modes of failures. On the other hand, community structure plays a significant role in balancing the power flow distribution and further slowing the propagation of failures. Guo et al. [44] found that the robustness of power grids with obvious small-world properties depends more on the generation nodes detected by community structure. Otherwise, the generation nodes with important influence on power flow are more critical in the network. Pepyne et al. [45] studied the topology of a synthetic network constructed using the WS small-world model and found that topologies with more disorder in their interconnection topology tend to be robust with respect to cascading line outages than more regularly interconnected topologies. However, when a cascade get started, the topologies with more disorder tend to be more fragile and break apart after fewer outages than more regularly interconnected topologies. Therefore, it is necessary to identify the most important components in the power grids and give priority to them, which can effectively prevent cascading failures.

Cascading failure occurs in power grids due to unbalanced load distribution and line congestion. At the same time, it will also occur under external attacks on links. Therefore, it is necessary to consider the impact of different link attack strategies on the power grids when studying the network structure. The classical link attack strategies tend to attack the links with the biggest degree or the highest load, while the lowest load attack is ignored. Wang and Rong [46] proposed two attack strategies, the attack on the links with the lowest load and the attack on links with the smallest proportion between the total capacities of the neighboring links and the capacity of the attacked links. They studied cascading failures of the western United States power grids under these attack strategies. And the numerical simulations show that the local characteristics of a breakdown link has an important impact on the effects of intentional attacks in different parameter circumstances. Many studies have shown that adding new physical shortcuts to the grids can enhance its resistance to cascading failures. However, the simulations of Wang et al. [47] show that there is also a Brass paradox in the power grids: adding additional lines to the power grids sometimes reduces the robustness of the power grids. And they identified the specific substructure that leads to the existence of the Brass paradox. Therefore, in the design and expansion of power grids, we should avoid the Brass paradox in the system and optimize the robustness of the power grid structure.

The smart power grid model is a relatively novel concept in power grids based on advanced monitoring, controlling and communication technologies. It is not only designed to effectively utilize resources in the power system, but also to provide reliable, secure power supply services [48]. Cuadra et al. [49] used genetic algorithms to optimize the structure of smart grids. They coded the upper triangular matrix of the adjacency matrix of each potential network structure as its chromosome, and proposed a domain-specific initial population that includes both small-world and random networks, helping the algorithm converge quickly. The experimental work points out that the proposed algorithm can generate the optimum, synthetic, small-world structure that leads to beneficial properties such as improving both the local energy exchange and the robustness. Cascading failures in the power grids are not only caused by malicious attacks in the limited case of a single, non-interacting network. Actually, power outages are often caused by a series of failures between interdependent networks [50].

In practical applications, smart grids are often coupled with communication networks to form interdependent systems. Chai et al. [51] evaluated the robustness of large-scale medium-voltage distribution grids for cascade failures caused by different types of faults, and found that a communication networks with small world properties can improve the robustness of interdependent systems, and the formation of hub hierarchies, which is known to enhance independent network robustness, actually has adverse effects against cascading failures. Kang et al. [52] proposed a smart grid with two-way coupling link consists of a power grid with small-world properties and a communication network with scale-free topology. And they found that the Assortative Coupling in Subnets mode [52] applied to the bottom-up coupling link is beneficial in enhancing the robustness of the smart grids. Their work shows the relationship between load, subnet structure, coupling mode and cascading failures in the smart grid.

2.2.1.4 Transportation Networks

Transportation network planning is a complicated process. While there are many traditional methods of analyzing transportation networks, emerging complex network theories are particularly valuable for traffic planners and operators. Derrible et al. [53] studied 33 metro systems in the world and found that most metro systems have both scale-free and small-world properties. And they suggest that small-scale networks should focus on creating transfer stations to make the network more clustered, thus generating cycles to offer alternative routes. For large-scale networks, it is important to establish additional transfers at the periphery of the city centers. That will further improve the overall robustness of the transportation network. Zhang et al. [54] analyzed traffic networks with small-world and scale-free properties, such as the Shanghai Metro network, which have strong connectivity robustness under random failures and strong vulnerability under malicious attacks. They presented a framework that assesses the resilience of a large metro system, which provides an immediate basis for determining the optimal recovery sequence and optimal repair time.

For the analysis of the transportation networks, it is necessary to represent street networks in the city. The most direct way is via planar graphs, which are defined as a set of vertices and edges $\{V, E\}$ embedded in a two-dimensional surface. However, more and more studies have shown that in order to understand the dynamic characteristics of the transportation networks in cities, the dual representation of a street network is critical. The dual representation of a planar graph is a network where the nodes or vertices are the transportation units, i.e., an assemblage of individual street segments belonging to the same road. It is also called information space, which reflects a coding system of symbolic information. Masucci et al. [55]

used a new hybrid technique, the hierarchical interactive continuity negotiation principle, to extract the dual representation from the planar graph. They found that the small world model is a stable property of the London street network in the past two centuries, highlighting that the navigability in the information space of this city is a robust property of the transportation system.

The train flow network is an important part of the urban transportation networks, and its stability and service capability are the basis for the stable operation of modern society. Meng et al. [56] analyzed the train flow network by using the real data from China railway, and proved that the network has both small world and scale-free network properties. They suggest the junction station is most important in railway transportation organization, so much attention must be paid to the operation of the junction station to keep the train flow network robust. When conducting robustness analysis of urban public transit networks (PTNs), it is necessary to consider the occurrence of cascading failures and the dynamic behaviors of passengers. Huang et al. [57] conducted a complex weighted network analysis for Beijings bus stop network and multimodal transit network coupled with bus and urban rail systems. They show that the dynamic flow redistribution can significantly improve the tolerance of small-world or scale-free PTNs against random faults. And Because of the coupling of bus and rail systems, the cascading failures of the multimodal network with scale free topology and flow distribution structures will be much more intense once the failure is triggered. Therefore, They found some thresholds of topology and flow coupling strength in the spreading process,which can be exploited to develop strategies to control cascading failures.

2.2.1.5   P2P Networks

Many real-world networks are robust to random attacks, but vulnerable to malicious attacks. The hierarchical unstructured peer-to-peer (P2P) networks can be tolerant to churn, i.e., the dynamics of peer participation and departure. But it still faces the problem of being vulnerable to denial of service (DoS) attacks [58]. Therefore, how to design a P2P network structure that is simultaneous robust to random attacks and malicious attacks is critical. Tanizawa et al. [59] studied the robustness of the network to multiple waves of simultaneous (i) malicious attacks against nodes with the highest degree and (ii) random attacks with partial nodes failures. And they found that the robust network has a bimodal degree distribution, with a fraction r of the nodes having degree $k_2 = (\langle k \rangle - 1 + r)/r$ and the remainder of the nodes having degree $k_1 = 1$, where $\langle k \rangle$ is the average degree of all the nodes. Sonawanea et al. [60] proposed a model for constructing a network with bimodal degree distribution. And they studied the standard quantities which characterize the networks, like average path length and clustering coefficient and show that the bimodal degree distribution is in the small world family.

Networks with bimodal degree distribution are most robust to random and malicious attacks [60]. Suto et al. [58] introduced the bimodal degree distribution to unstructured P2P networks and accordingly developed a peer joining procedure to construct and maintain a two-tier unstructured P2P network close to the optimal topology. And they demonstrated that the network can offer high network connectivity and increase the tolerance of DoS attacks and churn. This method has great potential in applications such as file sharing systems, multimedia streaming.

2.2.2   Robustness Optimization Based on Scale-Free Model

Many real-world networks have the characteristics of scale-free networks, and the degree distribution follows the power-law distribution $p(k) \sim ck^{-\alpha}$, where $\alpha \in (2, 3)$. These networks are a type of heterogeneous network, and their node communication capabilities are incredibly robust under the affect of high failure rates. However, these networks have high fault tolerance for random failures, but they are very vulnerable to external malicious attacks [33]. Therefore, how to design a scale-free network modeling method and reconfiguration strategy to maintain the network performance under malicious attacks has become a research hotspot. We summarize the relevant research work in the past 10 years. And the topology modeling and optimization strategies, attack strategies, network robustness metrics, whether the topology distribution unchanged after optimization, the type of the largest scale network used in the simulation, and the size of the network (number of edges/nodes) are listed in the Table 2.2 respectively.

2.2.2.1   Onion-Like Structure Resistant to Malicious Attacks

In 2010, Xiao et al. [61] studied the relationship between the robustness of scale-free network and its assortative level. They proposed a simple rewiring method that slightly reduced the assortatively coefficient [73] without changing any node degree to enhance the robustness of the network. In 2011, Herrmann et al. [62] proposed a scale-free network structure optimization method, hill-climbing method, which based on swapping edges. The optimization process significantly improves the robustness of the scale-free network against the high degree adaptive attack (HDA), which corresponds to the attack on the node with the highest degree in each time, and the degree of nodes is recalculated before next attack. And they discovered the topology of the robust network has an onion-like structure, where high degree nodes are connected to each other, hierarchically surrounded by rings of nodes of decreasing degree. This experimental result is of great significance to future research work. The onion-like structure is shown in Fig. 2.2.

In 2012, Tanizawa et al. [65] were inspired by the onion-like structure, and proposed an onion-like candidate for a nearly optimal structure against simultaneous random attacks and HDA. And they defined the total robustness metric R_{tot} as the sum of the robustness measure R [6] for HDA and that for random attacks. Experiments show that the nearly optimal structure, hierarchically interconnected random regular graphs can significantly improve the robustness of scale-free net-

Table 2.2 Robustness optimization strategies for scale-free networks

Work	Optimization strategy	Attack strategy	Robustness metric	Degree distribution fixed	Sample network type	Number of nodes/edges
[61] 2010	A simple rewiring method	Intentional attacks without recalculating	The largest clustering size and cluster diameter	Yes	The random scale-free network	10,000/-
[62] 2011	The hill climbing algorithm	High degree adaptive attacks (HDA)	R	Yes	The Internet at the level of autonomous system	18,124/37,357
[63] 2011	The simulated annealing algorithm	HDA	R	Yes	BA scale-free network	300/-
[64] 2010	Randomized local rewiring	Simultaneous random and targeted disruptoins	Supply Availability, Network Connectivity and Delivery Efficiency	Yes	The military logistic network	1000/1815
[65] 2012	Hierarchically interconnected random regular graphs	Simultaneous random and targeted high degree node attacks	R_{tot}	–	The synthetic scale-free networks	6993/-
[66] 2013	A bayesian game clustering algorithm	Random and deliberate attacks	Network coverage	No	The synthetic scale-free networks	–

(continued)

Table 2.2 (continued)

[22] 2013	Smart rewiring strategy	HDA	R	Yes	The entire World Air-transportation network	1326/16001
[67] 2014	A memetic algorithm	HDA	R	Yes	The Internet at the level of autonomous system	7671/27951
[68] 2016	Two novel self-organizing schemes	HDA	The number of nodes connected to the sink node	No	The Synthetic scale-free Networks	2000/-
[23] 2016	A two-phase multiobjective evolutionary algorithm	High degree/betweeness adaptive node/link attacks	R	Yes	The U.S.-Air network	332/2126
[69] 2017	ROSE	HDA	R	Yes	The synthetic scale-free Networks	300/-
[21] 2017	A multi-population genetic algorithm	HDA	R	Yes	The synthetic scale-free Networks	300/-
[70] 2018	The great deluge algorithm	HDA	R	Yes	The synthetic scale-free Networks	500/-
[71] 2018	A heuristic algorithm based on edge classification	High degree/betweeness adaptive node attack	R and the betweenness centrality C_B	Yes	The synthetic scale-free networks	1000/-
[72] 2018	A regular hexagonal-based clustering scheme	The energy exhaustion and random failure of nodes	The number of nodes in the largest connected component	–	The synthetic scale-free networks	–

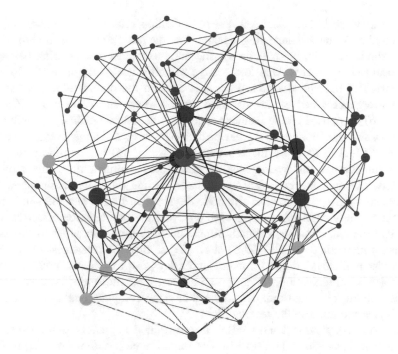

Fig. 2.2 The onion-like structure of a robust network with $N = 100$ nodes and $M = 200$ edges obtained from the work of Qiu et al. [21]. The size of nodes is proportional to their degree, and the nodes of similar degree have the same color

works under malicious attacks without affecting the robustness to random attacks. In 2013, Louzada et al. proposed a smart rewiring method based on the evolution of the network's largest components [22], which promoted the formation of a highly modular structure called a 'modular onion-like structure'. Compared with random rewiring [6], this method lowers the computational cost necessary to improve robustness by several orders of magnitude. The onion-like structure optimizes the robustness of the network to malicious attacks without changing the resistance of the scale-free network to random attacks. In future research work, many scholars and researchers have proposed robust optimization strategies for the evolution of onion-like structures [23, 63, 67, 69, 71].

2.2.2.2   Robustness Optimization Strategies for Scale-Free Networks

(1) Strategies with R as robustness metric

In 2011, Buessor et al. [63] designed a rewire strategy based on simulated annealing optimization heuristic. When the rewiring operation reduces the robustness of the network, this operation still has a certain probability of being accepted. The simulations show that when the number of nodes in the network is less than 300, the optimization effect of the rewire strategy based on simulated annealing is better than the hill-climbing method [62]. The optimization algorithms based on the edge-exchange and rewiring belong to local search process. Due to the large search space of the network structure design, if only local search process is used in the optimization process, the convergence speed of the algorithm will be very slow. Therefore, Zhou et al. [67] proposed a new memetic algorithm called MA-RSF$_{MA}$ combining a crossover operator which can perform global search and a local search operator in 2014. And they use the robustness metric R [6] as the fitness function. In the comparison experiments, the robustness optimization of the synthetic networks and the real-world networks is carried out. The results show that the MA-RSF$_{MA}$ guarantees the node degree distribution and the single node connectivity unchanged in the topology, and the optimization effect is better than the hill-climbing method, simulated annealing strategy and the smart rewiring method. In 2017, Zhou et al. [23] studied the robustness of networks under malicious attacks on nodes and edges from the perspective of multi-objective optimization, and proposed a two-stage multi-objective evolutionary algorithm. The algorithm can well balance the computational cost of the two targets and improve the search efficiency.

Nodes deployment in the WSNs is constrained by actual requirements, such as communication range and maximum node degree thresholds. Qiu et al. [69] proposed a scale-free network modeling method that takes into account constraints in homogeneous WSNs, and also proposed a new scale-free WSNs robustness optimization algorithm ROSE. The algorithm combines the degree difference operation and the angle sum operation to make the scale-free network topology quickly approach the onion-like structure without changing the node degree distribution. Compared with the hill-climbing method and the simulated annealing algorithm, ROSE can achieve a better robustness optimization effect and consume fewer computing resources. WSN is mostly used to monitor the environment, especially in mountainous terrain. In 2018, Qiu et al. [74] used Gauss Integration to build a three-dimensional (3D) terrain to simulate the mountain terrain, and then constructed an initial scale-free network based on the characteristics of WSNs in 3D terrain. In addition, they proposed a genetic algorithm with a novel crossover operator and mutation operator for robust optimization in 3D terrain [21, 75]. This algorithm uses co-evolution of multi-populations to avoid falling into the local optimal solution. Paterson et al. [70] used another heuristic algorithm, the great deluge algorithm, to optimize the robustness of scale-free networks. In each iteration of this algorithm, when the robustness is greater than a certain threshold, the network is accepted and the threshold increases over time. The experimental results show that the optimization effect of the algorithm is greatly improved compared with the simulated annealing algorithm. In 2018, Rong et al. [71] proposed an edge classification method, which divides the edges in the network into valid edges, invalid edges and flexible edges. And a heuristic robustness optimization algorithm is proposed that changes the connection relationship of the same type of edges by adjusting the number of each type of edges while keeping the node degree distribution unchanged. The simulations show that the robustness optimization effect of the algorithm is better than the memetic algorithm when the network size is less than 1000 nodes.

(2) *Strategies with practical requirements as robustness metric*

The above-mentioned robustness optimization strategies of scale-free networks are mostly designed with robustness metric based on the largest connected component of the network. In other practical networks, the robustness is often measured according to the actual application scenarios and functional requirements of the network. In 2011, Zhao et al. [64] used supply availability, network connectivity and delivery-efficiency as measures of robustness in supply and distribution networks. Meanwhile, they also proposed a new rewiring method called randomized local rewiring to optimize the robustness of a military logistic and a retailer's distribution network with scale-free properties. The results show that the optimized network structure is more robust to both random and malicious attacks. In the topology evolution algorithm, some clustering and self-organizing methods have received extensive attentions, and they have made great progress in the topology optimization and energy efficient utilization. In 2013, Zheng et al. [66] used bayesian game clustering algorithm to achieve a uniform clustering, and carried out the evolution of scale-free networks among cluster heads according to random walk. In the process of topology evolution, the residual energy, node fitness, node saturation and communication range of the nodes are taken into account. And the generated heterogeneous WSN model is very uniform in degree distribution. When this model dose not strictly follow a power law distribution, it will have a better survivability.

The large-scale WSNs have more stringent requirements for energy consumption and topology robustness. The more important the nodes in the network, the more traffic will be delivered and aggregated. Therefore, these nodes consume more energy, causing node failures and affecting network topology connectivity. To tackle this problem, Peng et al. [68] proposed two self-organizing schemes, energy-aware common neighbor scheme (ECN) and energy-aware low potential-degree common neighbor scheme (ELDCN), which balance the degree and energy consumption of the nodes according to the intrinsic characteristics of the large-scale WSNs, the topology information of the common neighbors, such as potential degree. These methods can construct clustering-based and scale-free-inspired large scale network against cyber-attacks. However, the ELDCN is more robust to malicious attacks due to its hub-nodes without more links.

In order to balance the energy consumption and fault tolerance, Hu et al. [72] proposed a regular hexagonal-based clustering scheme and a scale-free network topology evolution mechanism in 2018. Their work exploits the synergy between reliable clustering schemes and topology evolution to make network structure tolerate energy exhaustion and random failures.

      Robustness optimization of network structure has become a critical research field, and the complex network theory has been widely used. Researchers and scholars use different heuristic and optimization algorithms to enhance the robustness of network structure. These strategies have different performances for different types of networks such as power grids, transportation networks and wireless networks. The network structure needs to be more accurately modeled, and the more suitable robustness optimization methods considered different attack strategies should be designed. And the distributed robustness optimization of network structure will become an important research direction.

References

1. Bauer, D., Boesch, F., Suffel, C., & Tindell, R (1981). Connectivity extremal problems and the design of reliable probabilistic networks. In *The Theory and Application of Graphs* (pp. 89–98).
2. Harary, F. (1983). Conditional connectivity. *Networks, 13*(3), 347–357.
3. Fiedler, M. (1973). Algebraic connectivity of graphs. *Czechoslovak Mathematical Journal, 23*(2):298–305.
4. Jamakovic, A., & Uhlig, S. (2007). Influence of the network structure on robustness. In *2007 15th IEEE International Conference on Networks* (pp. 278–283). New York: IEEE.
5. Wu, J., Barahona, M., Tan, Y.-J., & Deng, H.-Z. (2011). Spectral measure of structural robustness in complex networks. *IEEE Transactions on Systems, Man, and Cybernetics-Part A: Systems and Humans, 41*(6):1244–1252.
6. Schneider, C. M., Moreira, A. A., Andrade, J. S., Havlin, S., & Herrmann, H. J. (2011). Mitigation of malicious attacks on networks. *Proceedings of the National Academy of Sciences, 108*(10):3838–3841.
7. Li, R., Yu, J. X., Huang, X., Cheng, H., & Shang, Z. (2014). Measuring the impact of mvc attack in large complex networks. *Information Sciences, 278*, 685–702.
8. Mishkovski, I., Biey, M., & Kocarev, L. (2011). Vulnerability of complex networks. *Communications in Nonlinear Science and Numerical Simulation, 16*(1):341–349.
9. Tizghadam, A., & Leongarcia, A. (2010). Autonomic traffic engineering for network robustness. *IEEE Journal on Selected Areas in Communications, 28*(1):39–50.
10. Scellato, S., Leontiadis, I., Mascolo, C., Basu, P., & Zafer, M. (2013). Evaluating temporal robustness of mobile networks. *IEEE Transactions on Mobile Computing, 12*(1), 105–117.
11. Koç, Y., Warnier, M., Kooij, R. E., & Brazier, F. M. T. (2013). An entropy-based metric to quantify the robustness of power grids against cascading failures. *Safety Science, 59*:126–134.
12. Koc, Y., Warnier, M., Van Mieghem, P., Kooij, R. E., & Brazier, F. M. T. (2014). The impact of the topology on cascading failures in a power grid model. *Physica A: Statistical Mechanics and Its Applications, 402*:169–179.
13. Cuadra, L., Salcedo-Sanz, S., Del Ser, J., Jiménez-Fernández, S., & Geem, Z. (2015). A critical review of robustness in power grids using complex networks concepts. *Energies, 8*(9), 9211–9265.
14. Albert, R., Jeong, H., & Barabasi, A.. Error and attack tolerance of complex networks. *Nature, 406*(6794):378–382.
15. Callaway, D. S., Newman, M. E. J., Strogatz, S. H., & Watts, D. J. (2000). Network robustness and fragility: Percolation on random graphs. *Physical Review Letters, 85*(25):5468–5471.
16. Cohen, R., Erez, K., Benavraham, D., & Havlin, S. (2001). Breakdown of the internet under intentional attack. *Physical Review Letters, 86*(16):3682–3685.

17. Cohen, R., Erez, K., ben Avraham, D., & Havlin, S. (2000). Resilience of the internet to random breakdowns. *Physical Review Letters, 85*:4626–4628.
18. Wu, J., Deng, H., Tan, Y., & Zhu, D. (2007). Vulnerability of complex networks under intentional attack with incomplete information. *Journal of Physics A, 40*(11):2665–2671.
19. Zeng, A., & Liu, W. (2012). Enhancing network robustness against malicious attacks. *Physical Review E, 85*(6):066130.
20. Kasthurirathna, D., Piraveenan, M., & Thedchanamoorthy, G. (2013). On the influence of topological characteristics on robustness of complex networks. *Journal of Artificial Intelligence and Soft Computing Research, 3*(2):89–100.
21. Qiu, T., Liu, J., Si, W., Han, M., Ning, H., & Atiquzzaman, M. (2017). A data-driven robustness algorithm for the internet of things in smart cities. *IEEE Communications Magazine, 55*(12), 18–23.
22. Louzada, V. H. P., Daolio, F., Herrmann, H. J., & Tomassini, M. (2013). Smart rewiring for network robustness. *Journal of Complex networks, 1*(2):150–159.
23. Zhou, M., & Liu, J. (2016). A two-phase multiobjective evolutionary algorithm for enhancing the robustness of scale-free networks against multiple malicious attacks. *IEEE Transactions on Cybernetics, 47*(2):539–552.
24. Cohen, R., & Havlin, S. (2010). *Complex networks: Structure, robustness and function.* Cambridge: Cambridge University Press.
25. Watts, D. J., & Strogatz, S. H. (1998). Collective dynamics of small-worldnetworks. *Nature, 393*(6684):440–442.
26. Helmy, A. (2003). Small worlds in wireless networks. *IEEE Communications Letters, 7*(10):490–492.
27. Dixit, S., Yanmaz, E., & Tonguz, O. K. (2005). On the design of self-organized cellular wireless networks. *IEEE Communications Magazine, 43*(7):86–93.
28. Brust, M. R., Ribeiro, C. H. C., Turgut, D., & Rothkugel, S. (2010). Lswtc: A local small-world topology control algorithm for backbone-assisted mobile ad hoc networks. In *IEEE Local Computer Network Conference* (pp. 144–151).
29. Tan, M., Yang, T., Chen, X., Yang, G., Zhu, G., Holme, P., & Zhao, J. (2018). A game-theoretic approach to optimize ad hoc networks inspired by small-world network topology. *Physica A: Statistical Mechanics and its Applications, 494*:129–139.
30. Hawick, K. A., & James, H. A. (2010). Small-world effects in wireless agent sensor networks. *International Journal of Wireless and Mobile Computing, 4*(3):155–164.
31. Guidoni, D. L., Mini, R. A. F., & Loureiro, A. A. F. (2010). On the design of resilient heterogeneous wireless sensor networks based on small world concepts. *Computer Networks, 54*(8):1266–1281.
32. Guidoni, D. L., Mini, R. A. F., & Loureiro, A. A. F. (2012). Applying the small world concepts in the design of heterogeneous wireless sensor networks. *IEEE Communications Letters, 16*(7):953–955.
33. Liu, L., Qi, X., Xue, J., & Xie, M. (2014). A topology construct and control model with small-world and scale-free concepts for heterogeneous sensor networks. *International Journal of Distributed Sensor Networks, 10*(3):374251.
34. Huang, R., Chu, X., Zhang, J., & Hu, Y. H. (2017). Scale-free topology optimization for software-defined wireless sensor networks: A cyber-physical system. *International Journal of Distributed Sensor Networks, 13*(6):1550147717713626.
35. Toyonaga, S., Kominami, D., & Murata, M. (2015). Brain-inspired method for constructing a robust virtual wireless sensor network. In *2015 International Conference on Computing and Network Communications (CoCoNet)* (pp. 59–65). New York: IEEE.
36. Luo, D., Qiu, T., Deonauth, N., & Zhao, A. (2015). A small world model for improving robustness of heterogeneous networks. In *2015 IEEE Global Conference on Signal and Information Processing (GlobalSIP)* (pp. 849–852). New York: IEEE.
37. Qiu, T., Luo, D., Xia, F., Deonauth, N., Si, W., & Tolba, A. (2016). A greedy model with small world for improving the robustness of heterogeneous internet of things. *Computer Networks, 101*:127–143.

38. Huang, W.-Q., Zhuang, X.-T., & Yao, S. (2009). A network analysis of the chinese stock market. *Physica A: Statistical Mechanics and its Applications, 388*(14):2956–2964.
39. Li, X., Wang, Q., & Jia, S. (2017). Analysis of topological properties of complex network of chinese stock based on copula tail correlation. In *2017 International Conference on Service Systems and Service Management* (pp. 1–6). New York: IEEE.
40. Zhang, W., & Zhuang, X. (2019). The stability of Chinese stock network and its mechanism. *Physica A: Statistical Mechanics and its Applications, 515*:748–761.
41. Jin, Y., Zhang, Q., & Li, S.-P. (2016). Topological properties and community detection of venture capital network: Evidence from China. *Physica A: Statistical Mechanics and Its Applications, 442*:300–311.
42. Pagani, G. A., & Aiello, M. (2013). The power grid as a complex network: A survey. *Physica A: Statistical Mechanics and its Applications, 392*(11):2688–2700.
43. Ding, M., & Han, P. (2006). Reliability assessment to large-scale power grid based on small-world topological model. In *2006 International Conference on Power System Technology* (pp. 1–5). New York: IEEE.
44. Guo, W., Wang, H., & Wu, Z. (2018). Robustness analysis of complex networks with power decentralization strategy via flow-sensitive centrality against cascading failures. *Physica A: Statistical Mechanics and Its Applications, 494*:186–199.
45. Pepyne, D. L. (2007). Topology and cascading line outages in power grids. *Journal of Systems Science and Systems Engineering, 16*(2):202–221.
46. Wang, J.-W., & Rong, L.-L. (2011). Robustness of the western united states power grid under edge attack strategies due to cascading failures. *Safety Science, 49*(6):807–812.
47. Wang, X., Koç, Y., Kooij, R. E., & Van Mieghem, P. (2015). A network approach for power grid robustness against cascading failures. In *2015 7th International Workshop on Reliable Networks Design and Modeling (RNDM)* (pp. 208–214). New York: IEEE.
48. Colak, I., Sagiroglu, S., Fulli, G., Yesilbudak, M., & Covrig, C.-F. (2016). A survey on the critical issues in smart grid technologies. *Renewable and Sustainable Energy Reviews, 54*:396–405.
49. Cuadra, L., Pino, M., Nieto-Borge, J., & Salcedo-Sanz, S. (2017). Optimizing the structure of distribution smart grids with renewable generation against abnormal conditions: A complex networks approach with evolutionary algorithms. *Energies, 10*(8):1097.
50. Buldyrev, S. V., Parshani, R., Paul, G., Stanley, H. E., & Havlin, S. (2010). Catastrophic cascade of failures in interdependent networks. *Nature, 464*(7291):1025.
51. Chai, W. K., Kyritsis, V., Katsaros, K. V., & Pavlou, G. (2016). Resilience of interdependent communication and power distribution networks against cascading failures. In *2016 IFIP Networking Conference (IFIP Networking) and Workshops* (pp. 37–45). New York: IEEE.
52. Kang, W., Zhu, P., & Hu, G. (2018). Cascading failure based on load redistribution of a smart grid with different coupling modes. In *International Conference on Computational Science* (pp. 328–340). New York: Springer.
53. Derrible, S., & Kennedy, C. (2010). The complexity and robustness of metro networks. *Physica A: Statistical Mechanics and its Applications, 389*(17):3678–3691.
54. Zhang, D.-M., Du, F., Huang, H., Zhang, F., Ayyub, B. M., & Beer, M. (2018). Resiliency assessment of urban rail transit networks: Shanghai metro as an example. *Safety Science, 106*:230–243.
55. Masucci, A. P., Stanilov, K., & Batty, M. (2014). Exploring the evolution of london's street network in the information space: A dual approach. *Physical Review E, 89*(1):012805.
56. Meng, X., Jia, L., Xie, J., Qin, Y., & Xu, J. (2010). Complex characteristic analysis of passenger train flow network. In *2010 Chinese Control and Decision Conference* (pp. 2533–2536). New York: IEEE.
57. Huang, A., Michael Zhang, H., Guan, W., Yang, Y., & Zong, G. (2015). Cascading failures in weighted complex networks of transit systems based on coupled map lattices. In *Mathematical Problems in Engineering, 2015*.

58. Suto, K., Nishiyama, H., Kato, N., Nakachi, T., Fujii, T., & Takahara, A. (2013). THUP: A P2P network robust to churn and dos attack based on bimodal degree distribution. *IEEE Journal on Selected Areas in Communications, 31*(9):247–256.
59. Tanizawa, T., Paul, G., Cohen, R., Havlin, S., & Stanley, H. E. (2005). Optimization of network robustness to waves of targeted and random attacks. *Physical Review E, 71*(4):047101.
60. Sonawane, A. R., Bhattacharyay, A., Santhanam, M. S., & Ambika, G. (2012). Evolving networks with bimodal degree distribution. *The European Physical Journal B, 85*(4):118.
61. Xiao, S., Xiao, G., Cheng, T. H., Ma, S., Fu, X., & Soh, H. (2010). Robustness of scale-free networks under rewiring operations. *EPL (Europhysics Letters), 89*(3):38002.
62. Herrmann, H. J., Schneider, C. M., Moreira, A. A., Andrade, J. S. Jr., & Havlin, S. (2011). Onion-like network topology enhances robustness against malicious attacks. *Journal of Statistical Mechanics: Theory and Experiment, 2011*(01):P01027.
63. Buesser, P., Daolio, F., & Tomassini, M. (2011). Optimizing the robustness of scale-free networks with simulated annealing. In *International Conference on Adaptive and Natural Computing Algorithms* (pp. 167–176). New York: Springer.
64. Zhao, K., Kumar, A., & Yen, J. (2010). Achieving high robustness in supply distribution networks by rewiring. *IEEE Transactions on Engineering Management, 58*(2):347–362.
65. Tanizawa, T., Havlin, S., & Stanley, H. E. (2012). Robustness of onionlike correlated networks against targeted attacks. *Physical Review E, 85*(4):046109.
66. Zheng, G., & Liu, Q. (2013). Scale-free topology evolution for wireless sensor networks. *Computers & Electrical Engineering, 39*(6):1779–1788.
67. Zhou, M., & Liu, J. (2014). A memetic algorithm for enhancing the robustness of scale-free networks against malicious attacks. *Physica A: Statistical Mechanics and Its Applications, 410*:131 143.
68. Peng, H., Si, S., Awad, M. K., Zhang, N., Zhao, H., & Shen, X. S. (2016). Toward energy-efficient and robust large-scale wsns: a scale-free network approach. *IEEE Journal on Selected Areas in Communications, 34*(12):4035–4047.
69. Qiu, T., Zhao, A., Xia, F., Si, W., & Wu, D. O. (2017). Rose: Robustness strategy for scale-free wireless sensor networks. *IEEE/ACM Transactions on Networking, 25*(5):2944–2959.
70. Paterson, J., & Ombuki-Berman, B. (2018). Optimizing scale-free network robustness with the great deluge algorithm. In *International Conference on Industrial, Engineering and Other Applications of Applied Intelligent Systems* (pp. 434–446). New York: Springer.
71. Rong, L., & Liu, J. (2018). A heuristic algorithm for enhancing the robustness of scale-free networks based on edge classification. *Physica A: Statistical Mechanics and its Applications, 503*:503–515.
72. Hu, S., & Li, G. (2018). Fault-tolerant clustering topology evolution mechanism of wireless sensor networks. *IEEE Access, 6*:28085–28096.
73. Newman, M. E. J. (2002). Assortative mixing in networks. *Physical Review Letters, 89*(20):208701.
74. Liu, J., Qiu, T., Zhang, S., Qu, W., & Sun, Q. (2018). A three dimensions deployment model for internet of things. In *2018 IEEE 22nd International Conference on Computer Supported Cooperative Work in Design ((CSCWD))* (pp. 859–863). New York: IEEE.
75. Qiu, T., Liu, J., Si, W., & Wu, D. O. (2019). Robustness optimization scheme with multi-population co-evolution for scale-free wireless sensor networks. In *IEEE/ACM Transactions on Networking, 2019*

Chapter 3
Robustness Optimization Based on Self-Organization

This chapter discusses the robustness optimization problem of the network topology from the perspective of self-organization, which is the first step to construct a topology robustness optimization framework. Massive sensor nodes are deployed to establish a self-organizing network with neighbor nodes, and transmit the collected data to the data center for analysis through the multi-hop mode. How to make nodes spontaneously connect to high-quality nodes within the communication range is a problem to be studied in this chapter. According to the characteristics of node self-organization communication, this chapter introduces solutions to improve network robustness from three aspects: path planning, topology construction, and time synchronization.

3.1 Path Planning with The Greedy Principles

There are many types of heterogeneous networks in IoT [1]. How to make these networks run efficiently and stably is a hot research [2], especially for lightweight networks with limited energy. It is particularly important to study the topology robustness so that it can withstand node failures. The small world model in complex networks [3] has been proven to be an effective method for optimizing network topology. Aiming at the heterogeneous network composed of sensor nodes and sink nodes, this work designs and implements a robust and efficient topology based on the small world model, and long-range edges are introduced to implement shortcuts between nodes [4]. By judging the importance of nodes, a greedy model (GMSW) is proposed to plan the path [5]. GMSW uses the greedy principles for topological staining, and constructs a shortcut addition strategy by the local importance of nodes. This algorithm is suitable for heterogeneous topologies containing multiple

T. Qiu et al., *Robustness Optimization for IoT Topology*,
https://doi.org/10.1007/978-981-16-9609-1_3

types of nodes. GMSW can improve the efficiency of network data transmission and reduce the energy consumption of super nodes, thereby prolonging the life cycle of the network.

3.1.1 Overview of Topological Path Planning

The labeled sensing devices in the IoT are randomly deployed to collect environmental parameters, and the communication capability of these sensor nodes depends on the transmit power of the wireless transmission module. Therefore, in order to add shortcuts in the IoT, other devices must be used to increase the communication range. For example, Sharma et al. [6] introduced a few wired long range edges, and Dousse et al. [7] implemented remote communication through fixed base station. However, both wired connection and fixed base station will bring huge cost pressure. Due to the upgrading of hardware equipment, a better method is to equip the sensor nodes with different transmission power modules [8]. The node can not only work like a traditional ordinary node, but also achieve remote communication. However, long-distance communication inevitably bring greater energy consumption, which requires these high-load nodes to be equipped with better hardware. Guidoni et al. [9] referred to nodes with multiple transmission powers, more energy and stronger storage capacity as super nodes. The addition of shortcuts in this work is also based on the super nodes in the IoT.

Due to the high cost and energy consumption of super nodes, only a small number of super nodes are deployed in the IoT, while most other nodes are ordinary nodes. This makes how to efficiently use these super nodes become a problem. In the Random Addition Model (RAM) [3], shortcuts are added randomly. Considering the communication mode of the IoT (sink nodes are both the starting point and the end point of data transmission), it is not a good method. Guidoni et al. [10] proposed a Directed Angulation toward the Sink node Model (DASM), which adds shortcuts in the sector space toward the sink node and improves the quality of shortcuts. But it may construct some useless shortcuts at the two endpoints with few neighbors, although the orientations of these shortcuts satisfy the specified angle. Therefore, this section proposes a simpler and more efficient model GMSW by defining the local importance of nodes, which can greatly reduce the average shortest path length by adding a few shortcuts, and improve the robustness of network topology.

Node importance is a general concept, which has different measurement methods in many studies [11]. Callaway et al. [12] proposed that the importance of a node is related to the degree on this node. This is a simple and efficient method but not very accurate. Then, Newman [13] proposed a novel concept called "betweenness" to judge the node importance. On the basis of the previous works, Fang Hu et al. [14] proposed a new multi-index method for evaluating the node importance called Linear Discriminant Analysis (LDA), which can conduct a comprehensive multi-dimensional comparative analysis. The node importance judgments in the above works require global topology information, and consume a lot of node energy. Due to the limited battery capacity of wireless sensor devices in the IoT, the above methods make the node fail prematurely and reduce the stability of the network. Therefore, GMSW designed a metrics to measure the node importance with less energy consumption based on local information, which is called local importance.

3.1.2 Description of Greedy Principles

In the sensing layer of the IoT, the decisive factor to measure the node importance is the distance between the node and sink node in the topology. The reason is that the sensor nodes responsible for data collection will eventually transmit information to the sink node. When the initial energy of node is the same, the node close to the sink node has a greater probability of forwarding data from other nodes, which means that the node has more chances to appear on the data forwarding path of other nodes in the network. Based on the above considerations, two greedy principles are proposed to measure the importance of different nodes in the topology. The main reason for naming "greedy principle" is that greedy algorithm is used to determine the importance of neighbor nodes. That is, every choice is the local optimal solution. The details of two greedy principles are shown in Figs. 3.1 and 3.2. The "main" node is the super node, which needs to select a neighbor node as the next hop.

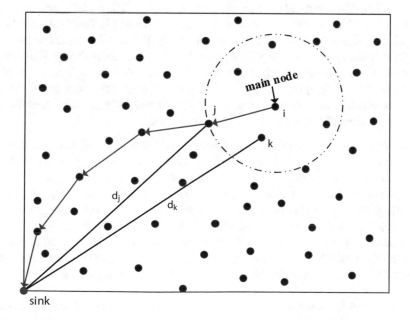

Fig. 3.1 Minimum hop route principle

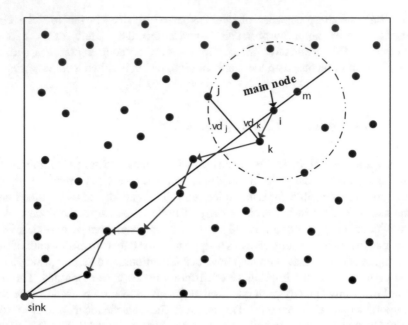

Fig. 3.2 Minimum distance route principle

(i) *The neighbor node closest to the sink node is preferentially selected.* The reason is that the number of hops for data forwarding is positively correlated with the straight-line distance to the sink node. The smaller the distance is, the fewer hops are theoretically forwarded. In Fig. 3.1, among all neighbors of the main node i, node j is closest to the sink node, that is, d_j has the smallest value. Therefore, node j is selected as the next hop. According to this greedy principle, the main node i can send data to the sink with the minimum number of hops through the red path. Proof is as follows.

Proof Assuming that the perception radius of node in the topology is r. Both nodes j and k can exchange data with the main node i, and $d_j < d_k$. MH_{js} and MH_{ks} respectively represent the minimum number of hops from nodes j and k to the sink node under ideal conditions, that is, $MH_{js} = \lceil d_j/r \rceil$ and $MH_{ks} = \lceil d_k/r \rceil$. Therefore, the hop number of node i forwarding data to sink node through node j is $\lceil d_j/r \rceil + 1$. For neighbor node k, the above value is $\lceil d_k/r \rceil + 1$. Since d_j is less than d_k, then $\lceil d_j/r \rceil + 1 \leq \lceil d_k/r \rceil + 1$. That is, the sink node can be reached with fewer hops through neighbor node j. $MH_{is} = \lceil d_{min}/r \rceil + 1$, d_{min} indicates the shortest straight-line distance between the neighbors of main node and the sink node. □

(ii) *The neighbor node closest to the straight line between sink node and main node is preferentially selected.* In other words, when the straight-line distances from multiple neighbor nodes to the sink node are equal, the node with the minimum vertical distance vd to the line has higher priority. The purpose is to shorten the Euclidean distance of the data transmission path. In Fig. 3.2,

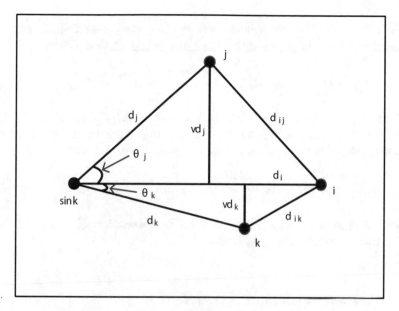

Fig. 3.3 Comparison of two path lengths under different vertical distances

among the neighbors of the main node i, $d_j = d_k$ and $vd_k < vd_j$, neighbor node k is chosen as the next hop. Compared with the second greedy principle, the first greedy principle is given priority. For example, the node m in Fig. 3.2. Even though $vd_m = 0$, node m will not be preferred since d_m is greater than d_j. According to this greedy principle, the local optimal solution is selected in turn, and the transmission path with the minimum Euclidean distance can be obtained. Proof is given below.

Proof The precondition is that nodes j and k satisfy $d_j = d_k$ and $vd_k < vd_j$, then the Euclidean distance between the main node and the sink node through j is $d_j + d_{ij}$, and the Euclidean distance through k is $d_k + d_{ik}$. To illustrate the priority of choosing node k as the next hop, $d_k + d_{ik} < d_j + d_{ij}$ needs to be proven. Since $d_j = d_k$, it only needs to verify $d_{ik} < d_{ij}$. The mathematical model shown in Fig. 3.3 is constructed to solve the above problems.   □

According to the label of the straight line, the angle formed by d_j and d_i is set as θ_j, and the angle formed by d_k and d_i is θ_k. Based on the cosines function, d_{ij} and d_{ik} can be expressed as the following forms.

$$d_{ij} = \sqrt{d_i^2 + d_j^2 - 2 * d_i * d_j * cos\theta_j} \tag{3.1}$$

$$d_{ik} = \sqrt{d_i^2 + d_k^2 - 2 * d_i * d_k * cos\theta_k} \tag{3.2}$$

Since $cos\theta_j = \sqrt{1 - sin^2\theta_j}$ and $cos\theta_k = \sqrt{1 - sin^2\theta_k}$, the following equation can be obtained by making the difference between Eqs. (3.1) and (3.2).

$$d_{ik}^2 - d_{ij}^2 = 2 * d_i * d_k * (\sqrt{1 - sin^2\theta_j} - \sqrt{1 - sin^2\theta_k}) \qquad (3.3)$$

Combining the sine function with Fig. 3.3, $sin\theta_j = vd_j/d_j$ and $sin\theta_k = vd_k/d_k$. Since $d_j = d_k$ and $vd_j > vd_k$, $sin\theta_j > sin\theta_k$ is true. Note that the values of $sin\theta_j$ and $sin\theta_k$ range from 0 to 1. The following result can be concluded.

$$(\sqrt{1 - sin^2\theta_j})^2 - (\sqrt{1 - sin^2\theta_k})^2 = sin^2\theta_k - sin^2\theta_j < 0 \qquad (3.4)$$

According to the result of Eq. (3.4), it can be known that $d_{ik}^2 - d_{ij}^2 < 0$ in Eq. (3.3) is true. Therefore, $d_{ik} < d_{ij}$ is proved. $\square$

3.1.3   Topological Staining Operation

In order to add shortcuts, this section simplifies the initial network topology by retaining the connection between nodes and some influential neighbor nodes. This process is called topological staining. Connections that need to be preserved are colored, while uncolored connections are deleted. Therefore, it is the most important to determine which neighbor nodes have greater influence. Combining the above two greedy principles, this section gives the definition of the influence coefficient of node v in the neighbor list.

Definition 3.1 The *influence coefficient (IC)* of one neighbor v in the network is defined as a linear combination of two greedy principles.

$$IC_v = 1 - [\alpha * \frac{d_v}{\sum d_v} + (1 - \alpha) * \frac{vd_v}{\sum vd_v}] \qquad (3.5)$$

As shown in Eq. (3.5), d_v is the straight-line distance between the sink node and the neighbor node v, and vd_v is the vertical distance between the neighbor node v and the straight line that passes through the main node i and the sink node. α is a sliding factor, which is used to adjust the importance of the two greedy principles. $\sum d_v$ and $\sum vd_v$ represent the sum of straight-line and vertical distances of all neighbors, respectively.

By calculating the ICs of all neighbor nodes, nodes are arranged in descending order. "Topological staining" means that we select n neighbor nodes with the larger IC and stain their connections with the main node i in different colors. Figure 3.4 shows a process of topological staining. By randomly deploying 500 sensor nodes in an area of $1000 * 1000 \, m^2$, these nodes form the initial topology shown in Fig. 3.4a

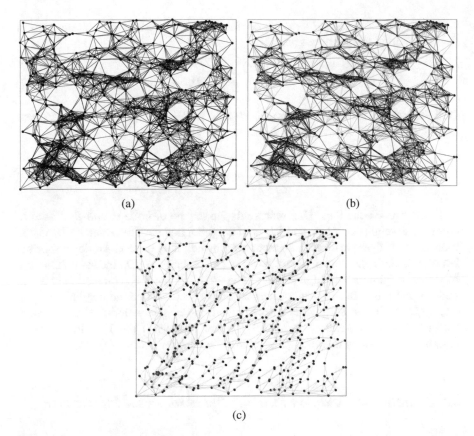

Fig. 3.4 The process of topological staining ($n = 2$). (**a**) Initial topology. (**b**) Stained topology. (**c**) Simplified topology

through self-organization. The location of the sink node is fixed and marked in red. The perception range of each node is $100\ m$, and it is connected to all neighbor nodes. When $n = 2$, Fig. 3.4b shows the effect of staining the initial topology. Each node selects two neighbor nodes according to IC and marks them as light green, that is, each light green line represents a stained edges. Figure 3.4c is the simplified topological subgraph after only the stained edges are retained.

According to the results of topological staining, this section proposes the *first importance degree (FID)* and *the second importance degree (SID)* of node. On this basis, the *local importance degree (LID)* of neighbor v is defined, which is an important criterion for the subsequent shortcut addition.

Definition 3.2 The *first importance degree (FID)* of one node v is defined as the node's degree after staining.

$$FID_v = De_v \tag{3.6}$$

Definition 3.3 The *second importance degree (SID)* of one node v is the sum of FID of k ordinary neighbor nodes.

$$SID_v = \sum FID_k \tag{3.7}$$

Definition 3.4 The *local importance degree (LID)* of one node v is a linear combination of FID and SID of k ordinary neighbor nodes.

$$LID_v = \beta * \frac{FID_v}{\sum FID_v} + (1 - \beta) * \frac{SID_v}{\sum SID_v} \tag{3.8}$$

In the above equations, De_v represents the degree of node v, and β is used to control the weights of FID_v and SID_v of neighbor node v. The larger FID_v is, the more stained edges are directly connected to the neighbor node v. Adding a shortcut between nodes i and v can benefit more nodes. A larger SID_v means that node v has many neighbors with high degrees. The establishment of a connection between nodes i and v improves the robustness of the shortcut. When the neighbor v fails, alternative node can be quickly selected from the neighbor node list to maintain the efficiency of shortcuts. β is a sliding factor between 0 and 1, and its value is determined according to the specific network topology.

3.1.4 Shortcuts Addition Strategy Based on Local Importance

Suppose the sink node in a fixed position broadcasts its coordinate information to all nodes in the topology. Super nodes and ordinary nodes in the topology are randomly deployed, and can obtain their own location information. In their communication range, super nodes select neighbor nodes to add some shortcuts with a probability p, which is related to the LID of the node. However, the calculation of LID depends on the topological staining results. Therefore, the topology staining process needs to be completed in the initialization phase.

Note that when the super nodes are stained, the neighbor super nodes located below the sink node have a greater probability of being retained. The reason is that the distance between super nodes and sink node is much smaller than other ordinary nodes, which can obtain a larger IC. Therefore, we only select the optimal solution in the staining queue where the main node is the super node. This ensures the efficiency of shortcuts, and the value of n can also control the maximum number of shortcuts added between super nodes. In addition, we maintain a *local importance degree threshold (LIDT)* for each super node. Only when the LID of neighbor node is larger than $LIDT$, it is allowed to establish a shortcut with main node. The specific calculation method is as follows.

$$LIDT = LID_{min} + \gamma * (LID_{max} - LID_{min}) \tag{3.9}$$

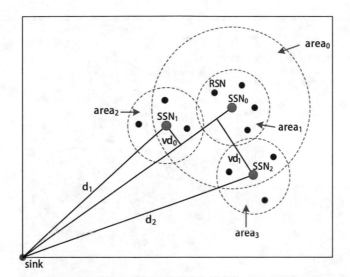

Fig. 3.5 The strategy of shortcuts addition

The value of $LIDT$ is determined by the sliding factor γ. By setting the value of γ (that is from 0 to 1), we can control $LIDT$ to change between LID_{min} and LID_{max}. Figure 3.5 further illustrates the process of adding shortcuts. SSN_i and RSN represent the super node i and ordinary node, respectively. The maximum communication area of SSN_0 is expressed as $area_0$, and $area_1$ contains all RSN neighbor nodes of SSN_0. In addition, $area_2$ and $area_3$ contain all RSN neighbor nodes of SSN_1 and SSN_2, and the SSN neighbor nodes of SSN_0 are located between $area_0$ and $area_1$. Since d_1 and d_2 are much smaller than the distance between all $RSNs$ in $area_1$ and the sink node, when $n \geq 2$, SSN_1 and SSN_2 must be in the staining node set of SSN_0. Before adding the shortcuts, we need to calculate the LID_1 and LID_2 of SSN_1 and SSN_2, and obtain the $LIDT$ of SSN_0 by the neighbor nodes and parameter γ. When SSN_i is in the staining set of SSN_0 and LID_i of SSN_i is greater than $LIDT$, a shortcut can be established between nodes SSN_0 and SSN_i.

Figure 3.6 is the specific example to find the optimal solution by using this strategy, which gives the stained topological subgraph when $n = 2$. When super node i performs the shortcut addition operation, there are three neighbor super nodes m, j and k in its communication range. According to Fig. 3.6, $FIDs$ of three super nodes are 4, 6 and 6. Meanwhile, $SIDs$ of three super nodes are 17, 21 and 18. When $\beta = 0.8$, the above data are substituted into Eq. (3.8) to calculate LID, that is, $LID_m = 0.26071$, $LID_j = 0.3750$, $LID_k = 0.36428$. Since $n = 2$, node m is not included in the staining queue of node i. Therefore, node m is not considered for shortcut addition. The value of γ is set as 0.8, it can be seen from Eq. (3.9) that $LIDT$ of node i is $LID_k + 0.5 * (LID_j - LID_k) = 0.36964$. Due to $LID_j > LIDT > LID_k$, the shortcut e' between nodes i and j is added in

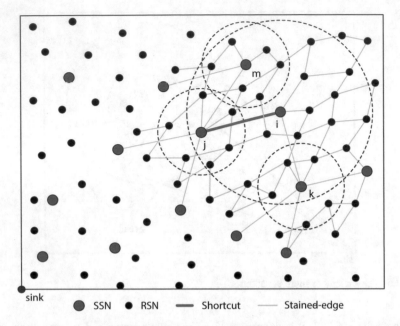

Fig. 3.6 Description of shortcuts addition in the topology ($n = 2$)

preference. In addition, whether the shortcut e' can be added to the topology also depends on the probability p. The entire process of adding shortcuts does not end until all super nodes have been searched.

3.1.5 Performance Evaluation

We conduct an experimental analysis on the small-world characteristics and robustness of the GMSW model. RAM and DASM models are chosen for comparison. The reason is that GMSW and DASM models all use the "random reconnection method" from the RAM model to add shortcuts. In addition, GMSW and DASM have certain similarities. In the shortcut addition strategy, they all consider the direction angle, that is, the shortcut should be towards the sink node.

In order to intuitively compare the differences in topology optimization of multiple models, the topologies after adding shortcuts based on RAM, DASM, and GMSW models under a certain probability p are shown. A total of 500 sensor nodes included super nodes and ordinary nodes are deployed in an area of $1000 * 1000 \, \text{m}^2$, and the only one sink node is located in the lower left corner. The communication ranges of ordinary nodes and super nodes are 100 m and 300 m, respectively. Note that sink node also belongs to the super node. All experimental results are from the k ($k \geq 10$) simulations, and each topology is a connected graph. The values of different model parameters are listed below: in DASM model, $\theta = 30°$; in GMSW model, $\alpha = 0.8$, $\beta = 0.8$, $\gamma = 0.5$, and $n = 5$.

Figure 3.7a shows that the addition of shortcuts in the RAM model is random, and each blue line represents a shortcut. If a pair of super nodes are within communication range of each other, a shortcut can be established between them. Whether to add this shortcut depends entirely on the random probability p. Obviously, this is not a good shortcut addition strategy, because many useless shortcuts are introduced. Figure 3.7b is a shortcut addition strategy using the DASM model. The parameter θ is the angle between two straight lines. One straight line goes through the main node and sink node, and the other straight line is the shortcut. The smaller the value of θ is, the more the shortcut is biased towards the sink node. DASM is a better choice than RAM because the sink node is both the start and end points of data transmission in the IoT. Figure 3.7c shows the GMSW model. It can be seen that the shortcuts are also toward the sink node in the GMSW model. They are located in the area with dense nodes and show obvious clustering phenomenon. Through the

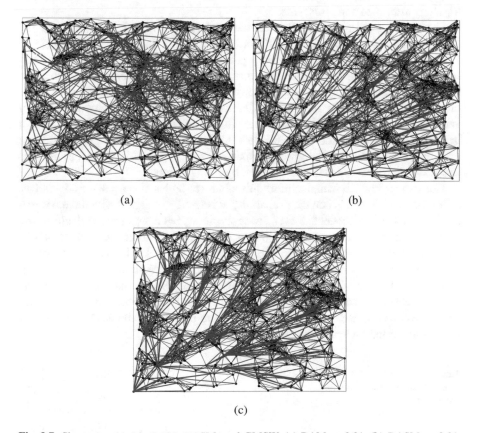

(a)   (b)

(c)

Fig. 3.7 Shortcuts added in RAM, DASM, and GMSW. (**a**) RAM, p=0.01. (**b**) DASM, p=0.01, $\theta = 30°$. (**c**) GMSW, p=0.01, n=5

comparative analysis of these three models, it can be seen that GMSW and DASM have certain similarities. The reason is that the two greedy principles in GMSW are both related to the location of the sink node. Compared with DASM, GMSW considers the importance of the nodes at both ends of the shortcut in the topology, not just the direction of the shortcut. In this case, DASM may choose a super node with small angle but sparse location to add a shortcut. However, GMSW picks out the nodes for constructing shortcuts according to the local importance of the nodes, so that the quality of the shortcuts is further improved. The number of shortcuts added by the three models with the probability p is shown in the Table 3.1.

Next, this section will conduct comparative experiments on the small-world characteristics of RAM, DASM and GMSW models. The shortest path of the network L and the network clustering coefficient C are used to measure the small-world characteristics of the network. $C(0)$ and $L(0)$ represent the value of the initial topology on two indicators. $C(p)$ and $L(p)$ are the values on two indicators after adding some shortcuts according to the probability p. By analyzing the values of $C(p)/C(0)$ and $L(p)/L(0)$, it can clearly reflect the impact on the entire network topology after the shortcut is added.

Figure 3.8 shows the variation curves of $C(p)/C(0)$ and $L(p)/L(0)$ of the three models when the shortcut addition probability p increases from 0.0001 to 1. It can be seen that as the probability p increases, all models can exhibit small-world characteristics, that is, they have a smaller average shortest path length and a larger network clustering coefficient. However, the decline rates of these two curves in different models are completely different. The reciprocal ratio of $C(p)/C(0)$ and $L(p)/L(0)$ is used to illustrate this situation. The specific results are shown in Tables 3.2 and 3.3 for $p = 0.1$ in GMSW, the reciprocal of $L(p)/L(0)$ is $1/0.29091 = 3.4375$. Therefore, compared to the initial topology, the average shortest path length of GMSW is reduced by 3.4375 times.

Combining Fig. 3.8 with the information in three tables, it can see the advantages of the GMSW model. When the probability p is fixed, compared with the other two models, the GMSW model achieves fewer shortcuts, but a larger network clustering coefficient and a smaller average shortest path length. This means that GMSW's shortcut addition strategy is more efficient, which can make the network topology easier to present and maintain the characteristics of the small world. For example, when $p = 0.01$, the GMSW model only introduces 294.04 shortcuts on average, but the clustering coefficient and average path length are reduced by 1.0271 times and 2.5705 times, respectively. These values are better than the RAM and DASM models under the same conditions.

Table 3.1 Number of shortcuts added with different probabilities p

p	RAM	DASM	GMSW
0.001	41.33	30.67	29.33
0.01	456.52	308.10	294.04
0.1	1094.27	516.33	483.67
1	2239.56	530.54	492.83

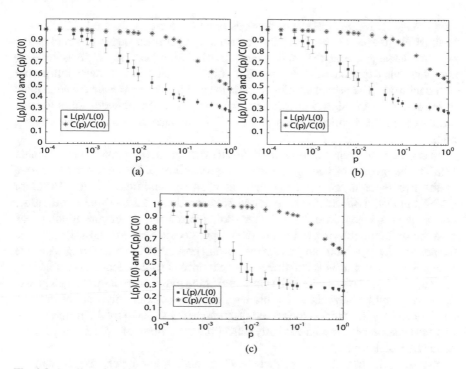

Fig. 3.8 Small-world characteristics on different models. (a) RAM. (b) DASM, $\theta = 30°$. (c) GMSW, n=5

Table 3.2 Reciprocal of $C(p)/C(0)$ with different probabilities p

p	RAM	DASM	GMSW
0.0001	1.0010	1.0006	1.0005
0.001	1.0134	1.0086	1.0072
0.01	1.0351	1.0316	1.0271
0.1	1.2066	1.1477	1.1059
1	2.0936	1.8207	1.7189

Table 3.3 Reciprocal of $L(p)/L(0)$ with different probabilities p

p	RAM	DASM	GMSW
0.0001	1.0020	1.0021	1.0022
0.001	1.1112	1.1744	1.3090
0.01	1.6454	1.7660	2.5705
0.1	2.5713	2.7764	3.4375
1	3.5014	3.5888	3.9809

The previous experiment shows that the GMSW model has good small-world characteristics. Then this section will continue to discuss the robustness of the GMSW model. This experiment no longer compares with RAM, but only chooses DASM. The reason is that Guidoni et al. [10] have compared DASM with RAM in previous work. Experimental results show that DASM has better robustness than RAM. Therefore, GMSW only needs to be compared with the DASM model to illustrate its robustness. Since the robustness experiment needs to simulate the network latency in the real data packet transmission process, $NS2$ is used to complete this experiment. Only one sink node is located in the lower left corner of the network. The packet sending node is located in the upper right corner, which is furthest from the sink node. So that more nodes in the network topology can participate in the data forwarding process. There is also only one packet sending node.

In addition, different from the small-world experiment, this experiment no longer restricts the process of adding shortcuts by probability p. In other words, as long as the two super nodes meet the shortcut addition conditions of the DASM or GMSW model, a shortcut can be added between them. Instead, the node failure rate p' is introduced. In order to better show the impact of network topology on data transmission, the simplest flood routing protocol is used to forward packets at the network layer, which can prevent the routing protocol from interfering with data transmission. The reason is that there is no influence of route selection on the result, as long as two nodes are within the communication range of each other, data packet forwarding can be carried out. In this way, the transmission efficiency of network data completely depends on the topology structure constructed by different models, and the experimental results can fully reflect the robustness of different topologies under the attack state.

In each simulation, the packet sending node periodically sends data to the sink node. As in the previous comparison experiment, results adopt $Latency(P')/Latency(0)$ to better reflect the impact of adding shortcuts on the whole network data transmission. Each simulation cycle is set to $120s$, and the packet sending node starts from $20s$ and sends a 512-bit data packet to the sink node every $10s$. Note that the $20s$ is to allow each model to have enough time to add shortcuts according to the addition strategy.

In order to verify the robustness of network topology, experiments use two different methods to generate network node failures, namely random network failures and malicious attacks. In random network failures, node failures are randomly generated in the entire network topology according to the probability p at intervals of $10s$. The failed node will lose all communication links. The malicious attack simulates the situation where the core backbone nodes in the real network topology are attacked by enemies or hacker groups, so the failure only occurs on the super nodes.

Figure 3.9 shows the change of data transmission latency of DASM and GMSW models under two different random failure probabilities p'. When $p' = 0.01$, there will be no large-scale super node failures. However, with the prolongation of the simulation time, the increase of failed nodes makes the transmission latency of DASM and GMSW gradually increase. When $p' = 0.1$, there will occasionally be a large-scale failure of the super node, which causes the obvious fluctuation of the network latency. On the whole, the robustness of the DASM and GMSW models under random failures is similar, and the data transmission latency is maintained

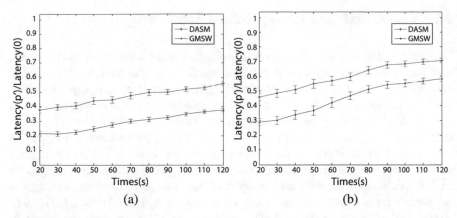

Fig. 3.9 Network data transmission latency under random failures. (a) $p' = 0.01$. (b) $p' = 0.1$

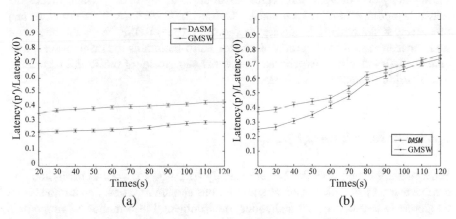

Fig. 3.10 Network data transmission latency under malicious attacks. (a) $p' = 0.01$. (b) $p' = 0.05$

at a low level. However, network latency of GMSM model is always smaller than DASM model. That is to say, GMSW model has better data transmission capability than DASM model under random failure. Figure 3.10 shows the network latency of different models under a malicious attack. Compared with the case of $p' = 0.01$, the network latency fluctuation at $p' = 0.05$ is larger, because the higher failure probability seriously destroys the shortcut constructed by the super nodes. Combining random failures and malicious attacks, we can see that the network topology constructed by GMSW model is more robust.

3.2 Construction of Highly Robust Topology

Section 3.1 discusses the path planning problem based on the small world model, and improves the robustness of network topology by constructing two greedy principles. In order to further construct the high robust topology, the properties of the IoT topology need to be studied in depth. The scale-free model in complex networks has good robustness against random attacks. This section first presents a novel modeling strategy to construct the scale-free topology, which takes into account the communication limitations of the nodes in the sensor network and the upper limit of the degree on each node. However, scale-free networks are easily damaged by malicious attacks, especially some important target nodes. Therefore, this section proposes a novel robustness enhancing algorithm for scale-free networks, namely ROSE [15]. For the initial scale-free network, ROSE rearranges the edges in the topology according to the degree distribution of the nodes, which makes the network topology similar to a stable "Onion-like" structure. This structure can effectively resist malicious attacks. At the same time, ROSE keeps the degree of node unchanged, and the optimized topology still maintains the original scale-free characteristics. Multiple experiments show the superiority of the ROSE algorithm. The algorithm details are as follows.

3.2.1 Research Background

Emerging applications in the IoT are usually based on network transmission and environmental perception, such as smart homes and smart cities. Sensor nodes can cooperate to monitor, detect and collect environmental information in geographic areas, and complete designated tasks autonomously. They transmit the collected data in a multi-hop form. However, due to the increase in the scale of devices and the ubiquity of network attacks, enhancing the robustness of large-scale network topologies has become a hot issue. Sensor nodes in the IoT are often deployed in complex natural environments, and their storage, communication, power and processing capabilities are limited. Therefore, the nodes are often damaged due to different reasons, for example, man-made damage, battery energy, software and hardware failures. We regard the phenomenon that network nodes are unusable due to external or self influence as the attacks on network topology. After a node is attacked, it loses not only the node itself, but also all the links connected with it. These damages to the topology are unpredictable. Figure 3.11 shows the node failure on the topology.

Figure 3.11a is the initial network topology. The black solid dots represent the nodes in the topology, and the blue solid lines refer to the corresponding connections. In Fig. 3.11b, suppose that the nodes N_3, N_4, N_5, N_6 and N_7 are destroyed due to network attacks, the remaining topology can still maintain good connectivity, and the network can continue to work normally. In Fig. 3.11c, it is

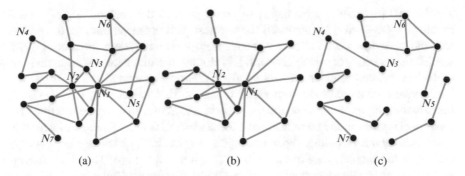

(a)   (b)   (c)

Fig. 3.11 Node failure in IoT

assumed that only a few nodes fail, such as N_1 and N_2. Because these two nodes have many edges, a large number of connections are lost when the two nodes fail. The network topology is divided into multiple small pieces and no longer connected, which seriously reduces the stability of the topology. The above example shows that the robustness of the topology is particularly fragile when some "important" nodes fail. In addition, the failure of a node will also increase the load of the neighbor node, because the tasks that need to be processed by this node will be assigned to its neighbor node. The increase of load leads to excessive energy consumption, which affects the survival time of node and causes cascading failure [16].

Attacks on the network topology are usually divided into random attacks and malicious attacks [17, 18]. In the actual deployment environment, network attacks are universal, and it needs to ensure that the network topology can maintain connectivity after being attacked. Of course, the connectivity of a fully connected network is not damaged. When any node fails, the remaining nodes can still be connected. However, the disadvantages of building such a network topology in the IoT are very obvious. There is a limit on the communication ranges of sensor nodes. In addition, full connection means that data packets are repeatedly forwarded, and the energy consumption of the node increases. Therefore, how to design and deploy a highly robust network topology is a very necessary and urgent task. When some sensor nodes are attacked, the remaining nodes in the topology can still maintain connectivity and the network can continue to provide the original services [19]. Robustness is always an extremely important feature of various network topologies, and it is even more necessary in the deployment and application of actual topologies. However, in existing research, there are still many challenges to construct a highly robust topology that can resist various types of attacks.

3.2.2 Preliminaries

With the advent of graph theory and complex network theory [20], scale-free networks have gradually been accepted for their high robustness against random attacks, and researchers have begun to apply them to the construction of robust topologies. Du et al. [21] analyzed the shortest path characteristics in the scale-free model and proposed a more effective transportation system. Ebel et al. [22] studied the topology of e-mail network. It is similar to social network, with obvious scale-free characteristics in structure and small-world characteristics in behavior. Virus emails are more prone to spread in this network. Eguiluz et al. [23] explored the structure of the brain functional network, and found that the connections of functional regions in the brain also have the scale-free feature. Compared with the traditional network topology, the sensor topology is limited by hardware and battery, and needs to complete data transmission through multiple hops. Therefore, sensor nodes can only communicate with neighbor nodes and forward appropriate packets.

The traditional robust network construction scheme needs to be improved to be suitable for the IoT topology. Jian et al. [24] proposed an energy-aware topology model based on the BA model (EABA). This model used an adjustable coefficient to reduce energy consumption of the scale-free network topology. Zhu et al. [25] proposed an energy-saving scale-free topology construction scheme, which can balance the energy consumption on node according to the remaining energy and the number of connection. All of the above strategies can construct a scale-free topology in the IoT. But the energy balance and other factors they consider have an impact on subsequent robustness optimization of malicious attacks, and there is no restriction on the order of nodes joining the network, which will lead to the instability of the network structure. The scale-free topology has opposite characteristics in terms of robustness. The nodes with small degrees are widely deployed in the topology, and only a few nodes have more connections. The overall degree of nodes presents a power-law distribution. Under a random attack, the small-degree nodes, which occupy a large proportion of total nodes, are more vulnerable to attacks. Therefore, only a few communication links will be broken. However, the malicious attack destroys the node with the highest degree, and the topology will lose many links, which will quickly paralyze the entire network. Researches have paid much attention on improving the ability of scale-free topology to resist malicious attacks.

Schneider et al. [26] proposed a novel index R based on the percolation theory, which evaluates the robustness of the topology by maximum connected subgraph after each attack. Based on the R value, Herrmann et al. [27] proposed hill climbing algorithm (HC) to optimize the robustness of scale-free network against malicious attacks. Two edges in the topology are randomly selected to cross, and the connection with a larger R value is reserved. However, since the HC algorithm optimizes topology robustness from one direction, there is a multi-peak problem and only local optimal values can be obtained. Therefore, Buesser et al. [28] designed a simulated annealing algorithm (SA) whose edge-swapping operation is consistent with the HC algorithm. The SA algorithm accepts some edge-swapping operations with the lower R value, which can avoid the multi-peak problem to a certain extent. However, it requires multiple rounds of edge-swapping operations, which causes the running time of the algorithm to increase exponentially. Zhou et al. [29] proposed a memetic algorithm that integrates global and local searches to improve the robustness of scale-free topology against malicious attacks without changing the degree distribution. However, the communication capability of sensor node is not considered, and it is not suitable for IoT topology. Therefore, this section proposed the robustness enhancement strategy ROSE, which transforms the initial scale-free network to a more stable "Onion-like" structure, and greatly improves the robustness of IoT topology against malicious attacks.

3.2.3 Scale-Free Topology Deployment Strategy

Compared with the Internet and social networks, due to the limitation of node communication range and energy, the BA model proposed by Barabsi and Albert [30] is not suitable for constructing scale-free topology in the IoT. Each node has its own communication range, and can only communicate with other nodes within this range, and cannot communicate beyond this range. Therefore, the newly joined node can only choose a suitable node from the neighbor nodes to establish a connection. When the number of neighbor nodes is insufficient, the node will not be able to join the network. The following three principles are used to deploy the initial scale-free topology.

- The preferential attachment is restricted to the neighbor nodes. Two nodes in a traditional scale-free topology can be directly connected regardless of their position. However, in the IoT, the communication between any two sensor nodes is restricted within the communication radius.
- The degree of the node is limited to avoid premature failure of some nodes. The node with a high degree will forward and process heavy data, which causes faster energy consumption.
- Determine the attack scheme for the network topology. This section focuses on the construction method of highly robust scale-free topology for malicious attacks.

Therefore, in order to construct a highly robust scale-free topology in the IoT, this section considers three aspects of improvement according to the generation rules of BA network topology. First, there must be enough nodes to connect to in the communication range of the newly joined node. Therefore, instead of placing nodes one by one according to growth characteristics in BA model, all nodes are densely placed in the topology. At this time, each node has a sufficient number of neighbor nodes, and no node is an isolated node.

To simulate the growth characteristics in the BA model, each node needs to be added to the network in a certain order. It means that the process of adding the connections is asynchronous. Assume that all nodes within the communication range of the newly joined node constitute a candidate space. The degree and coordinate information of each node needs to be recorded. In addition, the neighbor node that has been connected with the newly joined node or reaches the maximum degree no longer belongs to the candidate space. The order in which all nodes join the topology is expanded from the center of topology to the periphery. Nodes newly added to the topology tend to connect with the higher degree nodes in the candidate space. $P_{Local}(i)$ is used to represent the probability that the newly joined node connects with neighbor node i.

$$P_{Local}(i) = d_i / \sum_{j=1}^{n} d_j \qquad (3.10)$$

In Eq. (3.10), d_i is the degree of node i, and n is the total number of nodes within the communication range of node i. Figure 3.12 describes the steps for nodes to join the network during the establishment of a scale-free topology. It takes into account the multiple situations, and can be summarized into the three types of nodes i, j and k in Fig. 3.12. The blue lines show the connections added during the topology construction process. The degrees of four candidate nodes in the candidate space of node i are all 0, which means that they are all isolated. When node i initiates a connection request, m nodes will be selected with equal probability to establish connections. However, the degrees of the five neighbor nodes in the candidate space of node j are 7, 5, 3, 2, and 1, respectively. According to Eq. (3.10), the connection probabilities of neighbor nodes are 0.3888, 0.2777, 0.1677, 0.1111, and 0.0555, respectively. Then, node j selects m nodes to connect through the roulette method among the neighbor nodes. In the roulette method, the connection probability of neighbor nodes is normalized, and nodes with high connection probability occupy

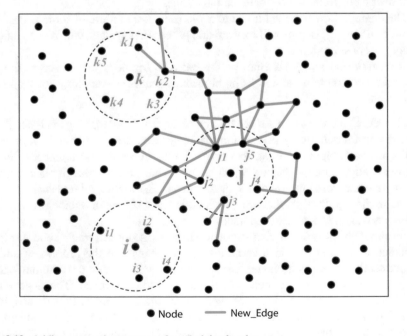

● Node   ▬▬ New_Edge

Fig. 3.12 Adding connection process of newly joined nodes

a larger selection area. Then, a random number in the range of 0 to 1 is generated, and node j will select the nodes in the area to which the random number belongs to connect.

In Fig. 3.12, there are both isolated nodes and connected nodes within the communication range of node k. The degrees of nodes $k1$ and $k2$ are 1 and 3. Node k will give priority to establishing connections with nodes $k1$ and $k2$ whose degrees are not 0. But the specific connection scheme is related to the number of connections m. If $m > 2$, except for the $k1$ and $k2$, it also needs to select $m - 2$ nodes from the remaining nodes with equal probability. If $m = 2$, nodes $k1$ and $k2$ are directly selected for connection. If $m < 2$, the model calculates the probabilities of nodes $k1$ and $k2$, respectively. Then, the roulette method is used to choose node. In an extreme case, if a node cannot find enough m neighbor nodes to establish connections when joining the network, the operation to join the network will be cancelled. The IoT is a dense network, each node has a sufficient number of neighbor nodes, and the probability of a large-scale node adding connection failure is close to 0. In contrast, the failure of individual nodes to join the network will not affect the scale-free characteristics of the entire topology.

Second, in the process of topology construction, it needs to limit the maximum number of edges that each node can connect. This section sets an appropriate maximum degree for nodes according to different network sizes and densities. When node i joins the topology, it can obtain the degree information of other neighbor nodes by broadcasting. If there are some neighbor nodes whose degrees reach the maximum value, node i will remove these nodes with the maximum degree from its candidate space, and only choose nodes from the remaining neighbor nodes when adding connections. Therefore, the nodes that reach the maximum degree will no longer establish connections with other nodes, which prevents the degree of these nodes from further increasing.

Third, the order in which each node joins the network is determined to make the scale-free network closer to the "Onion-like" structure during the construction process. Therefore, a node named "Starting node" is placed in the topological center of Fig. 3.13. The establishment of the network topology will start from this node. Suppose that m is 2, which means that each node will construct two new connections (as shown by the blue solid line in Fig. 3.13). Then, the "Starting node" broadcasts a data packet to its neighbor nodes, which contains its coordinates. The node that receives the data packet will set a timer. The $Timer$ is shown in Eq. (3.11).

$$Timer = q * \sqrt{(r_x - s_x)^2 + (r_y - s_y)^2} \tag{3.11}$$

Among them, r_x, r_y, s_x and s_y are the position of the receiving and sending nodes, and q is a factor that controls the size of the timer, which is set according to the actual topology. Assuming that the timer of node $n1$ is reset to zero, node $n1$ will add a new connection as shown by the green solid line in Fig. 3.13. After the addition operation, node $n1$ will forward the data packet to its neighbor after receiving the initial data packet for the first time, and the node that receives the data

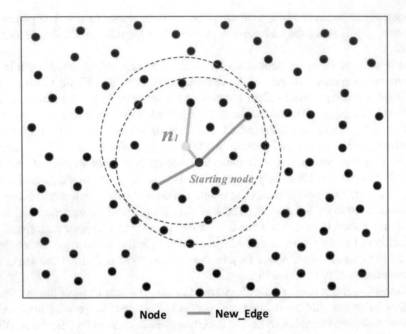

Fig. 3.13 Adding connection order of the nodes

packet will repeat the above process. In addition, each node receives the initial data packet only once. If there is duplicate data packet, it will be discarded. Through this strategy, the nodes close to the "Starting node" can join the network earlier. This process is repeated N times so that each node can perform the operation of adding connections and become part of the topology. It conforms to the trend that nodes with high degrees are distributed near the center of the topology, and nodes with low degrees are distributed at the edge of the topology. In this way, the initial scale-free topology is more similar to the "Onion-like" structure.

3.2.4 Highly Robust Topology Optimization Strategy

The basic idea of topology optimization is to gradually transform the initial scale-free topology structure into a stable "Onion-like" structure by changing edges. The reason why the "Onion-like" structure is relatively stable is that interconnected nodes have equal or similar degrees. When a node with a larger degree is damaged, the node communicating with it still has a larger degree, which can maintain topology integrity to a great extent. Before the ROSE is executed, each node transmits its own degree, coordinates, connection and other information to the sink node through multiple hops. After the robustness optimization process is completed, the sink node will send the adjusted connection information to each node in a multi-hop manner. ROSE mainly includes two parts: degree difference operation and angle sum operation. Both operations select independent edges in the topology to swap edges. Therefore, this section first introduces the concept of independent edges, and then explains these two important operations in detail.

The robustness index R value requires N iterations to obtain the result, which requires a relatively large amount of calculation. In the traditional robustness enhancement strategy, when local optimization is achieved, each edge needs to calculate and compare its R value with other qualified edges. However, this strategy has poor timeliness for large-scale topology. In order to improve the optimization effect and timeliness of the strategy at the same time, the scope of "qualified edges" is more strictly limited. The number of edges for swapping operation can be reduced, which greatly reduces the comparison times of R value. For a scale-free topology, i, j, k, and l are used to represent the four nodes in the network, and e_{ij} and e_{kl} are independent edges when they meet the following conditions.

- One node is within communication range of the other three nodes, which ensures that the four nodes can be connected to each other.
- There are no other edges among nodes i, j, k, and l, except for edges e_{ij} and e_{kl}.

Figure 3.14 shows three different connections between nodes i, j, k, and l. Figure 3.14a is the initial connection: e_{ij} and e_{kl}. Figure 3.14b and c show the other two alternative connections, respectively. The robustness of the scale-free topology is mainly improved by exchanging independent edge connections. That is, the best connection is chosen from the above three modes. The edge swapping operation is accepted only if the R value increases. Note that the degree of each node remains unchanged when the connections of nodes i, j, k, and l are changed. In the degree difference and angle sum operation, only when a pair of edges meet the conditions of independent edges, they will be selected for the swapping operation. Otherwise, no operation is performed. This not only satisfies the limitation of the communication radius in the IoT, but also greatly reduces the number of edge swapping, which makes the strategy more efficient.

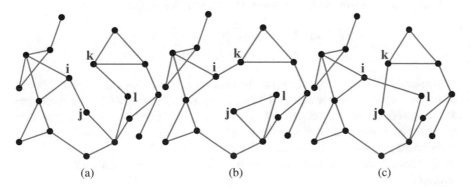

      (a)   (b)   (c)

Fig. 3.14 Three connection modes of independent edges

The following describes the degree difference operation. By connecting nodes with similar degrees, the scale-free network topology can be closer to "Onion-like" structure. The "Onion-like" structure was proposed by Schneider [26], and experiments have shown that the structure is very stable. Later, Tanizawa [31] proved its robustness against malicious attacks through mathematical analysis. The main feature of this structure is to connect nodes with the same or similar degrees in the network as much as possible, that is, the degree difference between the two nodes of each edge should be as small as possible. Due to the randomness of connection, the initial network established according to the scale-free rule is quite different from "Onion-like", and the network is prone to failure due to malicious attacks. Therefore, the highly robust topology construction strategy needs to make the initial topology structure closer to the "Onion-like" structure.

In the degree difference operation, ROSE calculates the degree difference of all three connections of independent edges, which are expressed by Eqs. (3.12), (3.13), and (3.14). Then, this section compares and selects the connection with the smallest degree difference. If this connection is the initial connection, no other operations are performed and the next round of edge swapping is performed. If the connection changes, two aspects of verification are required. On the one hand, the connection can maintain the fully connected state of the scale-free topology. On the other hand, the robustness index R value does not decrease. If the above verifications are passed, the edge swapping will be accepted.

$$SUB_0 = |d_i - d_j| + |d_k - d_l| \tag{3.12}$$

$$SUB_1 = |d_i - d_k| + |d_j - d_l| \tag{3.13}$$

$$SUB_2 = |d_i - d_l| + |d_j - d_k| \tag{3.14}$$

In order to improve the robustness of topology, ROSE further limits the extent of degree difference reduction, which is represented by parameter p. In this way, only when the degree difference is reduced to a certain proportion, the edge swapping operation can be performed. The range of p value is from 0 to 1.

$$p = max(\frac{|d_i - d_k| + |d_j - d_l|}{|d_i - d_j| + |d_k - d_l|}, \frac{|d_i - d_l| + |d_j - d_k|}{|d_i - d_j| + |d_k - d_l|}) \tag{3.15}$$

As shown in Eq. (3.15), only when the degree difference between a pair of nodes is less than a certain percentage of the initial degree difference, ROSE compares the R values of different connection methods. Finally, algorithm chooses the connection method that satisfies the parameter p and increases the R value. By setting an appropriate p value, the robustness of the network can be greatly improved, and many unnecessary R value comparison and edge swapping operations can be reduced.

In the "Onion-like" structure, there is another obvious feature besides the interconnection of nodes with similar degrees. Nodes closer to the center of the

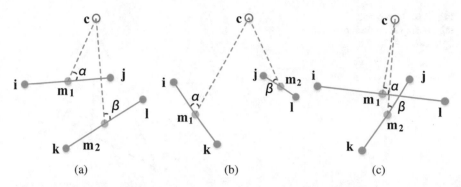

Fig. 3.15 Calculation methods of angle sum operation

topology have larger degrees. In the topology, there are a large number of edges perpendicular to the center of the network, which make nodes with similar degrees form a ring-like structure. Since the degree of the node generally decreases from the center to the edge, two nodes on the same ring are likely to have the same or similar degrees. Therefore, after degree difference operation, ROSE performs angle sum operation to further highlight the "Onion-like" characteristics of the scale-free network, and enhance the robustness of the network against malicious attacks.

The execution process of angle sum operation is as follows. First, the coordinates of "Starting node" is used as the center of topology. For each edge e_{ij}, an angle named "surrounding angle" is used to evaluate the angle between this edge and the center of topology. Figure 3.15 gives the definition and calculation of surrounding angles for all three connection methods of a pair of independent edges.

As shown in Fig. 3.15a, c is the center of the scale-free topology, and m_1 is the midpoint of the edge e_{ij}. The points c and m_1 are connected to form two complementary angles on the edge e_{ij}. In these two angles, the acute angle (or right angle in the vertical case) is selected as the surrounding angle between the edge e_{ij} and the center of the network, that is, the angle α in Fig. 3.15a. In addition, for any pair of independent edges e_{ij} and e_{kl}, ROSE calculates the surrounding angle between these two edges and the center of the network, and superimposes the two results. For example, in Fig. 3.15a, $\alpha + \beta$ represents the cumulative result of the surrounding angles of this pair of independent edges. In addition, this section discusses the other two connection methods of the independent edges e_{ij} and e_{kl} described in Fig. 3.15b and c, and calculates the cumulative results of their surrounding angles respectively.

$$\alpha = arccos\frac{len_b^2 + len_c^2 - len_a^2}{2 * len_b * len_c} \tag{3.16}$$

The angle sum operation uses the law of cosines to calculate the size of the surrounding angle. As shown in Eq. (3.16), len_b and len_c are the lengths of the two adjacent sides of the surrounding angle α, and len_a is the length of the opposite

Fig. 3.16 Geometric
relationship in angle sum
operation

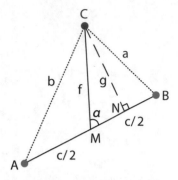

side. This section chooses the connection method with the largest cumulative result
of the surrounding angles. If this connection method does not break the connectivity
of the scale-free network and the robustness index R value is not reduced, the edge
swapping operation will be accepted. If an edge has a larger surrounding angle, the
distances from the nodes at both ends of the edge to the center of the network are
similar. Therefore, the node distance from the center of the network can be used to
complete the calculation of the angle sum.

As shown in Fig. 3.16, A and B are two nodes in the scale-free network, and C is
the center of network. M is midpoint of line segment AB, and CN is perpendicular
to AB. a, b, c, f, and g represent the lengths of corresponding line segments,
respectively. The following equations can be obtained by geometric methods.

$$(\frac{c}{2} - f\cos\alpha)^2 + g^2 = a^2 \tag{3.17}$$

$$(\frac{c}{2} + f\cos\alpha)^2 + g^2 = b^2 \tag{3.18}$$

Then, Eq. (3.17) is substituted into Eq. (3.18), and the relationship between a
and b can be obtained.

$$a^2 = b^2 - 2cf\cos\alpha \tag{3.19}$$

In Eq. (3.19), c and f are fixed parameters. The surrounding angle ranges from
$0°$ to $90°$. Therefore, when α approaches $90°$, a and b are close to equivalent.
At this time, the distances from node A and node B to the network center C are
almost equal. According to the characteristics of the "Onion-like" structure, A and
B have similar degrees, and there is a higher probability of establishing a connection
between them. On the contrary, the situation where α approaches $0°$ will have a
negative impact on the robustness of the topology.

3.2.5   *Performance Evaluation*

We conduct a comprehensive simulation and result analysis of all the strategies involved in this topic, which is mainly divided into two parts. First, experiments show the scale-free characteristics of the network topology deployed based on the construction strategy proposed in ROSE. Next, simulation results determine the most appropriate parameter p value in the degree difference operation, and further analyze the performance comparison and order selection of the degree difference and the angle sum operations in ROSE. Second, the robustness experiments are conducted between network topologies with different node sizes and edge densities, and the performance and timeliness of ROSE, HC [27], and SA [28] algorithms are compared.

The relevant basic parameters in the topology are set as follows. The nodes are randomly deployed in an area of 500 $*$ 500 m^2. Considering that in the network construction process, there must be a sufficient number of neighbor nodes around each node, the communication radius r of the node is set to 200 m, and the timer parameter $q = 10$. The maximum degree of each node cannot be specified as a fixed value, but can be limited according to the network size and edge density. In the scale-free network topology with $N = 100$ and $m = 2$, the maximum degree of nodes is limited to 25. On this basis, when the total number of nodes N increases by 50 or the number of added edges m increases by 1, the maximum degree threshold increases by 5. The above data are all based on the results of k ($k > 20$) independent repeated experiments.

Figure 3.17 shows the scale-free properties of topologies with different node sizes and edge densities. The red dots represent nodes in the topology. The size of the dot is used to distinguish the degrees of different nodes. The larger the dot

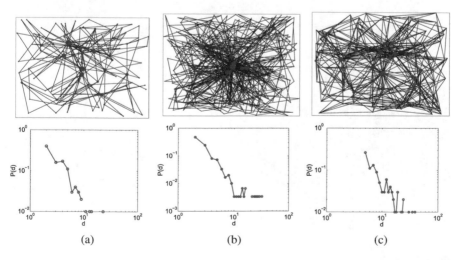

Fig. 3.17 Scale-free properties of network topology. (**a**) $N = 100$, $m = 2$. (**b**) $N = 300$, $m = 2$. (**c**) $N = 100$, $m = 5$

is, the higher the node's degree is. Only the nodes connected by black lines can communicate. In Fig. 3.17a, it is assumed that there are $N = 100$ nodes in the topology, and the number of edges that the nodes need to add is $m = 2$. The network topology shows that most nodes in the topology have small degrees and are scattered in the periphery of the topology. In addition, there are a small number of nodes with a large degree in the network. On the whole, the degree distribution of all nodes conforms to the characteristics of the power law distribution. Compared with Fig. 3.17a, Fig. 3.17b increases the number of nodes N to 300 and keeps m unchanged, while Fig. 3.17c increases the number of connections m to 5 and keeps N unchanged. It can be seen that no matter the size of the network or the density of the topology is changed, the scale-free topology constructed according to ROSE has good scale-free characteristics. The second row of Fig. 3.17 shows the degree of all nodes of these three topologies, and $P(d)$ represents the probability that the degree of the node is d. It can be seen that the degree of all nodes basically presents a downward sloping straight line, which conforms to the power law distribution.

Before evaluating the performance of ROSE, we need to determine the optimal value of the edge-swapping parameter p. Therefore, different p values are selected for robustness experiments, and the experimental interval of parameter p is set to 0.1. In order to ensure the comprehensiveness of the experiment, three network topologies with different node numbers and edge densities are used to measure the effect of p value on robustness optimization. As shown in Fig. 3.18, the x-axis is the value of parameter p, and the y-axis is the improvement of robustness index R after degree difference operation. $R(BA)$ represents the R value of the initial scale-free network, and $R(d)$ is the R value of the network after the degree difference operation. Since the R values of the three initial topologies are different, there is no comparison between the three network topologies, and the trend of each line needs to be noticed. When the value of the parameter is between 0.7 and 1.0, the

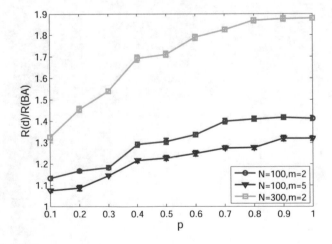

Fig. 3.18 Effect of parameter p in ROSE

improvement of the R value is relatively high among the three lines. In order to compare the performance of different strategies under a unified standard, the value of parameter p is fixed at 0.9.

Degree difference and angle sum operations are two components of ROSE. Both methods can improve the robustness of scale-free topology, but their implementation mechanisms are different. This section compares the performance of different combinations of these two operations in different scale-free network topologies. The number of connections added to each node is fixed at $m = 2$. The number of nodes in the scale-free network topology is set to 100, 150, 200, 250, and 300, respectively.

In Fig. 3.19, the x-axis is the number of nodes, and y-axis is the R value. ASO_DDO indicates that the angle sum operation is performed before the degree difference operation, while ROSE performs the degree difference operation first. $Initial - BA$ represents the initial topology deployed by the BA scale-free principle. The degree difference operation makes the scale-free network topology closer to the "Onion-like" structure by reducing the degree difference of independent edges. The angle sum operation is morphologically close to the "Onion-like" structure by selecting the maximum surrounding angle. Compared with the initial scale-free network topology, these two operations can improve robustness. However, due to the randomness of the initial network topology, the optimization effect of the degree difference operation is slightly better than the angle sum operation. In addition, ASO_DDO and ROSE combined the two operations in different order, which has a better robustness than a single operation. More importantly, when the degree difference operation is performed first, the robustness improvement effect is more obvious. Therefore, in ROSE, the execution order of these two operations is the degree difference operation and the angle sum operation.

Next, experiments evaluate the robustness optimization performance of ROSE in scale-free topologies of different sizes and different edge densities, and compare ROSE with existing HC and SA algorithms. In Fig. 3.20a, the number of connections

Fig. 3.19 Comparison of degree difference and angle sum operations on topology

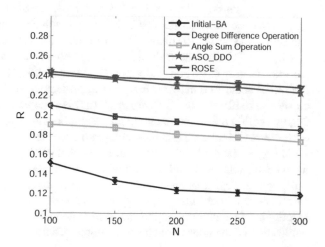

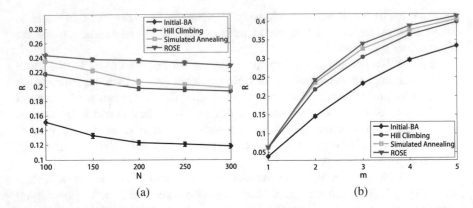

Fig. 3.20 Comparison between ROSE and other algorithms on the scale-free networks. (**a**) Different network sizes. (**b**) Different edge densities

added to each node is fixed at $m = 2$, which ensures that all scale-free network topologies have the same edge density. The number of nodes in the scale-free network is set to 100, 150, 200, 250, and 300, respectively. Each experiment runs a different strategy on the same initial scale-free topology. It can be seen that these three algorithms can significantly improve the robustness of the initial scale-free topology. As the number of nodes increases, the R value gradually decreases, which is caused by the fact that the network is farther away from the fully connected state.

Figure 3.20b shows the robustness optimization performance of ROSE in scale-free networks with different edge densities. The number of nodes in the network topology is fixed at $N = 100$, which ensures that all scale-free network topologies have the same size. The number of connections added to each node is set to 1, 2, 3, 4, and 5 respectively. It can be seen that the index R increases rapidly with the increase of nodes. The reason is that the number of edges in the network continues to increase, and the topology can maintain better connectivity. All three algorithms can significantly improve the R value. Since the SA can avoid the multi-peak problem, its performance is better than HC. Compared with the other two algorithms, ROSE can obtain the best performance in topologies with different edge densities.

Figure 3.21 shows the scale-free topology after ROSE optimization. The network parameters are $N = 300$ and $m = 2$. After ROSE, the connection of nodes in the initial scale-free network has been significantly changed, and the topology is closer to a stable "Onion-like" structure. In this structure, nodes with equal or similar degrees within the communication range can be connected and communicated with each other, which can maintain topological connectivity.

In Fig. 3.21a, the topology structure has changed significantly. Most of the edges have been exchanged, and only a few edges maintain the original connection. The position and degree of each node remain unchanged, which shows that the scale-free feature of the initial topology can be well inherited. Figure 3.21b uses the Depth First Search (DFS) algorithm to rearrange the positions of the nodes, and the connection of the nodes remains unchanged. There are many edges that are almost

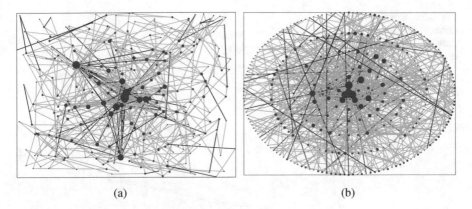

(a)   (b)

Fig. 3.21 Scale-free network topologies and degree distribution after ROSE when $N = 300$. (**a**) Scale-free network topology. (**b**) Redeployed location of nodes

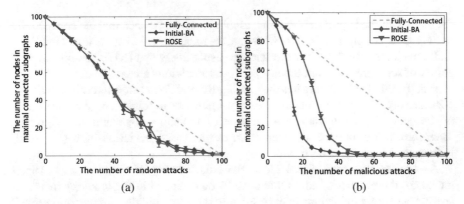

(a)   (b)

Fig. 3.22 Connectivity of scale-free network after different attacks. (**a**) Random attack. (**b**) Malicious attack

perpendicular to the network in the topology, which more directly indicates that the initial scale-free network is closer to the "Onion-like" structure.

ROSE can significantly improve the robustness of the scale-free topology against malicious attacks and maintain the robustness of the topology against random attacks. Figure 3.22 describes the connection situation of a scale-free topology under random and malicious attacks. The red and blue lines respectively represent the same topology before and after ROSE optimization. The x-axis is the number of attacks, and the y-axis is the number of nodes in the largest connected subgraph. The green dotted line represents the connection of the fully connected topology under different attacks. Figure 3.22a shows the random attacks. It can be seen that the red solid line basically overlaps with the blue solid line, which shows that ROSE has not destroyed the original power law distribution of the network topology, and the scale-free characteristics of the network topology have been well preserved. Figure 3.22b shows the malicious attacks. Compared with random attacks, malicious attacks can cause greater damage to the robustness of the network topology, because it removes

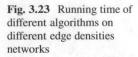

Fig. 3.23 Running time of different algorithms on different edge densities networks

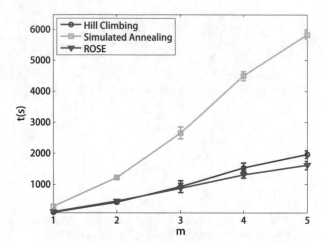

the node with the largest degree in the topology. It can be seen that the connectivity of the topology optimized by ROSE decreases more slowly than the initial topology under malicious attacks. The experimental results show that ROSE can improve the ability of scale-free network topology to resist malicious attacks.

Finally, this section compares the running time of these three algorithms with the edge density. Due to the randomness of the network topology and the uncertainty of the edge swapping, the execution time of the same algorithm varies greatly. Therefore, the errors are all taken from the standard deviation of k ($k \geq 20$) independent repeated experiments.

As can be seen from Fig. 3.23, as the edge density of the network topology increases, the number of edges that need to be swapped in the topology increases sharply, and the running time of each strategy increases rapidly. Among the network topologies with different edge densities, SA algorithm has the longest running time because it requires multiple rounds of edge swapping operations. When $m < 2$, the running time of ROSE and HC is basically the same. However, when $m \geq 3$, the efficiency of ROSE gradually emerges. The reason is that as the number of edges increases, the number of independent edges is relatively small. There are fewer edges to swap in ROSE, and the running time is reduced. In addition, the reduction of independent edges means that the calculation times of R value and the complexity of the algorithm are reduced. Therefore, ROSE can complete the optimization process of scale-free topology in a shorter time.

3.3   Robust Time Synchronization Scheme

In order to further improve the quality of service (QoS) of the IoT, except for constructing a highly robust topology structure, a robust and energy-efficient node time synchronization strategy is also crucial. It can synchronize some isolated nodes in the network to ensure the consistency of local clocks on multiple nodes. Finally, it can improve the quality of data transmitted on the network topology. Therefore, a robust time synchronization scheme for the network topology is proposed.

3.3.1   Research Background

For distributed wireless sensor networks, each sensor node runs on different microprocessors. In order to make the time difference between nodes not too large, time synchronization is required. For computers and large equipment, they can synchronize time with satellites through Global Positioning System (GPS), or connect to the Internet to obtain standard time. For distributed sensor nodes, it is necessary to select the time of a certain node as a reference, and periodically calibrate the respective local clocks of the nodes. The clock is counted by the internal crystal oscillator to obtain the system time. To make the two clocks fully synchronized, the vibration frequency of the crystal oscillator must be exactly the same, which is theoretically impossible. Therefore, the sensor nodes must adjust the clock.

In addition, time synchronization plays an important role in controlling the energy efficiency of the network [32]. The battery cannot be replaced after the wireless sensor node is deployed. The node is in an unsupervised state, and most operations are completed by time synchronization, such as the duty cycle of the sensor node during sleep and work. Since the energy consumption of the node in the sleep state is minimal, in order to control the energy consumption, nodes that do not collect data are put to sleep. However, the nodes in the IoT are distributed and cannot sleep or restart at a uniform time. Therefore, it is necessary to perform time synchronization operations on the nodes to ensure that the nodes can sleep or restart at the same time, which can achieve efficient management and save energy.

Time synchronization has many important applications in network scheduling protocols. For example, the Time Division Multiple Access (TDMA) protocol in the network divides a fixed communication time for each node according to the time slot after all nodes are synchronized. Otherwise, when multiple nodes send messages at the same time, it will cause network conflicts. By marking important events or messages with synchronized timestamp, these data can be processed more conveniently.

As early as 1991, Mills proposed the network time synchronization protocol (NTP) [33], which is suitable for complex network environments. However, due to the power consumption limitation, complex channel environment and dynamic topology of IoT, NTP has brought certain problems. At present, many time synchronization algorithms suitable for IoT have been proposed by researchers [34]. Elson et al. proposed the classic reference broadcasts synchronization (RBS) [35], which first proposed the receiver-to-receiver protocol (RRP). RRP randomly selects a node as the reference node and broadcasts a message to the neighbors. The neighbor nodes record the timestamp when the message is received and exchange the timestamp with each other. Then the initial time deviation and time drift rate are estimated according to the least square method.

RBS utilizes the feature of multiple nodes receiving the same message to improve the accuracy of synchronization. On the basis of RBS, the R^4Syn protocol proposed by Djenouri periodically changes the reference node to avoid the paralysis of the reference node due to excessive power consumption [36]. Gong et al. [37] proposed an energy-efficient coefficient exchange synchronization protocol (CESP), which can reduce broadcast power consumption, and improve the performance of RBS. The above protocols are based on the RRP synchronization model, and the time synchronization accuracy is improved. However, they all rely on the reference node. The synchronization process needs to exchange a large number of timestamps, which consumes more energy.

Another important time synchronization model is sender-to-receiver protocol (SRP), which completes synchronization by exchanging two broadcast messages. Since the number of broadcast messages in the SRP model is controllable, the energy consumption of nodes can be saved. Many time synchronization protocols that optimize and improve the SRP model appeared and were applied to different time synchronization scenarios. Ganeriwal et al. [38] proposed a time synchronization protocol based on spanning tree (TPSN). The model selects a node as the root node and expands the network in the form of spanning tree. The SRP model is used to synchronize the child nodes and the parent node from root node to each edge.

For energy consumption, Noh et al. [39] proposed pairwise broadcast synchronization protocol (PBS), which combines the RRP and SRP models. PBS absorbs the advantages of the high synchronization accuracy of these two models, and greatly reduces energy consumption. Furthermore, Noh et al. [40] presented groupwise pair selection algorithm (GPA) on the basis of PBS. By applying the PBS to a multi-hop network, GPA proposed a group synchronization method, which is also based on a spanning tree. The nodes of the entire network are grouped by spanning tree, and the child node with the largest degree in each group is selected. This node and the parent node use the SRP model to synchronize, and other neighbor nodes use the RRP model to passively synchronize. These methods can improve the accuracy of synchronization with low energy consumption, but lack a solution for isolated nodes. Therefore, this section proposes a robust time synchronization scheme based on the isolated nodes.

3.3.2 Motivation and Preliminaries

The above PBS, GPA, and TPSN protocols are all based on spanning tree and combined with RRP and SRP models for time synchronization. In these protocols, all nodes in the network are divided into undefined nodes (UN), backbone nodes (BN) and passive nodes (PN). During the time synchronization process, the node type can be changed. Figure 3.24 shows a spanning tree structure.

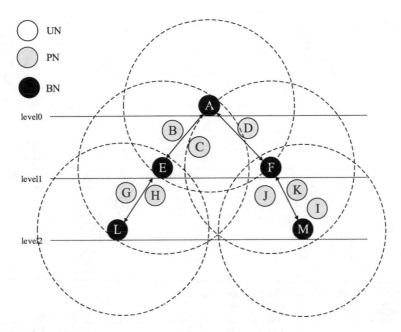

Fig. 3.24 Spanning tree structure

- UN: It is the initial state of each node, which can be changed to BN or PN.
- BN: The root node is the first BN. Multiple BNs actively exchange messages and use SRP model for synchronization.
- PN: The node does not send any broadcast messages, but passively receives messages from BN. PNs uses the RRP model to complete synchronization.

Since PN can only receive messages, some nodes close to PN but not to BN become isolated nodes in some algorithms. These nodes can neither use SRP nor RRP for synchronization. As shown in Fig. 3.25, nodes F, G, and H are neighbors of C whose node type is PN, but are not within the scope of any BN. They are isolated nodes, and the neighbor I is also an isolated node. Besides, in actual application scenarios, packet loss may occur due to factors such as channels and obstacles. For example, nodes K and L in Fig. 3.25, although they are within the broadcast range of BN, they are isolated due to packet loss. Since PNs that only receive messages use the RRP model to synchronize, when the number of PNs is large, the energy consumption of the whole network is reduced. Therefore, it is very meaningful to improve the synchronization accuracy as much as possible under the condition of low energy consumption. This section proposes the R-Sync to construct a robust and efficient time synchronization scheme [41].

Before introducing R-Sync, some assumptions and concepts need to be predefined. First, it is assumed that each node has a unique identification in the network, and each node can calculate the distance to the neighbor node. There are multiple distance estimation algorithms such as Received Signal Strength Indicator (RSSI)

Fig. 3.25 Isolated nodes

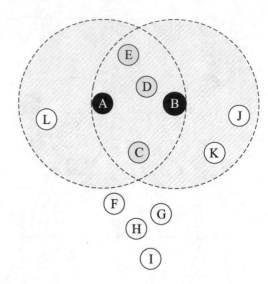

Table 3.4 Symbols and descriptions in time synchronization

Symbols	Descriptions	Symbols	Descriptions
T_i	The i_{th} timestamp	b_l	The l_{th} BN
$p_{l,i}$	The i_{th} PN whose parent node is l_{th} BN	$\Delta(x, y)$	The time deviation between nodes x and y
$LE(x)$	Local time error of node x	$GE(x)$	Global time error of node x
$LT(i)$	Local time of node i	$CT(i)$	Calibration time of node i

[42], Time Of Arrival (TOA) [43], and Time Difference Of Arrival (TDOA) [44].
Since RSSI is widely used in sensor networks, this section estimates the distance
based on the received signal power when the node receives the data packet.

$$P_{rcd} = c * P_{tx}/(d^{\alpha}) \tag{3.20}$$

In Eq. (3.20), P_{rcd} is the received signal power, and P_{tx} is the transmitted signal
power. d is the Euclidean distance, and the constants c and α are related to the
propagation model. According to this equation, when the transmitted signal power
is constant, the received signal power is inversely proportional to the distance. In
addition, each node has at least two built-in timers, and the timers do not affect each
other. The configuration of all nodes is the same, including transmission distance,
size, and crystal oscillator. The symbol descriptions in this section are shown in
Table 3.4.

Table 3.5 Message format

Fields	DestAddr	SrcID	Type	ParentID	RTS	STS	Level
Defaults	0xFFFF	0	NULL	0	NULL	NULL	0

There are six types of data packets in different scenarios, which are all broadcast messages. The format of the messages is shown in Table 3.5. The meaning of the different fields are as follows:

- DestAddr: Destination address of the packet.
- SrcID: The unique identifier of the sending node.
- Type: The type of the message including $ChRoot$ (selecting root node), $SetT$ (setting pulling timer), $Init$ (setting $Sync$ timer), $Sync$ (synchronization message), Ack (confirmation for $Sync$ message), $Pulling$ (synchronizing isolated node).
- ParentID: The parent node of the sending node, which is $NULL$ by default.
- RTS: The timestamp when the $Sync$ message is received. The default value is $NULL$.
- STS: The timestamp when the Ack message is sent. The default value is $NULL$.
- Level: The level of the sending node.

Time error is a key factor to describe the calibration time accuracy of synchronized node. The calibration time of a node is the sum of the local time and the measured time deviation. The local time is converted from the internal crystal oscillator count of the node, and the measured time deviation is calculated through the SRP or RRP model. Here, the time error is used to indicate the accuracy of the time synchronization algorithm.

Definition 3.5 The *local time error (LE)* refers to the difference between the calibration time of a node and the adjusted time of the parent node in the spanning tree (i.e., single-hop error).

$$LE(b_l) = |LT(b_l) + \Delta(b_{l-1}, b_l) - CT(b_{l-1})| \qquad (3.21)$$

$$LE(p_{l-1,1}) = |LT(p_{l-1,1}) + \Delta(b_{l-1}, p_{l-1,1}) - CT(b_{l-1})| \qquad (3.22)$$

Proof The local time error of the BN and PN are shown in Eqs. (3.21) and (3.22). Among them, LE represents the local time error, CT is the calibration time, and LT is the local time. For b_l that is BN and its parent node b_{l-1}, the measurement error $\Delta(b_{l-1}, b_l)$ is calculated by using the time stamp through the SRP model. Since $CT(b_l) = LT(b_l) + \Delta(b_{l-1}, b_l)$, the local time error is $LE(b_l) = |CT(b_l) - CT(b_{l-1})| = |LT(b_l) + \Delta(b_{l-1}, b_l) - CT(b_{l-1})|$. PN uses RRP model to calculate measurement error $\Delta(b_{l-1}, p_{l-1,1})$. For the $p_{l-1,1}$ that is PN and its parent node b_{l-1}, the following equation $CT(p_{l-1,1}) = LT(p_{l-1,1}) + \Delta(b_{l-1}, p_{l-1,1})$ is satisfied. Therefore, Eq. (3.22) is true. $\qquad\qquad \square$

Definition 3.6 The *global time error (GE)* of a node represents the difference of calibration time between the node and the root node in the spanning tree.

$$GE(b_l) = |LT(b_l) + \Delta(b_{l-1}, b_l) - LT(root)| \tag{3.23}$$

$$GE(p_{l-1,l}) = |LT(p_{l-1,l}) + \Delta(b_{l-1}, p_{l-1,l}) - LT(root)| \tag{3.24}$$

Proof The global time error of the BN and PN are shown in Eqs. (3.23) and (3.24). Among them, GE represents the global time error, and *root* is the root node of the spanning tree. For b_l, there is $CT(b_l) = LT(b_l) + \Delta(b_{l-1}, b_l)$. In a network with a spanning tree structure, the ultimate goal of all nodes is to synchronize with the root node, the root node does not need the calibration time, that is, $CT(root) = LT(root)$. Thus, $GE(b_l) = |CT(b_l) - CT(root)| = |LT(b_l) + \Delta(b_{l-1}, b_l) - LT(root)|$. In the same way, $GE(p_{l-1,l})$ can be derived.   □

3.3.3 Details of Time Synchronization Scheme

As mentioned earlier, the existing time synchronization algorithms still have some problems. The algorithm R-Sync in this section uses the PBS model to maintain low power consumption, and sets a pulling timer (PT) for each node to avoid isolated nodes. PT is used to push unsynchronized nodes to complete synchronization. The R-Sync algorithm mainly consists of three parts.

(1) Preparing time synchronization: The spanning tree is constructed using the flood protocol, and the start of PT is completed with the establishment of spanning tree. For the first round, a node is randomly selected as the root node. In each subsequent round, the neighbor with the most remaining energy in the original root node is selected as the new root node.

(2) Initializing synchronization process: Following the sequence from root to leaf in the spanning tree, the PBS model is used for synchronization. The root node is set as the BN, and select surrounding BN to exchange bidirectional path messages by another Sync Timer (ST).

(3) Isolation node synchronization process: When a node is not synchronized within a limited time, the PT will time out. The node will broadcast a synchronization request, and the neighbor nodes that have been synchronized will respond. The unsynchronized node preferentially selects the node with the earliest respond for synchronization.

The following figures are used to briefly describe the idea of synchronization. A straight line without an arrow indicates that two nodes are located within the communication range of each other. The dashed line with arrow represents the sending message. The dashed circle represents the communication range and the solid circle represents the synchronized area. In Fig. 3.26, all nodes are UNs in the initial state. Here, a node A is randomly selected as the root node. In the process of

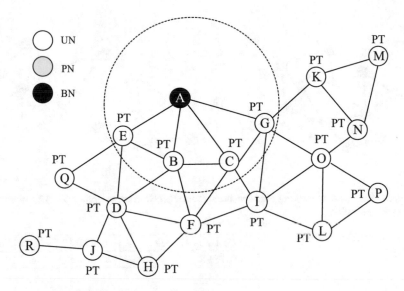

Fig. 3.26   Process of setting the PT

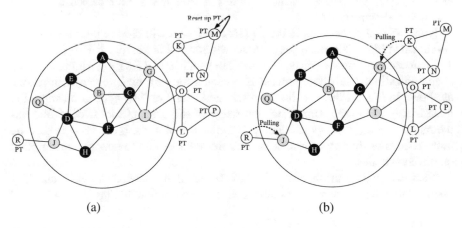

         (a)   (b)

Fig. 3.27   Process of initializing time synchronization. (**a**) Resetting the PT. (**b**) Broadcasting a *Pulling* message

initializing the topology, the root node A will broadcast a message to all neighbor nodes. Any node that receives the message starts the PT and continues to deliver the message until all nodes start the PT. The initial value of the PT is based on the level of the spanning tree where the node is located. When the nodes are synchronized, the PT that has not timed out will be closed.

Figure 3.27a shows the finished initial time synchronization. An unsynchronized node, such as node M, whose PT expires, sends a message to request synchronization. If there is no synchronized node in the surrounding neighbors or the message is lost due to poor signal, node M will reset the PT. Figure 3.27b shows another situation, that is, the message sent by the node can be received by a PN. For

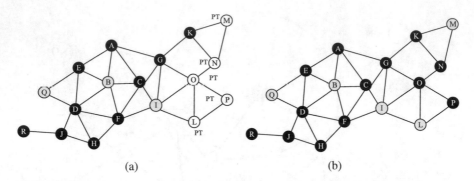

Fig. 3.28 Process of requesting time synchronization. (**a**) Converting node type. (**b**) Completing time synchronization

Table 3.6 Content of *SetT* message

DestAddr	SrcID	Type	ParentID	RTS	STS	Level
0xFFFF	A	SetT	NULL	-1	-1	0

example, *Pulling* messages sent by nodes K and R can be received by G and J whose node type is PN.

Nodes G and J that receive the *Pulling* message will change their node types. As shown in Fig. 3.28a, the types of these two nodes change from PN to BN. Since BN can exchange messages, these nodes can use SRP and RRP algorithms for time synchronization. The whole process is repeated until all nodes are synchronized, as shown in Fig. 3.28b. In addition, at the next round of time synchronization, the node that is within the communication range of the original root node A and has the most remaining energy is selected as the new root node. It can be seen that the more rounds of time synchronization, the more balanced the energy consumption on different nodes.

Next, the pulling mechanism with two timers is introduced in detail, and it is assumed that the deployment of sensor nodes is consistent with Figs. 3.26, 3.27, and 3.28.

(1) *Preparation time synchronization:* At the beginning of each round of time synchronization, all nodes are UNs, and each node needs to set a PT. Then the root node in the first round of synchronization is randomly selected from all the nodes. The type of this node is set to BN and the level is set to 0 (such as node A). This node broadcasts a message of type $SetT$. If a node that has not started the PT receives this message, it will set its own level to $L + 1$ (where L is the level of the message sender), start the PT, and forward this message. Nodes that have started the PT ignore this message. The content of the $SetT$ message is shown in Table 3.6. The $0xFFFF$ in the $DestAddr$ data represents that the destination address of this message is all nodes.

(2) *Initial time synchronization:* This process uses the PBS model to complete the synchronization, which is mainly divided into four steps.

Table 3.7 Content of *Init* message

DestAddr	SrcID	Type	ParentID	RTS	STS	Level
0xFFFF	A	Init	NULL	-1	-1	0

Step 1: After all nodes have set the PT, the root node broadcasts a *Init* message. The content of the message is shown in Table 3.7.

Step 2: For each UN that receives an *Init* message (such as node C), its PT is turned off. The sender is marked as the parent node, and the level of this UN is incremented by 1 on the basis of the parent node. Then the timer named ST is started to select BN. After the ST timer of any UN expires, the node type changes from UN to BN, and a *Sync* message is sent. The destination of the *Sync* message is its parent node, and the local timestamp Tl is recorded.

Step 3: For the node that receives the *Sync* message, it is processed separately according to the two cases.

- *Case 1:* The node is UN and the *DestAddr* of the message is its parent node, the ST of this node is turned off and the local timestamp is recorded as $T5$. The type of this node is converted to PN.
- *Case 2:* The node is BN and the *DestAddr* of the message is the node itself, the local timestamp is recorded as $T2$ when the message is received. The node will reply with an *Ack* message and the sending timestamp is recorded as $T3$. This *Ack* message contains the values of $T2$ and $T3$, which are stored in the RTS and STS of the data packet, respectively.

Step 4: For the node that receives the *Ack* message, it is processed separately according to the two cases.

- *Case 1:* The *DestAddr* of the message is the node itself, and the local timestamp is recorded as $T4$. Then the node can use the four timestamps Tl, $T4$, RTS, and STS (where RTS and STS store the timestamps $T2$ and $T3$) to estimate the time through the SRP model, which can be used to modify local time of the node. After the local time is modified, the node will broadcast the *Init* message.
- *Case 2:* The *DestAddr* of the message is not the node itself, and the node is PN. The RTS value in the message will be read. According to the timestamp $T5$ and RTS, the node can estimate the clock deviation between itself and the parent node through the RRP model. Then the node's own clock can be adjusted.

Steps 2 to 4 are executed cyclically in the topology. When no node responds to the *Init* message sent by the BN, the initial synchronization process ends. However, there are still some UNs not participating in the initial time synchronization. The reason is that these nodes are only within the communication range of PN or have not received messages. In order to synchronize these isolated UNs, the PT in *Step 1* begins to work.

(3) *Pulling process:* When the PT of node K expires, it must be UN. Then it broadcasts a *Pulling* message. If it doesn't receive any response (i.e., *Init* message), it will reset the PT. For the node that receives the *Pulling* message

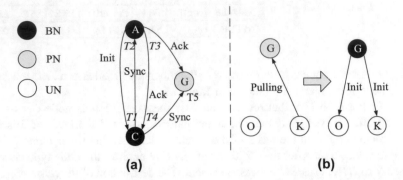

Fig. 3.29 Process of time synchronization. (**a**) Initial time synchronization. (**b**) Pulling process

(e.g., G), the node G converts itself from PN to BN, and broadcasts the *Init* message. Then it will continue to execute Steps 2 to 4. A time synchronization process and the corresponding timing chart are shown in Fig. 3.29.

(4) *Root node selection for next round:* After this round of synchronization is completed, the root node receives information about the remaining energy from the synchronized neighbor nodes. The root node selects the neighbor with the most remaining energy (such as node B) and sends a $ChRoot$ message to node B. Node B receives this message and becomes the new root node. The type of the node B becomes BN, and the level is 0.

The following describes the initialization of the timer. When the timer is started, a trigger period must be set to time a specific event. For the initial value of PT, R-Sync obtains the average time of each hop in the time synchronization process through simulation, which is denoted as AT_Period. The synchronization process starts when the parent node sends an *Init* message and ends when the child node receives an *Ack* message. The results of AT_Period are shown in Fig. 3.30.

This section uses $Init\_Time$ to represent the time required for the flooding process. The initial value of PT is determined according to the level of the node in the spanning tree, that is, $PT\_value = L * AT\_Period + Init\_Time$. In Fig. 3.31a, node A is the root node, and it does not need to set PT. The PT_value of node G is $1 * AT\_Period + Init\_Time$, and the PT_value of node H is $2*AT\_Period+Init\_Time$. Setting the initial PT value according to the spanning tree level can reduce the number of PT restarts and make the nodes synchronize as quickly as possible.

For the initial value of ST, if randomly selected, the two BNs may be very close. It may reduce the efficiency of the synchronization process, such as nodes A and B in Fig. 3.31b. Therefore, this section chooses two BNs that are far away from each other, which can cover more nodes. Since each node can calculate the distance from the sender to itself through the received message, the initial value of ST can be determined by the distance.

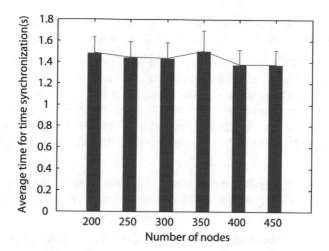

Fig. 3.30 Average running time of each hop

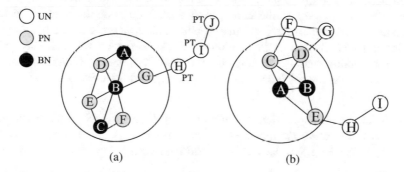

Fig. 3.31 Initial values for two timers. (**a**) Setting up PT. (**b**) BN selection for ST

3.3.4 Performance Evaluation

In this section, the network simulation tool NS-2 is used to compare and analyze R-Sync with TPSN [38], and GPA [40]. All sensor nodes are randomly deployed in $1000 * 1000\ m^2$ area to form a network topology. In order to broadcast over a long distance, a two-path ground reflection model is used to transmit messages. The energy model in NS2 is used to evaluate the energy consumption of nodes, where the transmitted power is $0.6w$, the received power is $0.3w$, and the idle power is $0.15w$. In order to improve the measurement accuracy, each experiment is run for $10,000$ cycles, and then the average value of all results is taken. The experiment mainly shows the performance of R-Sync from three aspects: the number of broadcast messages, energy balance, and time error.

First, the number of broadcast messages for different algorithms is studied. These messages are used to exchange timestamps and construct network topology.

Lemma 3.1 *Let M_{TPSN} denote the number of broadcast messages required by TPSN, then $M_{TPSN} = 4L - 3$, where L denotes the total number of nodes.*

Proof For the TPSN algorithm, each node broadcasts a message to construct a spanning tree network, which requires L messages. Since each node is connected to its parent node, except for the root node, there are a total of $L - 1$ edges in the spanning tree. In addition, three messages are required for each edge in the SRP model. Therefore, the number of messages that TPSN needs to broadcast is $M_{TPSN} = L + 3(L - 1) = 4L - 3$, which is only related to the number of nodes.   □

Lemma 3.2 *Let M_{GPA} denote the number of broadcast messages required by GPA, then $M_{GPA} = 3L + 3B - 5$, where B denotes the number of BN in each network group.*

Proof In GPA, all nodes need to be divided into several groups before synchronization, which can be achieved by simple flooding. It requires L messages. The parent node of each group has to master the connection information of each child node in the same group. In the same group, each child node needs to broadcast a message to other child nodes, and then sends another message to the parent node. A total of $2 * (L - 1)$ messages are required. Besides, each BN that uses paired broadcast synchronization (excluding the root node) requires 3 broadcast messages. Therefore, the number of broadcast messages required for GPA is $M_{GPA} = L + 2(L - 1) + 3(B - 1) = 3L + 3B - 5$.   □

Lemma 3.3 *Let M_{R-Sync} denote the number of broadcast messages required by R-Sync, which includes the topology initialization process. Then $M_{R-Sync} = L + 3(B - 1) + R$, where R is the number of Pulling messages.*

Proof The PT timer of each node is set and a spanning tree is constructed in the initial stage of the R-Sync. Each node needs one broadcast message. In the initial time synchronization phase, the number of broadcast messages is three times the number of BNs in the network. In addition, the synchronization process also needs to send *Pulling* messages. Therefore, the number of broadcast messages required by R-Sync is $M_{R-Sync} = L + 3(B - 1) + R$.   □

Because the number of BNs or *Pulling* messages in the network is much smaller than the number of nodes L, according to the above three lemmas, the number of messages required by R-Sync is less than the other two algorithms. Figure 3.32 is the result of the simulation experiment. Figure 3.32a shows the influence of the communication range on the number of messages. The number of nodes is set to 240, and the communication range varies from 85 to 160. It can be seen that as the transmission distance increases, the number of TPSN messages is basically stable. The reason is that M_{TPSN} is only related to the number of nodes. Besides, R-Sync decreases faster than GPA. The reason is that the number of *Pulling* messages decreases sharply. Figure 3.32b evaluates the number of broadcast messages under different numbers of nodes. The communication range is fixed at 85. The results show that the number of broadcast messages increases with

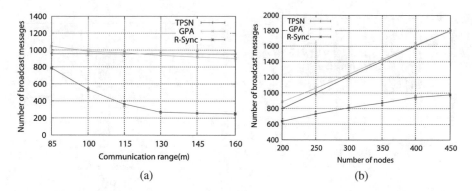

Fig. 3.32 Number of broadcast messages. (**a**) Different communication ranges. (**b**) Different number of nodes

the number of nodes. However, R-Sync always has the least number of messages among the three algorithms. Since nodes consume a lot of energy to broadcast messages, R-Sync with a smaller number of broadcast messages is an energy-efficient algorithm.

Second, the energy consumption of the network is analyzed. The communication range of the node is set to 100 m. The experimental results in Fig. 3.33 show that the energy consumption of TPSN and GPA are both distributed between 0.09–0.22 J, but the standard deviation of energy consumption in TPSN and GPA are 0.030 and 0.031, respectively. The energy consumption range of R-Sync is 0.07–0.15 J, and the standard deviation is 0.017. Therefore, the energy consumption distribution of R-Sync is more balanced.

Third, the time synchronization accuracy of the algorithm is discussed. Figure 3.34a shows the average local time error of TPSN, GPA, and R-Sync. The communication range of the node is 100 m, and the experiment is executed for 10, 000 cycles. It can be seen that the local time error of GPA and R-Sync is lower than TPSN. In TPSN, all nodes adopt SRP model to calculate the time error. Compared with GPA and R-Sync, the channel of TPSN is busier under same condition, especially in large-scale dense networks. This situation in TPSN increases the access time, and the send-side error becomes larger. Figure 3.34b describes the average global time error among three algorithms. Because the global time error is the hop-by-hop accumulation of the local time error, the trend is the same as the local time error. But the global time error of each algorithm is larger than the local time error under the same conditions. The experimental results show that the synchronization accuracy of R-Sync can maintain the same level as GPA, but is better than TPSN. In conclusion, R-Sync has a small time error and can ensure synchronization accuracy.

Finally, the R-Sync algorithm is tested on a hardware platform of the wireless nodes based on the ARM Cortex-M3 ($88MZ100$), 32MHZ high-precision crystal oscillator. In order to calculate the time error, a GPIO interface of the node is connected to an external measurement node. The measurement module is based on

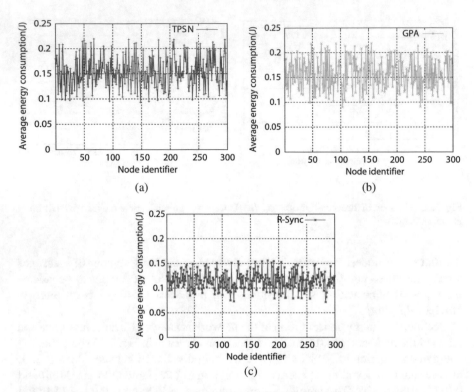

Fig. 3.33 Energy consumption distribution. (**a**) TPSN. (**b**) GPA. (**c**) R-Sync

the $STM32F103$ chip, which is designed to send a pulse regularly. After the sensor module receives the pulse, it triggers an external interrupt. The interrupt service function of the sensor module will immediately record the local timestamp and send it to the PC. PC collects the timestamps sent by all nodes, and calculates the difference between the timestamps, which is the synchronization error. Figure 3.35a shows the variation of the average global time error with the number of hops. Due to uncertain factors in the actual experiment, such as unstable channel conditions, hardware delay or some interference, the time error in the actual experiment is larger. But the difference is not more than 20%, and it is acceptable.

Figure 3.35b shows the local errors for PN and BN in simulation and hardware. Since the topology in the experiment is not a large-scale densely network, the time error of PN is very close to the time error of BN. Time synchronization error gradually increases with time, and clock drift appears in both hardware and simulation experiments. Due to the temperature, the local time error of the hardware experiment is almost 0 at the beginning, and the deviation rate of the simulation experiment is lower than the hardware experiment.

Fig. 3.34 Average time error.
(**a**) Local time error. (**b**)
Global time error

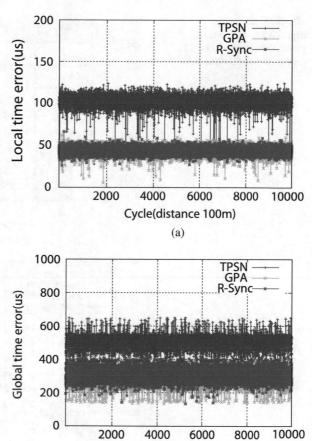

(a)

(b)

Fig. 3.35 Hardware
experiments. (**a**) Average
global time error. (**b**) Local
time errors of PN and BN

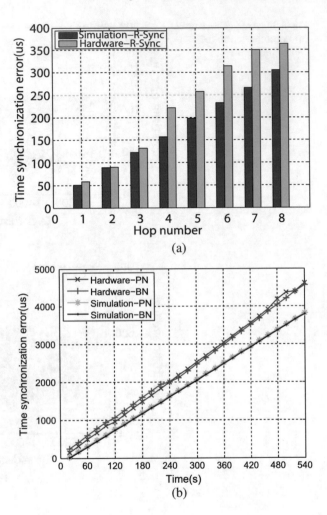

(a)

(b)

References

1. Watts, D. J. (2004). The new science of networks. *Annual Review of Sociology, 30*:243–270.
2. da Fontoura Costa, L., Oliveira, O. N. Jr., Travieso, G. (2011). Francisco Aparecido Rodrigues, Paulino Ribeiro Villas Boas, Lucas Antiqueira, Matheus Palhares Viana, and Luis Enrique Correa Rocha. Analyzing and modeling real-world phenomena with complex networks: A survey of applications. *Advances in Physics, 60*(3), 329–412.
3. Newman, M. E. J., & Watts, D. J. (1999). Renormalization group analysis of the small-world network model. *Physics Letters A, 263*(4–6), 341–346.
4. Watts, D. J., & Strogatz, S. H. (1998). Collective dynamics of small-world networks. *Nature, 393*(6684), 440–442.
5. Qiu, T., Luo, D., Xia, F., Deonauth, N., Si, W., & Tolba, A. (2016). A greedy model with small world for improving the robustness of heterogeneous internet of things. *Computer Networks, 101*:127–143.
6. Sharma, G., & Mazumdar, R. R. (2008). A case for hybrid sensor networks. *IEEE/ACM Transactions on Networking, 16*(5), 1121–1132.
7. Dousse, O., Thiran, P., & Hasler, M. (2002). Connectivity in ad-hoc and hybrid networks. In *Proceedings. Twenty-First Annual Joint Conference of the IEEE Computer and Communications Societies* (Vol. 2, pp. 1079–1088). New York: IEEE.
8. Cavalcanti, D., Agrawal, D., Kelner, J., & Sadok, D. (2004). Exploiting the small-world effect to increase connectivity in wireless ad hoc networks. In *International Conference on Telecommunications* (pp. 388–393). New York: Springer.
9. Guidoni, D. L., Mini, R. A. F., & Loureiro, A. A. F. (2010). On the design of resilient heterogeneous wireless sensor networks based on small world concepts. *Computer Networks, 54*(8), 1266–1281.
10. Guidoni, D. L., Mini, R. A. F., & Loureiro, A. A. F. (2012). Applying the small world concepts in the design of heterogeneous wireless sensor networks. *IEEE Communications Letters, 16*(7), 953–955.
11. Nardelli, E., Proietti, G., & Widmayer, P. (2003). Finding the most vital node of a shortest path. *Theoretical Computer Science, 296*(1), 167–177.
12. Callaway, D. S., Newman, M. E. J., Strogatz, S. H., & Watts, D. J. (2000). Network robustness and fragility: Percolation on random graphs. *Physical Review Letters, 85*(25), 5468–5471.
13. Newman, M. E. J. (2005). A measure of betweenness centrality based on random walks. *Social Networks, 27*(1), 39–54.
14. Hu, F., & Liu, Y. (2015). Multi-index algorithm of identifying important nodes in complex networks based on linear discriminant analysis. *Modern Physics Letters B, 29*(03), 1450268.
15. Qiu, T., Zhao, A., Xia, F., Si, W., & Wu, D. O. (2017). Rose: Robustness strategy for scale-free wireless sensor networks. *IEEE/ACM Transactions on Networking, 25*(5), 2944–2959.
16. Cai, Y., Cao, Y., Li, Y., Huang, T., & Zhou, B. (2015). Cascading failure analysis considering interaction between power grids and communication networks. *IEEE Transactions on Smart Grid, 7*(1), 530–538.
17. Li, R.-H., Yu, J. X., Huang, X., Cheng, H., & Shang, Z. (2012). Measuring robustness of complex networks under mvc attack. In *Proceedings of the 21st ACM International Conference on Information and Knowledge Management* (pap. 1512–1516).
18. Huang, X., Gao, J., Buldyrev, S. V., Havlin, S., & H. E. Stanley, H. E. (2011). Robustness of interdependent networks under targeted attack. *Physical Review E, 83*(6), 065101.
19. Wang, J., Jiang, C., & Qian, J. (2014). Robustness of interdependent networks with different link patterns against cascading failures. *Physica A: Statistical Mechanics and its Applications, 393*:535–541.
20. Cohen, R., & Havlin, S. (2010). *Complex networks: Structure, robustness and function.* Cambridge: Cambridge University Press.
21. Du, W.-B., Wu, Z.-X., & Cai, K.-Q. (2013). Effective usage of shortest paths promotes transportation efficiency on scale-free networks. *Physica A: Statistical Mechanics and Its Applications, 392*(17), 3505–3512.

22. Ebel, H., Mielsch, L.-I., & Bornholdt, S. (2002). Scale-free topology of e-mail networks. *Physical Review E, 66*(3), 035103.
23. Eguiluz, V. M., Chialvo, D. R., Cecchi, G. A., Baliki, M., & Apkarian, A. V. (2005). Scale-free brain functional networks. *Physical Review Letters, 94*(1), 018102.
24. Jian, Y., Liu, E., Wang, Y., Zhang, Z., & Lin, C. (2013). Scale-free model for wireless sensor networks. In *2013 IEEE wireless communications and networking conference (WCNC)* (pp. 2329–2332). New York: IEEE.
25. Zhu, H., Luo, H., Peng, H., Li, L., & Luo, Q. (2009). Complex networks-based energy-efficient evolution model for wireless sensor networks. *Chaos, Solitons & Fractals, 41*(4), 1828–1835.
26. Schneider, C. M., Moreira, A. A., Andrade, J. S., Havlin, S., & Herrmann, H. J. (2011). Mitigation of malicious attacks on networks. *Proceedings of the National Academy of Sciences, 108*(10), 3838–3841.
27. Herrmann, H. J., Schneider, C. M., Moreira, A. A., Andrade, J. S. Jr., & Havlin, S. (2011). Onion-like network topology enhances robustness against malicious attacks. *Journal of Statistical Mechanics: Theory and Experiment, 2011*(01), P01027.
28. Buesser, P., Daolio, F., & Tomassini, M. (2011). Optimizing the robustness of scale-free networks with simulated annealing. In *International Conference on Adaptive and Natural Computing Algorithms* (pp. 167–176). New York: Springer.
29. Zhou, M., & Liu, J. (2014). A memetic algorithm for enhancing the robustness of scale-free networks against malicious attacks. *Physica A: Statistical Mechanics and its Applications, 410*:131–143.
30. Barabási, A.-L., & Albert, R. (1999). Emergence of scaling in random networks. *science, 286*(5439), 509–512.
31. Tanizawa, T., Havlin, S., & Stanley, H. E. (2012). Robustness of onionlike correlated networks against targeted attacks. *Physical Review E, 85*(4), 046109.
32. Yao, Y., Cao, Q., & Vasilakos, A. V. (2014). EDAL: An energy-efficient, delay-aware, and lifetime-balancing data collection protocol for heterogeneous wireless sensor networks. *IEEE/ACM Transactions on Networking, 23*(3), 810–823.
33. Mills, D. L. (1991). Internet time synchronization: the network time protocol. *IEEE Transactions on Communications, 39*(10), 1482–1493.
34. Leng, M., & Wu, Y.-C. (2011). Distributed clock synchronization for wireless sensor networks using belief propagation. *IEEE Transactions on Signal Processing, 59*(11), 5404–5414.
35. Elson, J., Girod, L., & Estrin, D. (2002). Fine-grained network time synchronization using reference broadcasts. *ACM SIGOPS Operating Systems Review, 36*(SI), 147–163.
36. Djenouri, D. (2012). R^4Syn: relative referenceless receiver/receiver time synchronization in wireless sensor networks. *IEEE Signal Processing Letters, 19*(4), 175–178.
37. Gong, F., & Sichitiu, M. L. (2015). CESP: A low-power high-accuracy time synchronization protocol. *IEEE Transactions on Vehicular Technology, 65*(4), 2387–2396.
38. Ganeriwal, S., Kumar, R., & Srivastava, M. B. (2003). Timing-sync protocol for sensor networks. In *Proceedings of the 1st International Conference on Embedded Networked Sensor Systems* (pp. 138–149).
39. Noh, K.-L., & Serpedin, E. (2007). Pairwise broadcast clock synchronization for wireless sensor networks. In *2007 IEEE International Symposium on a World of Wireless, Mobile and Multimedia Networks* (pp. 1–6). New York: IEEE.
40. Noh, K.-L., Wu, Y.-C., Qaraqe, K., & Suter, B. W. (2008). Extension of pairwise broadcast clock synchronization for multicluster sensor networks. *EURASIP Journal on Advances in Signal Processing, 2008*, 1–10.
41. Qiu, T., Zhang, Y., Qiao, D., Zhang, X., Wymore, M. L., & Sangaiah, A. K. (2017). A robust time synchronization scheme for industrial internet of things. *IEEE Transactions on Industrial Informatics, 14*(8), 3570–3580.
42. Abouzar, P., Michelson, D. G., & Hamdi, M. (2016). RSSI-based distributed self-localization for wireless sensor networks used in precision agriculture. *IEEE Transactions on Wireless Communications, 15*(10), 6638–6650.

43. Laaraiedh, M., Avrillon, S., & Uguen, B. (2010). A maximum likelihood TOA based estimator for localization in heterogeneous networks. *International Journal of Communications, Network and System Sciences, 3*(1), 38–42.
44. Ble, F. Z., Lehtonen, M., Sihvola, A., & Kim, C. (2014). Power arcing source location using first peak arrival of rf-signal. *International Review of Electrical Engineering, 9*(4), 873–881.

Chapter 4
Robustness Optimization Based on Genetic Evolution

We discuss the self-organizing robustness optimization methods improving reliability of IoT topology in Chap. 3. In this chapter, we further improve the efficiency of optimization methods to solve multi-parameter and nonlinear problems. Researchers always pursue an optimal solution with less overhead and pay more attention to Genetic algorithm (GA). We analyze the topology structure characteristics from genetic evolution perspective, and propose an optimization method based on multi-population co-evolution to address the premature convergence problem in GA. Furthermore, in order to solve the problem that computational overhead is larger with the population size increasing, we present an adaptive optimization algorithm based on self-competition, which ensures the evolution direction and convergence speed of the population. This chapter rigorously demonstrates the correctness and effectiveness of the methods from a large number of experiment simulations.

4.1 Introduction

Robustness topology optimization of IoT is an NP-hard problem. The ability of self-optimization is significantly affected when the network size is increasing. In order to optimize the scale-free IoT topology, evolutionary algorithms are applied to obtain the global optimal solution. GA, as an evolutionary algorithm, is designed based on the core idea of Darwin's biological evolution theory–"Natural Selection and Survival of the Fittest", which searches the optimal solution of target problem through computer simulation of biological evolution process based on genetic mechanism in the real nature. However, in GA, "natural selection" is controlled by the user through fitness function. By constructing appropriate fitness function, the individual after each generation evolves is screened, so as to drive all the individuals in the population to evolve towards the direction we want to optimize, and finally find the optimal solution in the solution space [1–4].

The primary population represents the potential solution set of the problem, and each individual in the primary population has certain differences that ensure the diversity of genes. GA carries on the crossover operator to the population in the iterative way, that is, the father and mother individuals are selected. The daughter individuals are generated by the crossover of parents' gene codes. Then, several number of individuals produce genetic mutations, which are generally less likely to occur. Finally, the fitness function of the selection operation is used to determine which individuals will enter the next generation population. At the same time, some individuals that do not meet the optimization objectives are eliminated. After several generations of evolution, the ultimate result is an individual that meets the goal of optimization.

In practical application, many optimization problems are multi-parameter and nonlinear, and the GA shows exceptional search ability which has achieved outstanding results in many fields of application. However, a huge defect of GA is gradually exposed—i.e., premature convergence. Premature convergence is that the population does not produce an individual with higher fitness value than previous one when the global optimal solution has not been yet reached. The differences between individuals in a population are very small, and the genetic diversity of population decreases sharply. The crossover and mutation operators produce less good individuals, and the population will gradually lose evolutionary motivation. Finally, we will obtain an individual whose fitness value is not optimal in the population, as a result, the stagnation of the search for the optimal solution of GA is occurred. The evolutionary power of GA lies in maintaining the genetic diversity of the population. Once the population loses the genetic diversity, the optimization effect of GA will be greatly reduced, which is prone to appearing in the evolution process. GA will fall into evolutionary stagnation and the global optimization ability will soon lose when premature convergence occurs. It means that the GA will fall into premature convergence if there are the following two phenomena:

1. Most of the individuals in the population tend to be the same individual, and the population gradually stops evolving.
2. Individuals that are not optimal at present but may be close to the optimal solution in the future are always eliminated, and the evolutionary process gradually converges to a center individual.

Premature convergence generated by GA is stochastic, which is difficult to predict before algorithm optimization. Its occurrence is mainly related to the following aspects:

(1) In the evolution process of each generation of GA, individuals of the population are selected to participate in the crossover and mutation operators probabilistically. We assume that the probability of individuals participating in the two operators is defined as crossover probability P_c and mutation probability P_m. These two probabilities directly control the frequency of crossover and mutation

operators, which affects the balance between global search and local search. The final optimization performance of GA is dependent on the appropriate value of P_c and P_m that are not fixed law to determine. Before GA starts, it is impossible to predict the influence of the P_c and P_m on the final optimization results. Therefore, even similar values of P_c and P_m are likely to lead to completely different optimization results.

(2) After the individual evolution, the fitness value is screened whose value determines the probability of individual selection—i.e., the greater the fitness value, the greater the probability of individual selection. At this point, if the population occurs an exceptional excellent individual (i.e., whose fitness value is much higher than other individuals), the individual has a great probability to be selected in next generation. For many iterations of evolution, the individual not only again and again is selected, but there are more similar individuals in crossover operator. Finally, individuals in the population gradually converge to the one individual. The genetic diversity is lost, which leads to the loss of the evolutionary motivation and the topology robustness optimization problem falls into stagnation.

(3) Finally, the population size of GA also has an impact on the final optimization performance. Population size directly determines the population genetic diversity that is the basis of the search target solution in a bigger solution space. If the population size is small and genetic diversity is less, population evolution will soon converge and individuals have no differences. The probability of crossover operator to generate new individuals will be down to very low. However, if the difference of individuals is larger, the probability of crossover operator to produce new individuals is larger. Then, the mutation operator can only maintain the introduction of new genes in the population. Nevertheless, the occurrence probability of the mutation operator is limited to some extent, and the overall mutation rate needs to be controlled at a low level. Therefore, the evolution of the population soon stops. If the population size is large, the genetic diversity of the population is guaranteed. However, more crossover and mutation operators are involved in each generation, the evolution process is unusually slow, and the running time overhead of GA is bound to increase.

The rest of the chapter is organized as follows. In Sect. 4.2, a multi-population co-evolution genetic algorithm is proposed to solve the traditional premature convergence. Section 4.3 presents an adaptive robustness evolution algorithm with self-competition to further improve the optimization ability that digging the evolution of GA.

4.2 Robustness Optimization Scheme with Multi-population Co-evolution

Based on the shortcoming of GA in evolution algorithm, this chapter makes the following improvements and proposes a topology robustness optimization algorithm based on multi-population co-evolution (ROCKS):

i. Multi-populations are introduced to synchronously evolve during the algorithm running. By assigning different values of P_c and P_m to different populations, these populations are intentionally guided to have different balances in global search and local search. It is impossible to predict whether the current values of P_c and P_m will lead to premature convergence before ROCKS starts. Therefore, a number of different values are used to avoid the problem, and it can be observed that those populations are trapped in local optimum and stop evolving through comparison in the evolution process.

ii. When evolution of each generation in each population is completed, each population is communicated and co-evolved by migration operator. As mentioned above, although multi-populations of different P_c and P_m to avoid a single population fall into the predicament of the local optimum, the populations that are relatively backward in evolution or have fallen into the local optimum still occupy the computational resources. The migration operator can effectively prevent the waste of computing resources by introducing excellent individuals from other populations into these populations. Furthermore, each population exchanges genes in each generation by the migration operator to increase the diversity of genes, which also effectively ensures that the multi-population co-evolutionary motivation is inexhaustible. Finally, the optimal solution is obtained in the cooperative cooperation of each population.

iii. For each generation, the best individual will be selected to form an elite population that is the basis of the migration operator. In order to prevent the elite population from being destroyed, it is only treated with preservation rather than crossover and mutation operators. The optimal solution of each population in the whole evolutionary process will not be destroyed. Inserting genes from elite populations into evolving populations is easy to supplement genetic diversity, which is beneficial for fitness function to search for the optimal solution in a wider range.

4.2.1 Optimization Problem Model

The pattern theorem proposed by Holland is widely used to explain GA, which lays the mathematical foundation of GA [5]. This chapter uses the theorem to prove the topology robustness optimization algorithm of IoT based on multi-population co-evolution.

Proof After genetic mutation operator in each generation, the fitness function $f(G)$ is used to screen the individuals. Assume that $G_i (i = 1, 2, \cdots, n)$ is an individual topology for current population. Then, the probability of G_i being selected into the next generation is defined as follows:

$$P(G_i) = \frac{f(G_i)}{\sum_{j=1}^{NIND} f(G_i)} \tag{4.1}$$

Wherein, $NIND$ represents the number of individuals in current population, $f(G_i)$ denotes the fitness value of the individual topology G_i. According to the pattern theorem, assuming that m individuals from a population in current t generation match pattern α, represents $m(\alpha, t)$. In $t + 1$ generation, the number of individuals $m(\alpha, t = 1)$ that matched pattern α is defined as follows:

$$m(\alpha, t + 1) = MP \times NIND \times \sum_{G_i \in \alpha} P(G_i) \tag{4.2}$$

Wherein, MP represents the number of populations. Assuming that $f(\alpha)$ is the average fitness value of the individual matched pattern α, the following formula can be deduced from Eq. (4.2):

$$m(\alpha, t + 1) = MP \times NIND \times \frac{m(\alpha, t) \times f(\alpha)}{\sum_{j=1}^{NIND} f(G_j)} \tag{4.3}$$

The average fitness function value of all individuals in current population is defined as follows:

$$f' = \frac{1}{NIND} \times \sum_{j=1}^{NIND} f(G_j) \tag{4.4}$$

Based on Eqs. (4.3) and (4.4), the following formula is simplified:

$$m(\alpha, t + 1) = MP \times m(\alpha, t) \times \frac{f(\alpha)}{f'} \tag{4.5}$$

Assume that the average fitness function value $f(\alpha)$ of individuals matched by the pattern α can be represented by Eq. (4.6):

$$f(\alpha) = f' + cf' \tag{4.6}$$

where c is a constant value. And the following formula can be obtained:

$$m(\alpha, t + 1) = MP \times m(\alpha, t) \times \frac{f' + cf'}{f'} = MP \times m(\alpha, t) \times (1 + c) \tag{4.7}$$

If c is constant from $t = 0$, then Eq. (4.7) can be written as:

$$m(\alpha, t + 1) = MP \times m(\alpha, 0) \times (1 + c)^t \qquad (4.8)$$

From Eq. (4.8), if the average fitness function value of a certain mode is greater than the average fitness function value of the population, that is, $c > 0$, then the number of individuals matching this pattern will increase exponentially. Conversely, if the average fitness function value of a certain pattern is less than the average fitness function value of the population, i.e., $c < 0$, then the number of individuals matching this pattern will decrease exponentially. In addition, the optimization performance of multi-population GA is proportional to the number of population MP, and the larger MP is, the better the optimization performance is. □

Statistical research shows that: in the random search, to obtain a better feasible solution, we must ensure that the optimal solution of samples showed exponential growth. Through the above proof, the individual samples with higher fitness values will show exponential growth in the proposed algorithm. Therefore, ROCKS possesses the necessary condition to find the optimal solution from the search space.

4.2.2 Topological Data Processing

For the evolutionary GA, the goal of optimization problem should be set as coding of chromosome that is the carrier of individual feature information. Therefore, for topology robustness optimization, the IoT topology is encoded by binary code, and assembled to a chromosome that can be evolved by GA. Chromosome coding generally is a function that converts the optimized target solution corresponding data as a chromosome. This chapter outlines the IoT topology robustness optimization, which goal is achieved by changing the topology connection. As shown in Fig. 4.1, the IoT topology is converted to a binary-coded chromosome. The topology has five nodes, including i, j, k, l, m. In order to save more storage space, the upper triangular matrix of the adjacency matrix is able to completely represent the connections between nodes in IoT. Therefore, the shorted-length chromosome can improve the efficiency of GA and represent large-scale IoT topology as well as using less storage space.

4.2.3 Initialization Operation

Individual diversity is the factor that affects the performance of genetic evolution, which also influences the optimum search space. The bad situation is that all individuals are same, and the evolution of individuals only relies on the mutation operator, which leads premature convergence and obtains a local optimum solution

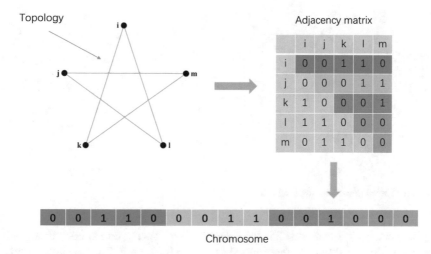

Fig. 4.1 The adjacency matrix is converted to a chromosome

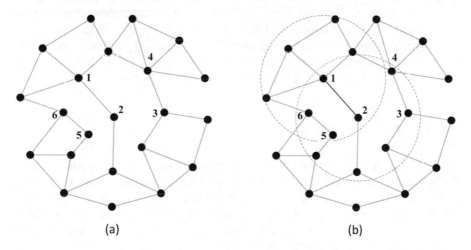

Fig. 4.2 Illustration of network structure. (a) Initial topology. (b) Selected edges for swapping

for robustness optimization. Therefore, it is very important to build a diverse initial topology population. The design of initialization operation is as follows.

In this algorithm, for the IoT topology, the location of each node is fixed and degree distribution is not changed. Firstly, a random probability is set up to control the frequency of edge swapping on the original topology as shown in Fig. 4.2. Then, for selected edges, there are three swapping methods as shown in Fig. 4.3. Thus, initial topologies with large difference are random and transformed from the original topology.

Figure 4.2a is an original scale-free WSNs topology, a new topology is generated by initialization operator that keeps degree distribution unchanged. An edge is selected by the random probability, as shown in Fig. 4.2b, for example, the edge

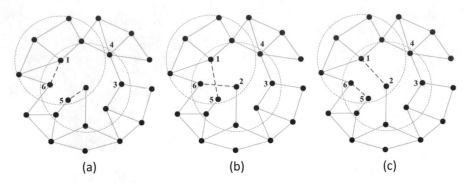

Fig. 4.3 Three edge-swapping methods

e_{12} between node 1 and node 2 is the selected edge. Then, another edge that can be swapped with e_{12} should be determined as shown in Fig. 4.3. The nodes on another edge can be communicate with nodes 1, 2. Therefore, e_{12} and e_{56} can conduct swapping operator. There are three candidate swapping operations respectively, as shown in Fig. 4.3. If edge e_{12} cannot find a matching edge after traversing all the edges of topology, the swapping operation for e_{12} will be abandoned. Then, the random selecting operations will be executed again. Finally, different initial topologies will be generated by using the initialization operation.

4.2.4 Crossover Operator

In order to increase the genetic diversity of populations, crossover operator is used that generates new offsprings. Generally, important structures of father and mother genes will be retained on new children topologies by using crossover operator. Besides, the initial degree distribution of each node in topologies is not changed that maintains the scale-free network model features. However, considering the limitations of IoT, the design details of crossover operator are as follows.

Suppose G_f and G_m are the father's topology and mother's topology, respectively. And G_s and G_d are the son's topology and daughter's topology, respectively. Firstly, the parents are chosen by the probability P_{cro} of crossover operator in a population. Then G_s inherits its father's topology G_f and G_d inherits its mother's topology G_m. Obtain the following sets of edges:

$$E_f^G = \{e_{ij} | e_{ij} \in G_f\} \tag{4.9}$$

$$E_m^G = \{e_{ij} | e_{ij} \in G_m\} \tag{4.10}$$

$$E_f = E_f^G - (E_f^G \cap E_m^G) \tag{4.11}$$

$$E_m = E_m^G - (E_m^G \cap E_f^G) \tag{4.12}$$

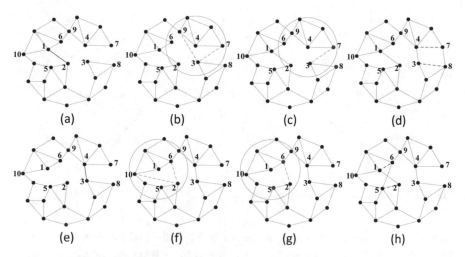

Fig. 4.4 The process of crossover operator

where, E_f^G is the set of the father's edges, and E_m^G is the set of mother's edges. E_f and E_m are the sets of father's exclusive edges and mother's exclusive edges respectively. Therefore, E_f is totally different from E_m. As shown in Fig. 4.4, the position of each node is fixed. The son's topology disconnects the existing edges to build every mother's exclusive edges E_m. The construction process of daughter's topology is similar to above operation.

Figure 4.4a–e illustrate the connections between nodes in the father's topology G_f and mother's topology G_m. e_{12} is the executive edge in G_f in Fig. 4.4a, and e_{34} is the executive edge in G_m in Fig. 4.4e. Based on crossover operator, the G_m's executive edge e_{34} is in the son's topology G_s in Fig. 4.4d, and also the e_{12} is in the daughter's topology G_d in Fig. 4.4h. Besides, when the father's topology G_f generates his son's topology G_s, if the node 3 cannot find an eligible node to match the node 7 which is the candidate neighbor of the node 4, another candidate node will be chosen until an eligible node matches the requirement. Otherwise, another edge is selected.

4.2.5   Mutation Operator

The mutation operator also produces individuals with high fitness values. First, an individual topology is selected by the mutation probability P_{mut}. The goal of the mutation operator is to adjust single individual topology to increase robustness by exchanging some edges. Mutation operator can find the optimal solution within the local area. According to the conclusion of Herrmann et al. [6], nodes with similarity degree are connected together to improve the robustness of network topology. Therefore, minimizing the adverse effects of failed nodes is the goal of this chapter.

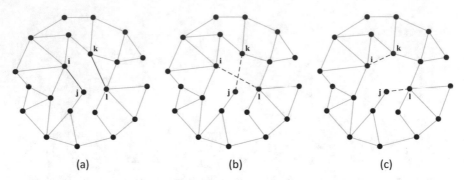

Fig. 4.5 Candidates for the topology connection

Based on initialization operator, two edges in the individual topology are selected to exchange each other that the four end nodes are in the communication range of each other. As shown in Fig. 4.5a, for edges e_{ij} and e_{kl} selected, a criterion to sort degree and swap edges as follows Eq. (4.13).

$$\frac{d_1 - d_2 + d_3 - d_4}{|d_i - d_j| + |d_k - d_l|} < P_{swap} \tag{4.13}$$

wherein, d_i, d_j, d_k, d_l are the degree of node i, node j, node k and node l respectively. They are sorted by descending order, and named as d_1, d_2, d_3, d_4. P_{swap} controls reduction ratio of degree difference. There are two candidate strategies in Fig. 4.5b and c.

Based on the criteria mentioned above, a topology that towards the onion-like structure [6] is generated. The swapping threshold P_{swap} is defined in [0, 1) that the efficiency of mutation operator by adjusting the value of P_{swap}. The appropriate swapping threshold P_{swap} can effectively avoid inefficient swapping edges operation.

4.2.6 Migration Operator

The goal of migration operator is to overcome premature convergence. Elite individuals actively communicate with other populations and leave important topological structures to avoid falling into a local optimum by introducing new individuals. Different mutation operator and crossover operator probabilities are assigned for every generation which extends the optimum search space. As shown in Fig. 4.6, first, individuals with the highest fitness are selected from each population, which will be grouped an elite population. Then, the elite individuals will replace the worst individual in a different population.

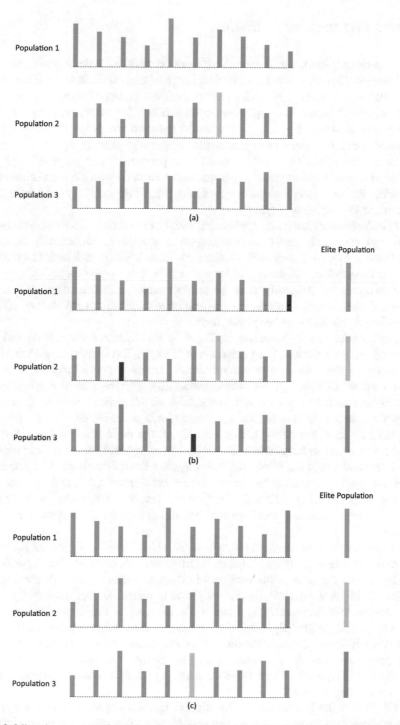

Fig. 4.6 Migration operator. (**a**) Select the optimal individual. (**b**) Identify the worst individual. (**c**) Replacement

4.2.7 Performance Evaluation

For experiment simulation, the monitoring area is a $500m*500m$ in which nodes are randomly deployed. The communication range of each node is set to 200 m which guarantees sufficient neighbors for each node. The number of populations is 10, the number of individuals in a population is 20. All detailed parameters are introduced in [7]. As shown in Fig. 4.7, a comparison between the proposed algorithm and conventional GA is executed to present the optimization trend of the best individuals of each generation. Obviously, from the experiments, the proposed algorithm achieves a great improvement in optimization compared with the conventional GA. Besides, the proposed algorithm can avoid premature convergence and a better optimized IoT topology is got.

In order to observe the attack effect intuitively, the maximum connected subgraph is always used to measure the robustness status of network connectivity encountering failed nodes. As shown in Fig. 4.8, random attack is that each node has the equal chance to be failed, and the malicious attack is that the important nodes have more probability to fail. To easily view the performance of random attack, one node is attacked each time until all the nodes have been failed in IoT. Moreover, different scale IoT topologies have been compared.

For random attack, as shown in Fig. 4.8a and b, one node and its links are removed in one iteration. The performance of ROCKS is consistent with the initial topology for the resistance to random attack, which is proved that the scale-free characteristic of topology has strong reliability. Different from random attack, malicious attack of network is a purposeful attack which refers to destroy the important nodes. In this algorithm, the bigger the degree of a node, the more important it is in the network. For simulation, the node with the biggest degree is the first target to be attacked. The initial topology and the optimized topology are compared under the same conditions against malicious attack. The number of nodes in maximal connected subgraph is recorded after each iteration. For malicious attack, as shown in Fig. 4.8c and d, the performance of the algorithm is closer to the fully connected network topology that has the most robustness against malicious attack.

Moreover, the algorithm is more robust than Hill Climbing algorithm [6] and the Simulated Annealing algorithm [8] under different edge densities. The edge density M represents the ratio of the number of edges to nodes in network topology. As shown in Fig. 4.9, all three algorithms promote metric R over the initial network topology with the increase of edge density. Besides, under different edge densities of network topologies, the algorithm always has a better optimization results compared with the traditional optimization algorithms. For different scale of network topology, the performance of the algorithm is also better than the two existing algorithms as shown in Fig. 4.10. All the three algorithms present a downward trend with the increase of network size.

Given that the limited communication range and limited node degree of network topology in real world, a multi-population co-evolution genetic algorithm

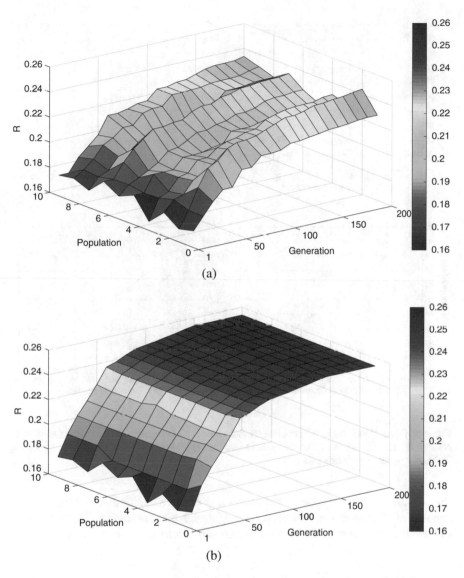

Fig. 4.7 Evolutionary process of multiple populations. (**a**) Conventional GA. (**b**) ROCKS

is proposed to improve the robustness and optimization efficiency. As we all know, the BA model is more robust against random attack while fragile against international attack. Therefore, we apply the BA model to promote its resistance against malicious attack. In this algorithm, two novel operators are designed, and all node degrees are unchanged which guarantees the scale-free property. Two existing algorithms are introduced to compare with the proposed algorithm for the optimization performance under different edge density and network size. Above all,

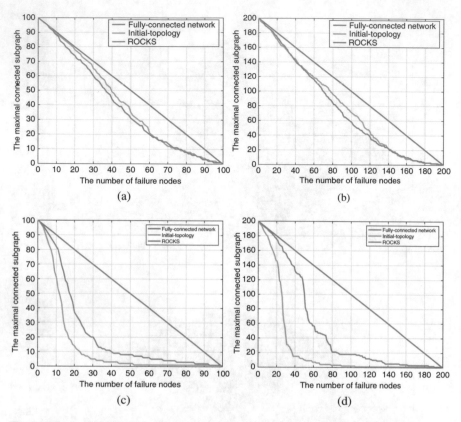

Fig. 4.8 Comparison on the network connectivity before and after ROCKS. (**a**) 100 nodes under random attacks. (**b**) 200 nodes under random attacks. (**c**) 100 nodes under malicious attacks. (**d**) 200 nodes under malicious attacks

the proposed algorithm is better than other algorithms and significantly improve the robustness of scale-free network topology against malicious attacks. With increasing of network size, the robustness of optimized network topology is still at a high level.

4.3   An Adaptive Robustness Evolution Algorithm with Self-competition

The traditional genetic algorithm has shown great advantages in seeking optimal solution in many fields. Its search ability is often linked with its initial population diversity. A single quantity of individuals in a population is limited that is easy to appear the phenomenon that difficult to produce superior to current population on the generation of individuals. Individuals are gradually in the direction of the current optimal solution convergent, and the population diversity declines or even

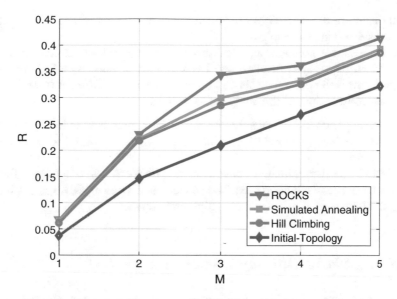

Fig. 4.9 Comparison between ROCKS and other algorithms in different edge densities

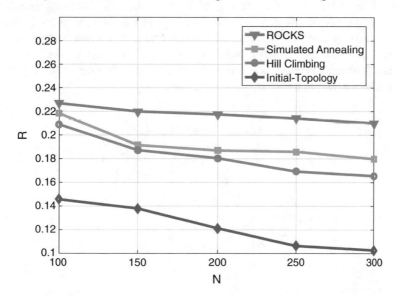

Fig. 4.10 Comparison between ROCKS and other algorithms in different network sizes

disappears. The crossover and mutation operators are very difficult to motivate the evolution of GA. This phenomenon is often refereed to as premature convergence. The prior work proposed a multi-population co-evolution algorithm (ROCKS) to solve the premature convergence. However, the increase in population size will greatly increase the amount of computation. Therefore, the above issues will be fully considered in this chapter.

To address this problem, an edge server is introduced which collects nodes' information. An Adaptive Robustness Evolution Algorithm (AREA) is proposed that performs well with only a single population, which is different from ROCKS. The main contributions of this study are as follows:

- Self-competition. AREA adaptively controls the evolution of individuals according to population state change, which also balances global and local search capabilities.
- Adaptive rate. The premature convergence is prevented with adaptively adjusting the crossover and mutation rates. The convergence speed of AREA is guaranteed by combing several excellent population individuals.

4.3.1   Population Diversity Measurement Method

In order to facilitate topological operations, we encode the IoT topology into a binary chromosome, as shown in Fig. 4.11. Each node has same communication range (r). We define effective gene positions (EGP) that refers to the two nodes that are in communication range with each other. A chromosome is used to represent the network topology. Besides, a new measurement method combining the gene position coverage ratio (GPCR) and gene distribution uniformity (GDU) are proposed to assess population diversity effectively.

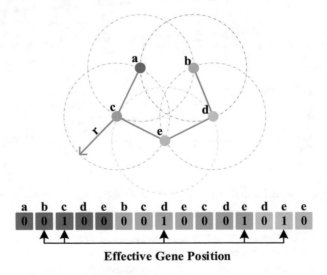

Fig. 4.11 Topological binary chromosome coding

4.3.1.1   Gene Position Coverage Ratio

GPCR refers to the ratio of the gene position encoded by the value 1 in the population of EGP, which represents connection diversity. The specific calculation is as Eq. (4.14).

$$
\begin{cases}
GPCR = \dfrac{Occ - E_{num}}{\min\{P_{num} \cdot E_{num}, |EGP|\} - E_{num}} \\[2mm]
Occ = \displaystyle\sum_{i=1}^{L} Occ_i
\end{cases}
\tag{4.14}
$$

wherein, L is the total number of gene positions in the chromosome of the individual. Occ_i represents whether the gene position i is occupied (0 is occupied and 1 is unoccupied). Occ is the total number of gene positions occupied by all individuals in the population. P_{num} is the number of individuals in the population. E_{num} is the number of edges in the topology. $|EGP|$ is the number of EGP. To ensure the validity of the evaluation method and consider the extreme cases [9], we use $(P_{num} \cdot E_{num})$ instead of $|EGP|$. The range of GPCR is [0, 1].

However, the GPCR can not estimate the diversity of a population comprehensively. Because even if the GPCR values of two populations are equal, the genetic position diversities of the populations may be different. Only when the gene distribution at each effective gene position is balanced, the operation at each gene position is average, and the operation of the individual is balanced. For example, in Fig. 4.12, there are two populations, each with four chromosomes ($P_{num} = 4$, $E_{num} = 5$ and $|EGP| = 10$). The number of gene positions occupied by these

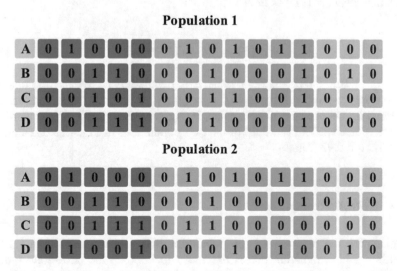

Fig. 4.12 Two populations with equal GPCR

two populations is the same ($Occ = 10$), but the individual gene distributions are different. The gene distribution in Population 2 is more uniform than that of Population 1.

4.3.1.2 Gene Distribution Uniformity

GDU, which can be measured by information entropy theory [10], is defined as Eq. (4.15).

$$
\begin{cases}
GDU = H_{P_{num}}(t)/\log_2 Occ \\[2mm]
H_{P_{num}}(t) = -\sum_{i=1}^{Occ} p_{k_{(i)}} \log_2 p_{k_{(i)}} \\[2mm]
p_{k_{(i)}} = \dfrac{1}{P_{num} \cdot E_{num}} \sum_{j=1}^{P_{num}} e_{k_{(i)} j}
\end{cases}
\tag{4.15}
$$

In Eq. (4.15), $H_{P_{num}}(t)$ represents the uniformity (diversity) of the gene distribution of a population with P_{num} individuals when it is iterated to the t-th generation by AREA. $\log_2 Occ$ is the maximum value of $H_{P_{num}}(t)$ (the proof is as follows). GDU is the result of $H_{P_{num}}(t)$ normalization and ranges in $(0, 1]$. $P_{k(i)}$ is the probability that the gene is encoded as 1 at the gene position $k_{(i)}$. $k_{(i)}$ represents the actual gene position. $e_{k_{(i)} j}$ is the value at the gene position $k_{(i)}$ of the individual j.

GDU describes the balance of gene distribution in covered areas, which compensates for the limitations of GPCR. We combine GPCR and GDU to measure population diversity (PD) as Eq. (4.16).

$$
PD(P) = \sqrt{GPCR \cdot GDU}
\tag{4.16}
$$

In Eq. (4.16), $PD(P)$ is the diversity of population P. When the population contains only two individuals, that is, $P = \{x, y\}$, PD can also be used to measure the similarity between x and y. Smaller $PD(x, y)$ values imply greater similarity between x and y. The PD values of the two populations in Fig. 4.12 calculated by Eq. (4.16) are 0.9732 and 1.

4.3.2 Adaptive Adjustment

To guarantee the diversity of the population and global search ability of the algorithm, a high mutation rate is necessary to improve the performance of the $PD(P)$ at the later stages of population evolution. Therefore, we add cosine iterative control to the mutation rate adjustment process. The iterative control $\psi(t)$, crossover rate $p_C^{x,y}$, and mutation rate p_M are as Eqs. (4.17), (4.18) and (4.19).

$$\psi(t) = \cos\frac{\pi(t-1)}{4(T-1)} \tag{4.17}$$

$$p_C^{x,y} = p_{Cmin} + (p_{Cmax} - p_{Cmin}) \cdot PD(\{x,y\}) \tag{4.18}$$

$$p_M = p_{Mmin} + (p_{Mmax} - p_{Mmin}) \cdot (1 - PD(P)) \cdot \psi(t) \tag{4.19}$$

In Eqs. (4.17), (4.18) and (4.19), p_{Cmax} and p_{Cmin} are the upper and lower limits of the crossover rate, respectively, p_{Mmax} and p_{Mmin} are the upper and lower limits of the mutation rate, respectively, t is the current number of iterations, and T is the maximum number of iterations.

4.3.3   Self-competitive Mechanism

In order to obtain the global optimal topology, a self-competitive mechanism is proposed that refers to the competition between individuals in P_t and individuals in P_{t+1} to the competition between the individuals in P_{t+1} and the global optimal individual G_{max}^{global}. As shown in Fig. 4.13, after the local search operation, a new population generation P_{t+1} is formed. We employ the *Tournament Selection* method

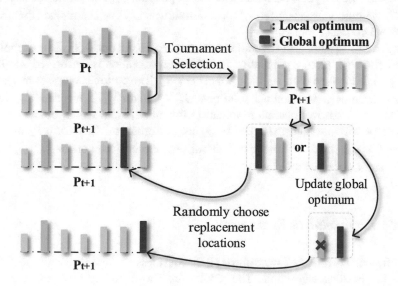

Fig. 4.13 Self-competitive mechanism

Algorithm 1 AREA

Require: G_0, P_{num}, p_{Cmax}, p_{Cmin}, p_{Mmax}, p_{Mmin}, p_{ls}, p_c, T.
Ensure: G_{max}^{global}, r_{max}^{global}
1: $[P_0, R_0] \leftarrow$ Population Initialization(G_0, P_{num});
2: $P_1 \leftarrow P_0$, $R_1 \leftarrow R_0$;
3: $[G_{max}^{global}, r_{max}^{global}] \leftarrow$ Optimal solution of P_1 and R_1;
4: **for** $t = 1$ to T **do**
5:      Get $p_C^{x,y}$ of P_t according to (4.18);
6:      $[P_{t+1}, R_{t+1}] \leftarrow$ Crossover Operation(P_t, P_{num}, $p_C^{x,y}$);
7:      Get p_M of P_{t+1} according to (4.19);
8:      $[P_{t+1}, R_{t+1}] \leftarrow$ Mutation Operation(P_{t+1}, R_{t+1}, P_{num}, p_M);
9:      $[P_{t+1}, R_{t+1}] \leftarrow$ Local Search(P_{t+1}, R_{t+1}, P_{num}, p_{ls});
10:     $[P_{t+1}, R_{t+1}] \leftarrow$ Tournament(P_t, R_t, P_{t+1}, R_{t+1});
11:     **if** $r_{max}^{local} > r_{max}^{global}$ **then**
12:         $r_{max}^{global} \leftarrow r_{max}^{local}$; $G_{max}^{global} \leftarrow G_{max}^{local}$.
13:     **end if**
14:     **for** $i = 1$ to $\lceil p_c \cdot P_{num} \rceil$ **do**
15:         $x \leftarrow$ Randomly select a position from P_{t+1};
16:         $G_x \leftarrow G_{max}^{global}$, $r_x \leftarrow r_{max}^{global}$;
17:         Add G_x to P_{t+1}, r_x to R_{t+1};
18:     **end for**
19: **end for**

---

to select individuals from P_t and P_{t+1}; then, we randomly select two individuals to compete and retain the best individual, and update P_{t+1}. To ensure the leading position of the global optimal solution in the population, regardless of whether the robustness of the optimal individual in the population P_{t+1} is greater or less than r_{max}^{global}, we randomly select $\lceil p_c \cdot P_{num} \rceil$ individuals in P_{t+1} and replace them with the global optimal solution.

Algorithm 1 presents the overall structure of AREA in detail. G_0 is the topology to be optimized. First, a population initialization operation is performed on G_0 to form an initial population P_0 and a robust set R_0. The optimal solutions in P_0 and R_0 are saved as global optimal solutions G_{max}^{global} and r_{max}^{global}, respectively. Then, T rounds of crossover operation, mutation operation, local search operation, and self-competitive mechanism (lines 11–19) are performed on P_0 to form P_T and R_T, where T is the maximum number of iterations. Finally, the obtained G_{max}^{global} and r_{max}^{global} are the optimal solutions.

4.3.4   Performance Evaluation

For different network size, we compare the robustness performance between AREA and other existing algorithms. The results are shown in Fig. 4.14, the proposed AREA has better performance than HC and SA in all respects.

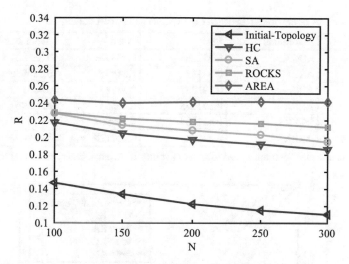

Fig. 4.14 Compare the optimization effects of AREA and other algorithms on scale-free IoT topologies with different number of nodes

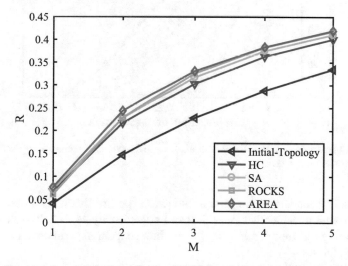

Fig. 4.15 Compare the optimization effects of AREA and other algorithms on scale-free IoT topologies with different edge densities

For different edge densities, the proposed AREA has better performance than HC and SA in robustness optimization as shown in Fig. 4.15, and Table 4.1 presents the details on the overlap between the ROCKS curve and the AREA curve. The bold values are the best optimized robustness values in different cases (i.e., worst and best). It can be seen that the robustness of the network topology increases as edge density increases. We conclude that AREA is better than the other algorithms.

Table 4.1 Results of the overlap between the ROCKS and AREA curves

M	Algorithms	Best	Worst	Average ± Variance
3	ROCKS	**0.351683**	0.303663	0.325861 ± 0.00021
	AREA	0.347327	**0.314752**	**0.330950 ± 0.00011**
4	ROCKS	0.391287	0.373267	0.383149 ± 0.00003
	AREA	**0.397525**	**0.375644**	**0.383901 ± 0.00004**
5	ROCKS	0.423267	**0.409901**	0.418287 ± 0.00002
	AREA	**0.428515**	0.407129	**0.419693 ± 0.00003**

The bold values are the best optimized robustness values in different cases, like worst and best.

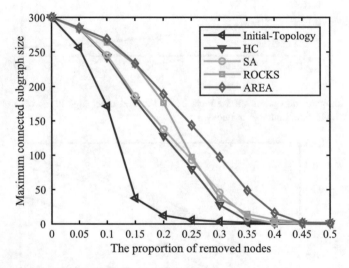

Fig. 4.16 Comparison of connectivity of scale-free IoT topologies optimized by various algorithms under malicious attacks

We conduct malicious and random attacks experiments on scale-free network topologies with node number $N = 300$ and edge density $M = 2$. The final results are the average of those from c ($c \geq 10$) independent experiments, as shown in Figs. 4.16 and 4.17.

For random attacks and malicious attacks, we compare the trends about the topological changes as shown in Figs. 4.16 and 4.17 for various algorithms. With the increasing of removed nodes, the size of the connected subgraphs decreases. AREA performs best among all algorithms. Besides, for random attacks, AREA curve deviates from the curve of the initial topology, but the overall deviation is not large. This implies that AREA-optimized topologies are still highly capable of resisting random attacks.

The communication range and energy limit of nodes in real-world IoT are considered. The scale-free BA model is applied for constructing IoT topology. To save storage space, a binary-coded chromosome is designed. A new population diversity measurement method is employed to adjust crossover and mutation operations that ensure the diversity of the early population. AREA combined with

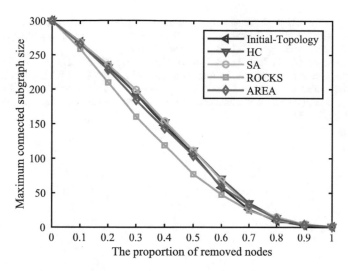

Fig. 4.17 Comparison of connectivity of scale-free IoT topologies optimized by various algorithms under random attacks

local search and self-competitive mechanism can effectively improve the robustness of individuals and prevent the loss of optimal individuals. The AREA-optimized scale-free IoT topology is far more capable of resisting malicious attacks than HC, SA, and ROCKS.

References

1. Ren, H., Huang, X., & Hao, J. (2015). Finding robust adaptation gene regulatory networks using multi-objective genetic algorithm. *IEEE/ACM Transactions on Computational Biology and Bioinformatics, 13*(3), 571–577.
2. Pandey, H. M., Chaudhary, A., & Mehrotra, D. (2014). A comparative review of approaches to prevent premature convergence in GA. *Applied Soft Computing, 24*, 1047–1077.
3. Wang, X., Han, S., Wu, Y., & Wang, X. (2012). Coverage and energy consumption control in mobile heterogeneous wireless sensor networks. *IEEE Transactions on Automatic Control, 58*(4):975–988.
4. Zheng, Z., Liu, A., Cai, L. X., Chen, Z., & Shen, X. (2015). Energy and memory efficient clone detection in wireless sensor networks. *IEEE Transactions on Mobile Computing, 15*(5):1130–1143.
5. Angel, O., Gorin, V., & Holroyd, A. (2012). A pattern theorem for random sorting networks. *Electronic Journal of Probability, 17*:1–16.
6. Herrmann, H. J., Schneider, C. M., Moreira, A. A., Andrade, J. S. Jr., & Havlin, S. (2011). Onion-like network topology enhances robustness against malicious attacks. *Journal of Statistical Mechanics: Theory and Experiment, 2011*(01):P01027.
7. Qiu, T., Liu, J., Si, W., & Wu, D. O. (2019). Robustness optimization scheme with multi-population co-evolution for scale-free wireless sensor networks. In *IEEE/ACM Transactions on Networking*, 2019.

8. Buesser, P., Daolio, F., & Tomassini, M. (2011). Optimizing the robustness of scale-free networks with simulated annealing. In *International conference on adaptive and natural computing algorithms* (pp. 167–176). New York: Springer.
9. Qiu, T., Lu, Z., Li, K., Xue, G., & Wu, D. O. (2020). An adaptive robustness evolution algorithm with self-competition for scale-free internet of things. In *IEEE INFOCOM 2020-IEEE Conference on Computer Communications* (pp. 2106–2115). New York: IEEE.
10. Shannon, C. E. (1948). A mathematical theory of communication. *Bell System Technical Journal, 27*(3):379–423.

Chapter 5
Robustness Optimization Based on Swarm Intelligence

This chapter introduces the application of swarm intelligence in robust topology optimization. Traditional greedy algorithms and evolutionary algorithms are easy to fall into the local optimum and cannot obtain the global optimum. The heuristic algorithm based on swarm intelligence can find an approximate optimal solution in polynomial time, which can meet the requirements of constructing a robust topology. In the swarm intelligence algorithm, ant colony and particle swarm are the two most widely used typical algorithms. Therefore, this chapter will discuss the topology robustness optimization problems of single-sink node network and multi-sink node network based on these two algorithms.

5.1 Topology Optimization Strategy with Ant Colony Algorithm

In Chap. 3.1, the GMSW algorithm [1] based on the greedy principle has been proposed to introduce the small-world model into the construction of the IoT topology and improve the ability of heterogeneous networks to resist attacks. Because the greedy principle is a locally optimal method, GMSW cannot get a global optimal solution. In order to further improve the optimization performance of topology robustness, this section proposes a global small-world topology optimization scheme for heterogeneous IoT based on GMSW. Through the ant colony optimization algorithm, the number of occurrences of nodes on all the shortest paths is obtained as the criterion for judging the importance of nodes. The shortcuts between important nodes in the network are added to build a global small-world model. Based on the above ideas, the TOSG algorithm [2] is proposed to optimize the topology of heterogeneous networks. The content of this algorithm is explained in the following sections.

© The Author(s), under exclusive license to Springer Nature Singapore Pte Ltd. 2022   117
T. Qiu et al., *Robustness Optimization for IoT Topology*,
https://doi.org/10.1007/978-981-16-9609-1_5

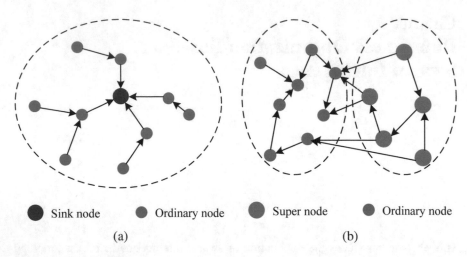

Fig. 5.1 Different types of topologies. (a) Homogeneous topology. (b) Heterogeneous topology

5.1.1 Statement of Research Problem

The topology of the IoT refers to a network structure composed of interconnections between nodes. Individuals in the network transmit messages through the network topology to maintain normal communication. The network topology of the Internet of Things is mainly divided into homogeneous topology and heterogeneous topology. Figure 5.1a is the structure of a homogeneous network. All nodes have the same communication range, initial energy, and computational capability. The homogeneous topology is simple in organization and stable in performance. Figure 5.1b is the topology of a heterogeneous network. The communication range, initial energy, and computational capability of nodes are different. network nodes are divided into ordinary nodes and super nodes. A super node has the larger communication range and more initial energy than the ordinary node. Heterogeneous networks are more complex than homogeneous networks, which have better flexibility but higher costs. This section focuses on the construction of heterogeneous network topology.

Since the work in Chap. 3.1 has compared GMSW and DASM [3], and overcomes the problems of DASM, this section only explains the problems with GMSW. The GMSW model is based on the greedy algorithm to add shortcuts. The greedy algorithm finds the local optimal solution every time, and it is easy to fall into the local optimal solution and the result is not the global optimal solution. Figure 5.2 is an example of adding shortcuts based on local optima and global optima, respectively. Area A, the largest dotted circle, is the maximum communication range of the super node, and the super nodes within the communication range can communicate with each other. Area B, the smallest dotted circle, is the maximum communication range of ordinary nodes. When the distance between the two nodes meets the smallest communication range of the two nodes, the ordinary node can communicate with the ordinary node or the super node. The communication

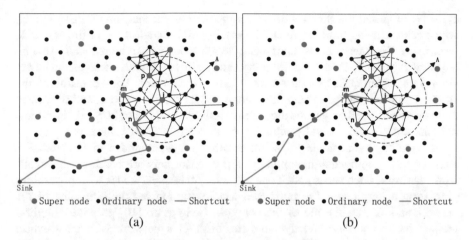

(a)   (b)

Fig. 5.2 Examples of local and global small worlds. (**a**) Local small world. (**b**) Global small world

relationship between nodes can be represented by connection lines, and only part of the node connections are shown in the figure.

Figure 5.2a is an example of shortcut addition using greedy algorithm. Super node i has three super nodes m, n and p within the communication range. A shortcut can be established between node i and node n with the largest local importance, and a short path from node i to sink node can be created. However, for the global optimal solution in Fig. 5.2b, node i chooses neighbor node m to add a shortcut. In comparison, the path length from node i to sink node in Fig. 5.2b is shorter, which makes the communication overhead smaller.

5.1.2 Preliminaries

For heterogeneous networks, many researchers have studied the construction of small-world characteristics in network topology. Helmy [4] first introduced the small-world model to wireless networks. By randomly adding a small number of shortcuts to the network, the average path length of the network is greatly reduced. Compared with adding shortcuts randomly, the DASM algorithm [3] uses the fan-shaped area limited by an angle to control the addition of shortcuts, which can reduce the number of invalid shortcuts. However, the importance of nodes in the topology is not considered. Therefore, Asif et al. [5] used the method of Neighbor Avoiding Walk (NAW) to calculate the betweenness of each node in the network, and then select the node with a larger betweenness to add shortcuts. By considering the energy consumption of nodes, Huang et al. [6] used a narrow-band search space to build a small-world model. This model can extend the life cycle of the network by periodically replacing the nodes at both ends of the shortcuts. In addition, Wang et al. [7] proposed the Small World Energy-Efficient mechanism (SWEE) model, which can use a few shortcuts to build a small-world model. By adjusting the node level in SWEE, energy consumption and network delays can be reduced. Also by adjusting the power, Zheng et al. [8] proposed an airborne health management power control algorithm (PCS) based on the small-world theory. They constructed the shortcuts between the power amplifier node and its neighbor nodes, and optimized these shortcuts based on genetic algorithm. Both SWEE [7] and PCS [8] algorithms built the small-world model by adjusting the power of a small number of nodes.

In addition, by deploying a small number of super nodes in the network, Kong et al. [9] optimized the topology of the sensor network based on the small-world network. Each super node connects with other super nodes with probability p to form a long edge. The optimized topology improves the efficiency of the network and extends the life of the network. Geng et al. [10] proposed a hybrid method based on static and dynamic to construct a network with small-world characteristics, which significantly improves the life of the network. Li et al. [11] deployed a small number of heterogeneous nodes that directly communicate with sink node to form the shortcuts. Pandey et al. [12] established a network model with small-world characteristics by adding new links between selected nodes and sink nodes. The network topology with small-world characteristics can reduce network energy consumption. The GMSW algorithm [1] mentioned in the previous chapter considers the local importance of super nodes when adding shortcuts. Although the GMSW has good small-world characteristics and robustness to node failure, there is still a local optimal problem. On the basis of these research works, this section uses ant colony algorithm to explore a more effective global optimization strategy for shortcut addition.

5.1.3 Path Search Process Based on Ant Colony

Ant colony algorithm [13] is a search algorithm that finds optimal paths in the graph. It is essentially a heuristic global optimization algorithm [14]. The ant colony can communicate information through pheromone. When the ant walks a path, it will leave a pheromone in the place where it walked. Other ants can follow the pheromone to search. Ants on a short path have a shorter round-trip time. In a unit time, the number of ants on a short path increases, and the concentration of pheromone left will gradually increase. This will attract more ants to follow this short path. After the accumulation of time, the entire ant colony will be concentrated on the best path under the effect of positive feedback.

Suppose this section needs to find the best path between the sensor node S and the sink node. In the initial stage, the pheromone on each edge is τ, that is, $\tau = C$ (C is a small constant). Then, m ants are placed on the sensor node S to find the best path to the sink node. In the process of ant movement, each ant selects the next hop node according to the size of pheromone and heuristic value until all ants reach the sink node. When the ant is on the node i, the selected probability of its neighbor node is calculated according to the following equations.

$$\begin{cases} \arg\max_{k \in L_i}\{[\tau_{i,k}]^\alpha[\eta_{i,k}]^\beta\}, (q \leq q0) \\ p_{ij} = \dfrac{[\tau_{i,j}]^\alpha[\eta_{i,j}]^\beta}{\sum_{w \in L_i}[\tau_{i,w}]^\alpha[\eta_{i,w}]^\beta}, (q > q0) \end{cases} \tag{5.1}$$

In Eq. (5.1), $\tau_{i,j}$ represents the pheromone concentration of the edge between node i and node j, L_i is the neighbor node list of node i, and $\eta_{i,j}$ is the heuristic function. The calculation method is as follows.

$$\eta_{i,j} = \frac{d_i}{d_j} \tag{5.2}$$

d_j is the distance between neighbor j of node i and the sink node, and d_i is the distance between node i and the sink node. It can be seen that the closer the distance between the node j and the sink node, the larger the value of $\eta_{i,j}$. The node j has a higher probability to be selected as the next hop node. Parameter α represents the relative importance of pheromone. The larger the value of α is, the more likely the ant is to choose the path that other ants pass. Parameter η represents the relative importance of heuristic value. The larger the value of η is, the closer the ant's path selection is to the greedy principle. p_{ij} represents the selected probability of node j as the next hop node. q is a random number between 0 and 1, and $q0$ is an adjustable parameter. If $q \leq q0$, the neighbor with the largest $[\tau_{i,w}]^\alpha * [\eta_{i,w}]^\beta$ value is selected as the next hop node. If $q > q0$, the roulette method is used to select the next hop node according to the selected probability of each node.

The most important parameter in the ant colony algorithm is the pheromone, which greatly affects the result of path search. There are two ways to update pheromone. The first method refers to that when the ant selects the next node, it needs to update the pheromone on the edge connected to the next node in real time. This operation is mainly used to prevent the algorithm from concentrating to the local optimal area too quickly and expand the search area. Path pheromone update means that after all ants complete the path search, TOSG selects the shortest path among all paths and updates the pheromone on each edge of the path. The shortest path is the path with the smallest number of hops. When multiple paths have the same number of hops, TOSG chooses the path with the shortest Euclidean distance.

$$\tau_{i,j} = (1 - \rho) * \tau_{i,j} \tag{5.3}$$

$$\tau_{i,j} = (1 - \rho) * \tau_{i,j} + \rho * \Delta\tau_{i,j} \tag{5.4}$$

Equations (5.3) and (5.4) are the calculation methods of the above two pheromone update, respectively. ρ is an adjustable parameter between 0 and 1, and $\Delta\tau_{i,j}$ is the pheromone increment. $\Delta\tau_{i,j} = 1/L^*$, and L^* is the number of hops on the shortest path. It can be seen that the real-time update will reduce the pheromone concentration of the edge, while the path update will increase the pheromone concentration of each edge on the shortest path. After many iterations, the pheromone concentration on the shortest path will be higher than the other paths, and all ants are concentrated on this shortest path.

5.1.4   Shortcuts Addition Strategy Based on Global Importance

Before adding shortcuts, it is necessary to define the global importance of each node in the entire network according to the best path obtained by the ant colony algorithm in the previous section. The global importance σ_i of node i indicates the number of times that node i occurs on the shortest path from all nodes to the sink node. The larger the σ of the node, the greater the influence it has on the network.

The shortcut is added based on the global importance of the node. First, TOSG finds all the super nodes within the communication range of node i and calculates the global importance of these nodes. Then, these nodes are sorted according to the value of σ, and the super node j with the largest value of σ and node i are selected to construct the shortcut. Preferentially connecting important nodes can directly benefit more nodes, which can reduce the number of hops for data forwarding.

The strategy of adding shortcuts is shown in Fig. 5.3. The large dotted circle is the maximum communication range of super node i, and the small dotted circle is the maximum communication range of regular nodes. The node is connected to the neighbor nodes within the communication range, and only the connections of some nodes are drawn in the figure. There are three super nodes m, n and p

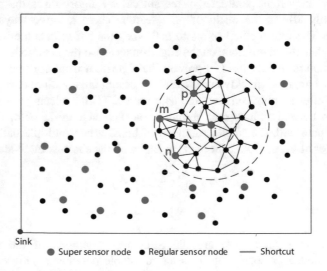

Fig. 5.3 Shortcuts addition strategy

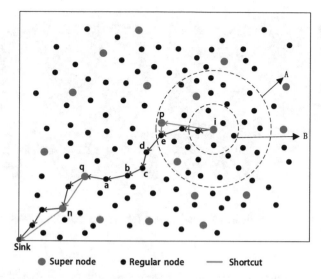

Fig. 5.4 Shortcuts addition strategy

within the communication range of super node i. Before establishing a shortcut, the shortest path from each sensor node to the sink node is found based on the ant colony algorithm. According to the global importance σ, the values of three super nodes are σ_m, σ_n, σ_p. Then, the three super nodes are sorted by global importance to find the node with the highest importance. Finally, the selected node is connected to super node i, which is the shortcut to add. Assuming that the value of σ_m in Fig. 5.3 is maximum, a shortcut is established between nodes i and m. This shortcut is represented by a blue line.

Figure 5.4 shows the change of the data forwarding method from node i to sink node after the shortcut addition. Before the shortcut is added, data packets need to pass through 13 nodes to reach the sink node from node i. This path is represented by the red arrows in Fig. 5.4. After the shortcut is added, data packets pass through nodes P, e, d, c, b, a, q, and n with a hop count of 9. It can be seen that the path length is greatly reduced when there are some shortcuts in the topology.

5.1.5 Performance Evaluation

This section carries out multiple simulation experiments to evaluate the performance of the TOSG algorithm, and compares it with the DASM and GMSW algorithms. The evaluation indexes are the average path length and clustering coefficient of the network, because these two indexes can reflect the characteristics of the small-world model. For parameter settings, 500 sensor nodes including super nodes and regular nodes are randomly deployed in the monitoring area. The size of this area is 1000 *

Fig. 5.5 Comparison of shortcuts addition between DASM and TOSG. (**a**) DASM, H=100. (**b**) TOSG, H=100

1000m^2. The communication radius of super node is 400 m, and that of regular node is 100 m. The network contains only one sink node, which is located at the lower left of the monitoring area. The topologies used in the experiment are all connected. In TOSG, the relative importance parameter α of pheromone is 3, and the relative importance β of heuristic value is set to 1. The pheromone update coefficient ρ is set to 0.1. The initial pheromone on each edge is 1, and the number of ants is 20. The threshold value $q0$ is set to 0.9. The maximum iteration number is 100. In DASM [3], $\varphi = 30°$. In GMSW [1], the values of parameters n, α, β and γ are 5, 0.8, 0.8 and 0.5, respectively.

First, the topology after adding shortcuts through different models is observed. Figure 5.5 shows the shortcut addition of TOSG and DASM models in the same topology with the same number of super nodes H. The blue edge is the shortcut, and H is 100. As can be seen from the Fig. 5.5, the DASM model strictly controls the deviation angle of shortcut towards the sink node, so that they are all oriented towards the sink node. TOSG and GMSW models, taking into account the importance of nodes in the whole network, present a clustering effect and further improve the quality of shortcuts. Although GMSW filters the endpoints of shortcuts according to their importance. However, GMSW only considers the local information of the topology. The addition of shortcuts may not have a large impact on the whole topology, and only reduces the path length from some local nodes to the sink node. TOSG considers global information of nodes, the quality of shortcuts can be improved compared to GMSW.

Next, the changes of average shortest path length (L) and clustering coefficient (C) in network topology are analyzed after shortcut is added through DASM, GMSW and TOSG. $L(0)$ is the average shortest path length of the initial topology, and $L(H)$ is the average shortest path length after adding shortcuts when there are H super nodes in the network. $C(0)$ is the clustering coefficient of the initial topology, and $C(H)$ is the clustering coefficient after adding shortcuts when there

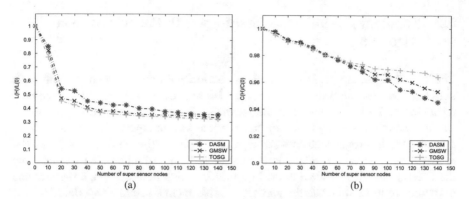

Fig. 5.6 Performance comparison of TOSG, DASM, and GMSW. (**a**) Average path length. (**b**) Clustering coefficient

are H super nodes in the network. By analyzing $L(H)/L(0)$ and $C(H)/C(0)$, it can clearly be seen the influence of shortcut addition on the average shortest path length and clustering coefficient of the entire topology. In addition, it can also analyze the influence of the number of different super nodes in the network on the two indicators.

As shown in Fig. 5.6a, the value of average shortest path length is decreasing as the number of super sensor nodes increasing. When $H = 0$, there is no super node in the network. $L(H)/L(0)$ of the three models are all equal to 1. When $H < 30$, the shortest path lengths of TOSG, DASM and GMSW decrease by 58%, 48% and 55%, respectively. When $H = 50$, the shortest path lengths of TOSG, DASM and GMSW decrease by 64%, 57% and 63%, respectively. When $H > 50$, the average shortest path lengths of both TOSG and GMSW models decrease slowly. By comparison, the TOSG model has a smaller shortest path length as the number of super nodes in the topology increases.

Figure 5.6b shows the change of clustering coefficient. As the number of super nodes in the network increases, the clustering coefficient of the network decreases. When $H \leq 50$, the clustering coefficient of TOSG is smaller than DASM and GMSW, and the value of TOSG gradually approaches DASM and GMSW with the increase of super nodes. When $H > 50$, the clustering coefficient of TOSG model is higher than DASM and GMSW. Although the clustering coefficients of the three models are constantly decreasing, the value of the clustering coefficient has always maintained a high level. When $H = 140$, the clustering coefficients of the three models are all reduced by less than 6%. Therefore, the TOSG model has a smaller average shortest path length and higher clustering coefficient compared with DASM and GMSW models, which shows good small world characteristics.

5.2 Topology Optimization Strategy with Particle Swarm Algorithm

The TOSG algorithm [2] in the previous section can optimize a single sink node network. However, in order to prolong the lifetime of the network, it is necessary to deploy multiple sink nodes in the network. Therefore, this section proposes a shortcut addition strategy based on the particle swarm algorithm (SAPS) [15] to optimize the heterogeneous network topology with multiple sink nodes. In SAPS, a fitness function is constructed to evaluate the quality of a particle by combining the average path length and the load on multiple sink nodes. Then, crossover and mutation are used to update the particles. Experimental results show that SAPS is superior to the other algorithms in terms of average path length, load and shortcut number.

5.2.1 Single Sink and Multiple Sink Networks

In the IoT, networks can be divided into single sink networks and multi-sink networks according to the number of sink nodes. Figure 5.7a shows the structure of single sink network. Multiple sensor nodes are dispersed in a detection area. These nodes form a network through self-organization and transmit the collected data to the sink node through one hop or multiple hops. In this network structure, sensor nodes around sink node tend to consume their own energy too quickly and form energy holes [16]. Since the sink node is both the end point and the starting point of data transmission in the IoT [17], the sensor nodes close to the sink node

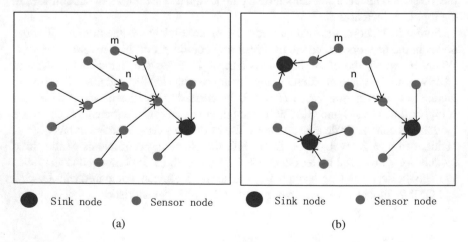

     (a)   (b)

Fig. 5.7 Network structures with single and multiple sink nodes. (**a**) Single sink network structure. (**b**) Multiple sink network structure

undertake more data transmission tasks than other nodes. When the sensor node is far from the sink node, the message needs to be forwarded by multiple hops to reach the sink node, and the transmission delay will be relatively large. The above-mentioned problems are more serious in large-scale networks. Deploying multiple sink nodes on the network can effectively solve these problems [18]. Figure 5.7b shows a network structure with multiple sink nodes.

In the multi-sink topology, each node chooses a sink node as the target of data forwarding, and those nodes with the same data forwarding target are divided into a cluster [19]. The sink node in the cluster is responsible for receiving the data collected by other sensor nodes. As the number of sink nodes increases, the probability that a sensor node has a sink node within a hop distance will increase. Therefore, the number of hops from a sensor node to the sink node will also be reduced.

For the same nodes m and n, in a single sink network (i.e., Fig. 5.7a), it takes 3 hops from node m to sink node and 2 hops from node n to sink node. But in a multi-sink network (i.e., Fig. 5.7b), it only takes 2 hops from node m to sink node. As can be seen that increasing the number of sink nodes can effectively reduce the number of hops required for data transmission from sensor nodes to sink nodes. Compared with a single sink network environment, a network with multiple sink nodes has the following characteristics:

- For data transmission in a multi-sink network, the number of nodes participating in a path is less than the single sink network.
- In a multi-sink network, if one sink node fails, the sensor node can select other sink nodes to transmit messages. Therefore, the failure of one sink node will not have a great impact on the performance of the entire network.
- Deploying multiple sink nodes can reduce the distance between the sensor node and the sink node, which can reduce the energy consumption of the node, and avoid the energy holes.

However, in multiple sink networks, when the number of nodes among clusters differs greatly, the load among multiple sink nodes is not balanced. Existing algorithm [20] set constraints while adding shortcuts to balance the load on multiple sink nodes, but there is a certain degree of randomness in the selection of nodes at both ends of the shortcuts. Therefore, this section uses the particle swarm algorithm to further improve the quality of the shortcuts by filtering endpoints.

Compared with the single sink network, there are a few studies on the application of the small-world model to the multi-sink network. Verma et al. [21] proposed Load-balanced Multi-Gateway Aware long link addition Strategy (LM-GAS). The number of hops is an important factor in determining the gateway to which each node belongs, and nodes under the same gateway form a cluster. Shortcuts are divided into the shortcuts within a cluster and the shortcuts between clusters. When adding a shortcut in the same cluster, any two nodes are selected from the cluster. If the relevant constraints are met, a connection is established between the two nodes. Shortcut addition between clusters needs to select two nodes from two different clusters and check whether the two nodes meet the constraints. The shortcut is established when the two nodes meet the constraints.

According to the idea of LM-GAS, this section applies the GMSW [1] to the multi-sink topology, which is compared with SAPS. In GMSW, the nodes in the topology are divided into multiple clusters, and each cluster is equivalent to a single sink topology. For the shortcuts in the cluster, shortcuts are added between nodes based on local importance. The method in GMSW is no longer suitable for adding inter-cluster shortcuts. Therefore, it adopts the strategy in LM-GAS. Finally, the effectiveness of the SAPS is verified by comparison with GMSW and LM-GAS.

5.2.2 Preliminaries

Before introducing the SAPS, it is necessary to introduce the basic process of particle swarm algorithm and the network model used in this section. The particle swarm algorithm [22] consists of a group of particles that move towards the optimal solution of the problem. The algorithm uses the particle's position and speed to represent motion, and iteratively updates the particle's position. The particle swarm moves toward a locally optimal position and eventually to a globally optimal position. This algorithm can search in a large candidate solution space without gradient information. Each particle has a position vector $X_i = (x_{i1}, x_{i2}, \cdots, x_{iD})$ and a speed vector $V_i = (v_{i1}, v_{i2}, \cdots, v_{iD})$, $i = 1, 2, \cdots, s$, where s is the population size and D is the dimensionality of the search space. The update method of the particles is as follows.

$$v_{ij}^t = \omega v_{ij}^{t-1} + c_1 r_1 (p_{ij} - x_{ij}^{t-1}) + c_2 r_2 (g_j - x_{ij}^{t-1}) \tag{5.5}$$

$$v_{ij}^t = \begin{cases} v_{max}, & (v_{ij}^t > v_{max}) \\ -v_{max}, & (v_{ij}^t < -v_{max}) \end{cases} \tag{5.6}$$

$$x_{ij}^t = x_{ij}^{t-1} + v_{ij}^t \tag{5.7}$$

Among them, p_{ij} is the optimal position found by the i_{th} particle, and g_j is the global optimal position currently found by the entire population. ω is the inertia weight, c_1 and c_2 are the acceleration coefficients, r_1 and r_2 are random numbers evenly distributed from 0 to 1. The algorithm repeatedly updates the position of each particle until the stop condition is satisfied.

Next, the network model is introduced, which mainly includes Euclidean distance, standard deviation of the number of nodes among clusters, neighbor node set, and next hop node set. Assuming that the network is fixed, and the nodes are randomly deployed on a two-dimensional plane. Euclidean distance represents the physical distance between two nodes. In Eq. (5.8), the coordinates of nodes v and

s are (v_x, v_y) and (s_x, s_y), respectively. $d(v, s)$ represents the Euclidean distance between node v and node s.

$$d(v, s) = \sqrt{(v_x - s_x)^2 + (v_y - s_y)^2} \tag{5.8}$$

$$S = \sqrt{\frac{1}{m} \sum_{i=1}^{m} (N_i - \frac{N}{m})^2} \tag{5.9}$$

The standard deviation S of the number of nodes among clusters shows the distribution of the total number of sensors in the network among sink nodes. Its calculation method is shown in Eq. (5.9). N_i represents the number of sensor nodes in the cluster to which sink node i belongs (each node chooses the sink node closest to itself based on the number of hops), and m is the number of sink nodes. When the standard deviation is smaller, it indicates that the number of sensor nodes in the cluster is more average, and the load on the sink node is more balanced.

In addition, the maximum communication radius of regular nodes and super nodes are r and R respectively, and $R > r$. In Fig. 5.8, nodes a and b in $area1$ belong to the set of short-range neighbor nodes of super node u, which is denoted as P''. The Euclidean distance between any node s and node u is less than r, that is, $\forall s \in P'', d(u, s) \leq r$. P' is the set of long-range neighbor nodes of super node u, which includes all super nodes p, q, and v in $area0 - area1$. The Euclidean distance between them and node u satisfies the relationship, that is, $\forall s \in P'$, $r < d(u, s) \leq R$. Therefore, the set of all neighbor nodes of super node u is $P = P'' + P'$. Moreover, the long-range neighbor node set P' of the super node is used as the next hop node set. Since regular nodes do not have long-range neighbor nodes, they do not have the next hop node set.

Fig. 5.8 An example of neighbor node set

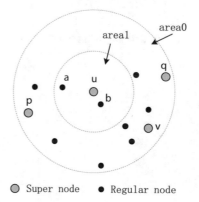

5.2.3 Particle Encoding and Fitness Function

This section introduces the encoding method of particles and the design of fitness function. In SAPS, each particle represents a shortcut addition scheme. The particles are encoded in the form of integers, which corresponds to an integer array of length $|V| * d$. $|V|$ represents the number of super nodes in the network. The position of $(i - 1) * d$ in the array represents the ID of super node V_i. The position of $(i - 1) * d + 1 \, i * d$ in the array is the ID of the node connected to the super node V_i, which indicates that a shortcut can be added between the super node V_i and these nodes. Here d is a sufficiently large integer, which can storage the IDs of all nodes connected to V_i. The encoding form of each particle is shown in Fig. 5.9.

It can be seen that n_j^i is the ID of the j_{th} node connected to super node V_i. When the number of nodes connected to V_i is less than $d - 1$, the value of the position $(i - 1) * d + N_i + 2 \, i * d$ is set to 0. In addition, if $n_j^i < 0$, the j_{th} node connected to super node V_i is the sink node.

Figure 5.10 is a simple example of topology conversion to individual encoding. The topology consists of nodes m, n, p, d, r, $sink1$ and $sink2$. The blue node is the super node, and the red node is the sink node. The black solid lines represent shortcuts added between nodes. The position marked in blue represents the ID of the super node, and three places are reserved behind each super node to store the ID

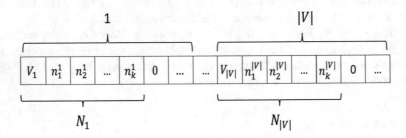

Fig. 5.9 Encoding of a particle

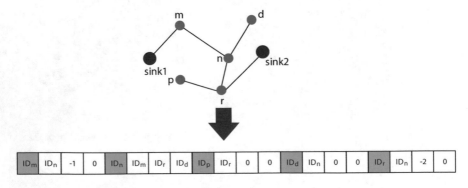

Fig. 5.10 Individual encoding in SAPS

of the node that can establish a shortcut with this super node. These three positions are called the associated positions of the super node. For example, if node n in the topology establishes shortcuts with nodes m, r, and d respectively, the ID of node m, r, and d is added to the associated position of node n. The -1 in the individual indicates that a shortcut is established between node m and $sink1$. Similarly, -2 means that a shortcut is established between node r and $sink2$.

In order to evaluate the solution represented by the particle during algorithm iteration, a fitness function is designed to calculate the fitness value of each individual. In a multi-sink network, the establishment of a shortcut only considers the path length, which may cause too many sensor nodes in some clusters. It will put more pressure on neighbor nodes of sinks with heavy load. Therefore, SAPS combines two factors, path length and load on sink node, to construct the fitness function.

$$Fitness = \gamma * \frac{L}{L_{initial}} + (1 - \gamma) * D \tag{5.10}$$

In Eq. (5.10), $L_{initial}$ is the path length from the node to the sink before adding the shortcut, and L is the path length from the node to the sink after adding the shortcut. γ is the sliding factor between 0 and 1. D is a variance function that evaluates whether the load between sinks is balanced. D can be calculated as follows.

$$D = \frac{1}{m} \sum_{i=1}^{m} (\frac{N_i - N_{avg}}{N_{avg}})^2 \tag{5.11}$$

$$N_{avg} = \frac{N}{m} \tag{5.12}$$

In Eqs. (5.11) and (5.12), N_i is the number of sensors in the cluster where the i_{th} sink is located, and the distance between these sensor nodes and i_{th} sink is small. N_{avg} is the number of nodes contained in each cluster under ideal conditions, and m is the number of sink nodes. N is the total number of sensor nodes in the network. When the number of nodes in the cluster is closer to N_{avg}, the value of D is smaller, and the load on sink nodes is more balanced. Conversely, the load on sink nodes is more unbalanced. Therefore, according to the fitness function, the smaller the fitness value of the particle, the better the solution.

5.2.4 Particle Update Strategy

This section introduces the particle update strategy. Since the particles in SAPS are encoded into discrete forms, the update method of the standard particle swarm optimization algorithm is no longer applicable. In order to update the discretely coded particles, SAPS introduces crossover and mutation of genetic algorithm. The partial information of current particle or optimal particle is saved through crossover, and new particle can be generated through mutation. Therefore, the particle update strategy includes initialization, crossover and mutation operations. The following describes the different operations in detail.

The first is initialization. In SAPS, the particles are randomly generated and each particle represents a solution. To ensure the feasibility of the solution, the node pair within the communication range is selected as the endpoint of the shortcut. That is, each super node randomly selects a node from its next hop node set P' to establish a connection. When all super nodes randomly select the next hop node and establish a connection, an initial particle is generated.

Next is the crossover operation. SAPS realize the crossover operation by exchanging the information of the particle and the current optimal particle. Suppose that α different super nodes, such as $v_1, v_2, \cdots, v_\alpha$, are randomly selected from $|V|$ super nodes. $Lis_1, Lis_2, \cdots, Lis_\alpha$ represent the shortcut set of the α super nodes in the current particle. The set of shortcuts corresponding to the α super nodes in the optimal particle is expressed as $Ls_1, Ls_2, \cdots, Ls_\alpha$. The first step is to delete the shortcut established by the super node v_i in the current particle and the nodes in the set Lis_i. The second step is establish a connection between the super node v_i and the nodes in the set Ls_i. After completing the crossover operation of α super nodes, a new reorganized particle is obtained. According to the elite retention strategy, only when the fitness value of the new particle is better than the old particle, the new particle can replace the old particle. Figure 5.11 illustrates the crossover operation.

Suppose that the super node v is selected for crossover operation, and the ID of node v is ID_v. In the current particle, the super nodes v and u are connected to each other. In the optimal particle, node v is connected to node m. During the crossover operation, the shortcut between nodes u and v is disconnected. ID_u is found and deleted from the associated positions of the super node v. If $ID_u < 0$, it means that the node u is a sink node. There is no associated position of the sink node in

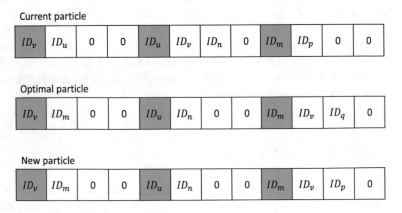

Fig. 5.11 Crossover operation in SAPS

Current particle

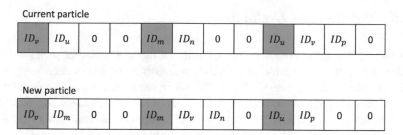

New particle

Fig. 5.12 Mutation operation in SAPS

the particle, and subsequent delete operations do not be performed. If $ID_u > 0$, ID_v is found and deleted from the associated positions of the super node u. Assume that neither node u nor m is a sink node. Then a shortcut is added between nodes v and m. The ID_m and ID_v are added to the associated positions of nodes v and m, respectively. A new particle can be obtained.

Finally, it is the mutation operation. Suppose that β different super nodes are selected as mutated nodes, and each super node is connected to $n_1, n_2, \cdots, n_\beta$ super nodes within the communication range. $Lis_1, Lis_2, \cdots, Lis_\beta$ represent the shortcut set of the β super nodes. When the super node v_i mutates, the shortcuts between v_i and n_i super nodes are disconnected, and then n_i super nodes are randomly selected from the next hop node set P' of v_i to connect to v_i. At this time, $Lis_i \neq Lst_i$. When the mutation of all β super nodes is completed, a new particle is obtained. Similarly, the elite retention strategy is used to screen for new particles. An example of a mutation operation is shown in Fig. 5.12.

Assume that node v is selected as a mutation node. In the current particle, node v is connected to node u. Node v disconnects from node u and adds connection to node m. The ID_u after ID_v and ID_v after ID_u are deleted from the current particle, ID_m and ID_v are added into the new particle. Therefore, the basic flow of SAPS is as follows. The particle swarm is initialized, and each particle represents a solution for adding shortcuts. After the initial solution is obtained, the fitness value of each individual in the particle swarm is calculated, and then the optimal particle of the population is updated according to the fitness value of the particle. Then new particle is obtained through the crossover of the current particle and the optimal particle and the mutation operation of the particle itself. If the condition for the algorithm termination is reached at this time, that is, the iteration is completed, the final shortcut addition scheme is obtained. Otherwise the next round of iteration is performed.

5.2.5 *Performance Evaluation*

This section first determines the optimal value of the sliding factor γ in the fitness function through experiments. Then, in the case of different sink nodes, the proposed SAPS is compared with LM-GAS and GMSW in terms of the average path length, the load on multiple sink nodes, and the number of shortcuts added. The size of the experimental area is $1000 * 1000\text{m}^2$, and the communication radii of super nodes and ordinary nodes are 450 m and 150 m, respectively. The number of sink nodes in the topology varies from 2 to 6, and they are randomly distributed in the network.

First, the effect of parameter γ on the average path length of the network and the standard deviation among clusters is evaluated. The number of sensor nodes is set to 200 in the experiment, and the number of super nodes is 20%. The number of crossover nodes α is 4, and the number of mutation nodes β is 1. The number of particles *num* is 40, and the maximum number of iterations NC_{max} is set to 400. Since the value of γ is in the range $[0, 1]$, the experiment is conducted with an interval of 0.1. Figure 5.13 is the influence curve of γ on the average path length and the standard deviation.

As can be seen from Fig. 5.13, when the number of sink nodes in the network remains unchanged, the value of average path length keeps decreasing while the value of standard deviation keeps increasing with the increase of γ. But when γ changes from 0.9 to 1, the standard deviation increases significantly. Since the main purpose of this paper is to reduce the average path length of the network, in combination with Fig. 5.13a and b, the value of γ is selected as 0.9.

Next, the performance of SAPS is evaluated. Table 5.1 is the comparison of shortcut addition quantity of the three algorithms under different number of sink nodes. The data in the table are the average value of multiple experiments. Compared with LM-GAS and GMSW, the number of shortcuts added by SAPS is relatively small. When the number of sink nodes is 2 and 3, the number of shortcuts

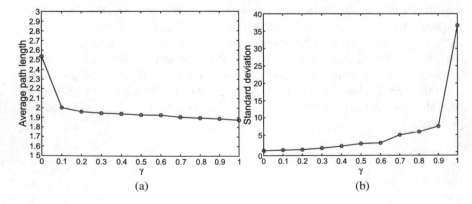

Fig. 5.13 The effect of parameter γ on the network topology. (**a**) Average path length. (**b**) Standard deviation

Table 5.1 Number of shortcuts for GMSW, LM-GAS, and SAPS with 200 nodes

Sink nodes	GMSW	LM-GAS	SAPS
2	60.1	66.1	58.8
3	67.1	66.5	58.4
4	66	70.8	56.5
5	68.1	72.8	54.1
6	68.1	73.3	51.2

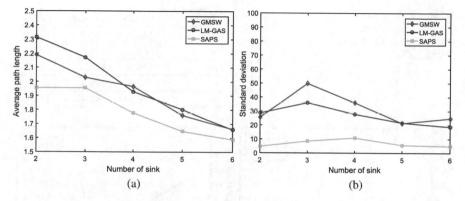

Fig. 5.14 Comparison of three algorithms under different sink nodes ($N = 200$). (**a**) Average path length. (**b**) Standard deviation

added by SAPS is similar to the LM-GAS and GMSW. When the number of sink nodes takes a larger value, the number of shortcuts added by SAPS is significantly less than the LM-GAS and GMSW.

Figure 5.14a shows the change curve of average path length when the total number of sensor nodes in the network is 200 and the number of sink nodes is from 2 to 6. It can be seen that the average path length decreases as the number of sink nodes increases. When the number of sink nodes is large, the total number of sensors in each cluster will be reduced, and it only takes less hops to reach the sink node from the sensor node. In addition, the average path length of SAPS is smaller than LM-GAS and GMSW in all cases. Combining Table 5.1 and Fig. 5.14a, when the number of sink nodes is fixed, SAPS can introduce fewer shortcuts to reduce the average path length more effectively.

Figure 5.14b shows the change curve of standard deviation value when the total number of sensor nodes in the network is 200 and the number of sink nodes is from 2 to 6. The results show that the standard deviation of SAPS is smaller than LM-GAS and GMSW. In other words, in SAPS, the number of sensor nodes in each cluster is relatively evenly distributed, which balances the load of sink nodes to a large extent. Figure 5.14 shows that in SAPS, there is a trade-off between the average path length of the network and the standard deviation of the number of nodes among clusters. While minimizing the length of the path from the sensor node to the sink node, it also ensures a balanced distribution of the number of nodes.

Table 5.2 Number of shortcuts for GMSW, LM-GAS, and SAPS with 300 nodes

Sink nodes	GMSW	LM-GAS	SAPS
2	94.2	94.2	90
3	97.2	109.3	94.7
4	102.7	113.7	84.3
5	101.8	113.9	84.8
6	98.9	108.9	80.1

Table 5.3 Number of shortcuts for GMSW, LM-GAS, and SAPS with 500 nodes

Sink nodes	GMSW	LM-GAS	SAPS
2	156.9	162.7	158.9
3	168.3	170.5	152.8
4	174.5	186.5	146.5
5	168.3	188.5	155
6	170.3	188.8	156.3

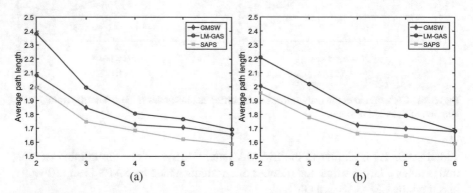

Fig. 5.15 Comparison of average path length under different sink nodes. (**a**) N=300. (**b**) N=500

The following analyzes the scalability of SAPS. By setting the number of sensor nodes to 300 and 500, the average path length of the network and the standard deviation of the number of nodes among clusters change with the number of sink nodes. In the above two cases, the number of shortcuts added by different algorithms is shown in Tables 5.2 and 5.3.

When the number of nodes is 300, the number of shortcuts added by the SAPS algorithm is still less than GMSW and LM-GAS. When the number of nodes is increased to 500 and the number of sink nodes is 2, SAPS increases the number of shortcuts more than GMSW. However, as the number of sink nodes increase, the number of shortcuts added by GMSW has exceeded SAPS. And the number of shortcuts added by SAPS has been less than the number of shortcuts added by LM-GAS. Figure 5.15 shows the change of the average path length when the total number of sensor nodes in the network is 300 and 500. It is well known that the longer the path, the higher the transmission delay. Therefore, reducing the number of hops in message transmission is a common technique in network communication.

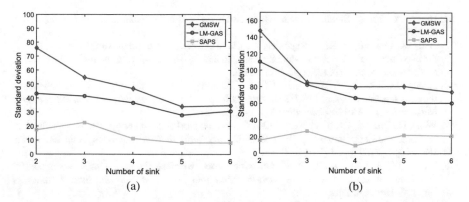

Fig. 5.16 Comparison of standard deviation under different sink nodes. (**a**) N=300. (**b**) N=500

It can be seen from these two figures that the average path length of these three algorithms decreases as the number of sink nodes increases. As the increase in the number of Sink nodes reduces the coverage of each cluster, the number of nodes contained in each cluster will also decrease. Only a few hops are needed from the source node to the sink node, which can reduce the number of message forwarding. In addition, the results of Fig. 5.15 show that with the same number of sink nodes, SAPS can still maintain the average path length of the network at a lower level than the LM-GAS and the GMSW algorithms.

Figure 5.16 shows that when the total number of sensor nodes is 300 and 500 respectively, the standard deviation of the number of nodes among clusters changes with the number of sink nodes. The experimental results show that the standard deviation of SAPS is smaller than LM-GAS and GMSW algorithms under the fixed number of sink nodes. Therefore, in the network topology constructed by SAPS, the number of sensor nodes in each cluster is relatively evenly distributed, which can balance the load on sink nodes. Through the analysis of several comparative experiments, SAPS has been significantly optimized in terms of shortcut addition number, average path length and load on sink nodes in multi-sink network topology.

References

1. Qiu, T., Luo, D., Xia, F., Deonauth, N., Si, W., & Tolba, A. (2016). A greedy model with small world for improving the robustness of heterogeneous internet of things. *Computer Networks, 101*, 127–143.
2. Qiu, T., Li, B., Qu, W., Ahmed, E., & Wang, X. (2018). Tosg: A topology optimization scheme with global small world for industrial heterogeneous internet of things. *IEEE Transactions on Industrial Informatics, 15*(6), 3174–3184.
3. Guidoni, D. L., Mini, R. A. F., & Loureiro, A. A. F. (2012). Applying the small world concepts in the design of heterogeneous wireless sensor networks. *IEEE Communications Letters, 16*(7), 953–955.

4. Helmy, A. (2003). Small worlds in wireless networks. *IEEE Communications Letters, 7*(10), 490–492.
5. Asif, W., Qureshi, H. K., & Rajarajan, M. (2013). Variable rate adaptive modulation (vram) for introducing small-world model into wsns. In *2013 47th Annual Conference on Information Sciences and Systems (CISS)* (pp. 1–6). IEEE.
6. Huang, J., Xie, Q., & Huang, B. (2012). Creating small-world model for homogeneous wireless sensor networks. In *2012 8th International Conference on Wireless Communications, Networking and Mobile Computing* (pp. 1–4). IEEE.
7. Wang, D., Wu, M., Lv, B., & Wen, J. (2013). A small world-based energy-efficient mechanism in wireless ad hoc networks. In *2013 IEEE International Conference on Communications Workshops (ICC)* (pp. 447–451). IEEE.
8. Zheng, W., & Luo, D. (2014). Small world-based wireless sensor network power control algorithm for airborne phm. In *Advanced Technologies in Ad Hoc and Sensor Networks* (pp. 177–186). Springer.
9. Kong, P., Fang, G., He, C., & Liu, Z. (2017). Topology optimization of port wireless sensor network based on small-world network. In *2017 International Conference on Circuits, System and Simulation (ICCSS)* (pp. 157–161). IEEE.
10. Geng, P., Liu, Y., & Yang, J. (2016). A dynamic energy balance method for wireless sensor networks with small world characteristics. In *Proceedings of the Fifth International Conference on Network, Communication and Computing* (pp. 287–291).
11. Li, C., Li, L., & Wang, X. (2017). An optimal clustering routing algorithm for wireless sensor networks with small-world property. *Wireless Personal Communications, 96*(2), 2983–2998.
12. Pandey, O. J., & Hegde, R. M. (2018). Low-latency and energy-balanced data transmission over cognitive small world wsn. *IEEE Transactions on Vehicular Technology, 67*(8), 7719–7733.
13. Dorigo, M., Birattari, M., & Stutzle, T. (2006). Ant colony optimization. *IEEE Computational Intelligence Magazine, 1*(4), 28–39.
14. Kennedy, J. (2006). Swarm intelligence. In *Handbook of Nature-Inspired and Innovative Computing* (pp. 187–219). Springer.
15. Qiu, T., Li, B., Zhou, X., Song, H., Lee, I., & Lloret, J. (2019). A novel shortcut addition algorithm with particle swarm for multisink internet of things. *IEEE Transactions on Industrial Informatics, 16*(5), 3566–3577.
16. Ammari, H. M. (2013). Investigating the energy sink-hole problem in connected k-covered wireless sensor networks. *IEEE Transactions on Computers, 63*(11), 2729–2742.
17. Rajesh, M. & Gnanasekar, J. M. (2015). Congestion control in heterogeneous wanet using frcc. *Journal of Chemical and Pharmaceutical Sciences ISSN, 974,* 2115.
18. Nagamalar, T. & Rangaswamy, T. R. (2015). Energy efficient cluster based approach for data collection in wireless sensor networks with multiple mobile sink. In *2015 International Conference on Industrial Instrumentation and Control (ICIC)* (pp. 348–353). IEEE.
19. Doostali, S., & Babamir, S. M. (2020). An energy efficient cluster head selection approach for performance improvement in network-coding-based wireless sensor networks with multiple sinks. *Computer Communications, 164,* 188–200.
20. Jain, T. K., Saini, D. S., & Bhooshan, S. V. (2015). Lifetime optimization of a multiple sink wireless sensor network through energy balancing. *Journal of Sensors, 2015.*
21. Verma, A., Verma, C. K., Tamma, B. R., & Manoj, B. S. (2010). New link addition strategies for multi-gateway small world wireless mesh networks. In *2010 IEEE 4th International Symposium on Advanced Networks and Telecommunication Systems* (pp. 31–33). IEEE.
22. Kennedy, J., & Eberhart, R. (1995). Particle swarm optimization. In *Proceedings of ICNN'95-International Conference on Neural Networks* (vol. 4, pp. 1942–1948). IEEE.

Chapter 6
Robustness Optimization Based on Multi-Objective Cooperation

The previous chapter uses the swarm intelligence algorithms to study the topology optimization problems of single sink and multi-sink networks, and verifies that the multi-sink network has better performance and can avoid the energy holes. However, in the $5G$ scenario, large-scale IoT devices are deployed densely to increase the peak value of traffic. This poses a greater challenge to the optimization of the IoT topology. The improvement of a single performance can no longer meet the needs of users for IoT services. Therefore, this chapter introduces a multi-objective cooperative optimization scheme for network topology on the basis of the previous multi-sink network to improve the energy efficiency and robustness of the networks.

6.1 Statement of Problem

In order to meet the requirements of the IoT for high traffic density in large-capacity scenarios, ultra-dense networking technology is proposed to achieve higher peak traffic [1], and the spectrum efficiency of the network is improved by reducing the communication range between intelligent devices and adopting dense deployment [2]. However, the problem is that the high density node connection makes the topology more complex and it is difficult to ensure the energy efficiency and stability of the network. In addition, the unbalanced energy load makes the super nodes close to the sink nodes become the bottleneck of network performance improvement, and users no longer meet the single performance improvement of the network, but pursue the comprehensive performance of the whole network system. Therefore, how to jointly optimize network topology in ultra-dense deployment environment based on multiple performance indicators is an important research issue while balancing the energy load of multiple sink nodes.

Network energy efficiency and robustness have always been key performance indicators for topology optimization problems [3]. In the IoT, the intelligence and

T. Qiu et al., *Robustness Optimization for IoT Topology*,
https://doi.org/10.1007/978-981-16-9609-1_6

number of connected devices will generate more energy consumption [4]. The complexity of the node deployment environment and the ubiquity of network attacks put forward higher requirements for the reliability of the network. In order to reduce the energy consumption of data transmission, Guidoni et al. [5] proposed the sink node directed angle model (DASM) by constructing the long path between super nodes. Different from long paths, Fathy et al. [6] proposed an adaptive data reduction method (AMDR). By reducing the amount of data transferred between nodes, the energy consumption of the network can be reduced. In addition, for network robustness optimization problems, the R value [7] provides a numerical index for robustness measurement, and the measurement methods of different node centrality also provide different granular attack modes for malicious attacks. Zhou et al. [8] proposed a two-stage evolutionary algorithm to optimize the robustness of scale-free networks against a variety of malicious attacks. In addition to the R value, Peng et al. [9] proposed a tabu search algorithm based on natural connectivity to optimize the robustness of the network. The above algorithm only optimizes a single index of the network, but the QoS of the IoT is often restricted by various factors.

Therefore, this chapter proposes a multi-objective cooperative optimization scheme based on Non-dominated Sorting Genetic Algorithm II (NSGA-II) [10] to solve the above problems. First, the initial network is preliminarily optimized to reduce redundant connections under the dense deployment of devices. Then the calculation methods of energy consumption on different types of nodes and load balancing on multiple sink nodes are designed respectively. As the objective function of multi-objective optimization process, the above indexes guide the direction of evolution. Then the optimal Pareto solution set [11] is obtained by crossover, mutation and Pareto layers. In addition, in order to avoid premature convergence [12] of NSGA-II algorithm in the multi-objective evolution process, this chapter also designs a layered cooperation mechanism between multiple populations to solve this problem. The following section describes the above operations in detail.

6.2 Network Topology Initialization

This section introduces the initialization operation of the network, which mainly includes the deletion of redundant edges and the determination of super nodes. It makes the network cluster structure more obvious and reduces interference between nodes by deleting redundant edges. The entire initialization operation provides a topological basis for subsequent optimization. In order to avoid deleting important edges, clustering coefficient (CC) and edge betweenness (EB) are used to jointly judge redundant edges. The calculation of the clustering coefficient CC can be geometrically expressed as the ratio of the number of triangles connected to node i to the number of triples connected to node i. EB reflects the number of times an edge appears on the shortest path between any pair of nodes in the network. Combined with Fig. 6.1, the edges in the network are divided into three types: isolated edges ($e1$), edges in triangles ($e2$), edges in quadrilaterals or polygons ($e3$).

Fig. 6.1 Three types of
edges in network topology

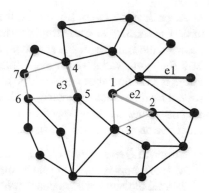

In order to judge redundant edges, the following symbols are defined. CC'_i
represents the clustering coefficient of node i after deleting associated edges. n_i
is the number of nodes that can be connected within the communication range of
node i, m_i is the number of triangles connected to node i, and the threshold of edge
betweenness is represented as EB_t. These three types of edges are discussed below.

- $e1$ is not deleted. After the deletion, the network is disconnected and communication is interrupted.
- The deletion of $e2$ will affect the clustering coefficients of nodes 1, 2 and 3.
Therefore, it is necessary to calculate the changes of clustering coefficients of
the three nodes before and after deletion.

$$CC_i = \frac{m_i}{C^2_{n_i}}(i = 1, 2, 3), \quad CC'_j = \frac{m_j - 1}{C^2_{n_j - 1}}(j = 1, 2), \quad CC'_3 = \frac{m_3 - 1}{C^2_{n_3}}$$

$$(6.1)$$

In Eq. (6.1), C is the permutation and combination symbol. If $CC_1 + CC_2 +
CC_3 > CC'_1 + CC'_2 + CC'_3$, $e2$ is not deleted. Otherwise, the edge betweenness
EB_{e2} of $e2$ is further calculated and compared with threshold EB_t. If $EB_{e2} <
EB_t$, $e2$ can be deleted.

- The deletion of $e3$ will affect the clustering coefficient of nodes 4 and 5, so it is
necessary to compare the clustering coefficient changes of these two nodes.

$$CC_k = \frac{m_k}{C^2_{n_k}}, \quad CC'_k = \frac{m_k}{C^2_{n_k - 1}}(k = 4, 5) \qquad (6.2)$$

In Eq. (6.2), since $CC_k < CC'_k$, that is, $CC_4 + CC_5 < CC'_4 + CC'_5$, the sum
of clustering coefficients of nodes always increases after edge deletion. It is only
necessary to judge the relationship between edge betweenness EB_{e3} of $e3$ and
threshold EB_t. Edge $e3$ is deleted only if $EB_{e3} < EB_t$.

After deleting redundant edges, the location of super nodes needs to be determined according to clustering coefficient and closeness centrality of nodes. K controls the number of super nodes, and N is the total number of sensor nodes. The following variables are predefined to select super nodes. Node density Den refers to the number of nodes within a hop of a node, and D refers to the hop matrix solved by the adjacency matrix. CC represents the set of clustering coefficients of all nodes, and CC is arranged in descending order. $Isvisit$ is used to mark nodes that have been processed. The specific process of loop calculation is as follows:

- Compare $Den(i)$ with $(N/K) - 1$: If $Den(i) < (N/K) - 1$, except for the node with one hop, it needs to select some nodes with hops $2, 3, \cdots$ from hop matrix D until the number of nodes is $(N/K) - 1$.
- Calculate the closeness centralities of N/K nodes: It needs to calculate the closeness centralities of $(N/K) - 1$ nodes and node i. The node with maximum value is set as super node.
- Select the next unmarked node j and assign it to i: The N/K nodes in above two steps are marked in the $Isvisit$. The next unmarked node j is selected from the matrix D. Repeat the above steps until all nodes are marked in the $Isvisit$.

Through the loop calculation of the above three steps, K super nodes can be obtained. In the whole process, the nodes with the larger clustering coefficient and surrounding nodes are regarded as a cluster, and the center of cluster is determined by closeness centrality. The advantage of this design is that all super nodes can be evenly distributed in the entire network topology and the distance between super nodes and other nodes in the cluster is shorter. This distribution is beneficial for ordinary nodes to transmit data through super nodes.

6.3 Multi-Objective Functions

Energy efficiency and robustness are commonly used performance indicators to evaluate the IoT topology. This section will give a calculation method to measure the energy efficiency of the entire network. In addition, load balancing on multiple sink nodes will also affect the performance of the network topology. Therefore, by constructing three objective functions, it can guide the direction of topology optimization, and finally obtain an efficient, robust, and load-balanced network topology. Since the robustness is measured by the R value, this indicator has been introduced in the previous chapters, and it is no longer introduced here.

6.3.1 Energy Efficiency on Network

In order to calculate the energy efficiency of the network, the types of nodes in the network and the tasks undertaken by each node in data transmission must be identified. This section makes the following assumptions: data is transmitted in the network in the form of k-bit packets, and the ID of ordinary node is set as N_i. The ID of super node is H_j. S is the sink node. There are four types of nodes in the network:

- Edge node: sending data (ordinary node).
- Relay node: receiving and forwarding data (ordinary node).
- Super node: receiving, aggregating and forwarding data.
- Sink node: receiving data (without energy limitation).

In order to refine the energy consumption of sensor nodes, according to the radio model [13], the energy consumption of sending or receiving one bit data within distance d can be expressed as:

$$E_{Tx}(d) = \begin{cases} E_{elec} + d^2\xi_{fs}, & (d \le d_0) \\ E_{elec} + d^4\xi_{mp}, & (d_0 < d \le R_0) \end{cases} \quad (6.3)$$

$$E_{Rx}(d) = E_{elec}, \quad d_0 = \sqrt{\frac{\xi_{fs}}{\xi_{mp}}} \quad (6.4)$$

In Eqs. (6.3) and (6.4), E_{elec} represents the energy consumption of sending or receiving one bit data in the communication module. For two different channel states, namely free space channel and multi-path fading channel, ξ_{fs} and ξ_{mp} respectively represent the energy consumption coefficient generated by amplifying the communication power. d_0 is the distance threshold to distinguish different channel models, and R_0 is the maximum communication distance of the node. The above two formulas can perform specific numerical calculations on the energy consumption of nodes receiving or sending data. In addition, the super node also needs to aggregate the received data, and E_{Ag} is used to represent the energy consumption of aggregated data. $Num(H)$ is the number of child nodes of super node H, which refers to the neighbor nodes of the first super node H on the shortest path. In order to limit the number of edges increased between super nodes, the energy consumption of establishing new connections between super nodes is set as β.

According to the classification of nodes and the definition of symbols, the energy consumption of nodes on three types of data transmission paths is analyzed as follows:

(1) None super node: $N_1 \rightarrow N_2 \rightarrow S$

$$E_{N_1} = kE_{Tx}(d_1), \quad E_{N_2} = kE_{Rx}(d_1) + kE_{Tx}(d_2) \quad (6.5)$$

Since the transmission path does not contain super nodes, no energy is consumed for data aggregation. N_1 is an edge node and only sends data. N_2 is responsible for receiving and forwarding data. Therefore, the energy consumption of N_1 and N_2 is shown in Eq. (6.5). d in the two formulas represents the distance between two nodes, which affects the choice of data transmission channel model. This type of data transmission mostly occurs on ordinary nodes close to the sink node.

(2) A super node: $N_1 \rightarrow H_1 \rightarrow S$

$$E_{H_1} = Num(H_1)kE_{Rx}(d_3) + Num(H_1)kE_{Ag} + kE_{Tx}(d_4) \qquad (6.6)$$

There is only one super node on the transmission path, energy consumption of H_1 is shown in Eq. (6.6). H_1 requires additional energy to aggregate data compared to N_2. $Num(H_1)$ indicates the number of child nodes of super node H_1. This type of data transmission occurs on nodes not far from the sink node.

(3) Two or more super nodes: $N_1 \rightarrow H_1 \rightarrow H_2 \rightarrow S$

$$E_{H_2} = [Num(H_2) + 1]kE_{Rx}(d_5) + Num(H_2)kE_{Ag} + 2kE_{Tx}(d_6) \qquad (6.7)$$

There are more super nodes in the data transmission path, the super node only receives the data packets aggregated by the previous super node. That means it only aggregates data from its child nodes. The energy consumption of H_2 is shown in Eq. (6.7), and "1" indicates the data packets aggregated by node H_1. This type of transfer mainly occurs at nodes far from the sink node.

Through the above three data transmission paths, the energy consumption of each node in one round can be calculated when the edge node sends data to the sink node. In order to evaluate the energy efficiency of the entire network, this section calculates First Node Died Time (FNDT) to measure the network [13].

6.3.2   Load Balancing on Multiple sink nodes

For the measurement of load balancing on multiple sink nodes, Chap. 5.2 only used the standard deviation to estimate the load of multiple sink nodes, which is a rough measurement. Therefore, this chapter proposes a more fine-grained method for measuring load balancing on multiple sink nodes. In the network topology, the data on the node is transmitted through the shortest path. The load on the sink node can intuitively calculate the number of edges connected to the sink node. When the number of edges on each sink node is equal, it can be said that load balancing on multiple sink nodes is achieved. Based on the above ideas, this section introduces information entropy [14] to measure the load balancing on multiple sink nodes. Entropy is an excellent mathematical description of uncertainty, and information entropy is a measure of uncertainty in the process of information transmission. Suppose there are n basic events with probabilities $p_1, p_2, \cdots, p_n$, and the sum of these probabilities is equal to 1. F stands for a function. Information entropy has the following three properties:

- Determined upper bound: When the probabilities of n basic events are equal, the information entropy can obtain the maximum value, that is, $F(p_1, p_2, \cdots, p_n) \leq F(\frac{1}{n}, \frac{1}{n}, \cdots, \frac{1}{n})$.
- Monotonicity: $F(p_1, p_2, \cdots, p_n)$ is a strictly increasing function of the natural number n.
- Additivity: $F(p_1, p_2, \cdots, p_n) = F(p_1) + F(p_2) + \cdots + F(p_n)$.

In this section, the number of sink nodes is set as n, and the ratio of the number of edges on each sink node to the total number of edges is used as the probability of an independent basic event. The following formula is used to calculate the load balancing (LB) of the entire network system.

$$LB(x) = -\sum_{i=1}^{n} p(x_i) \log p(x_i) \tag{6.8}$$

In Eq. (6.8), x_i represents the basic event about load balancing on the i_{th} sink node. According to the property of information entropy, when the probability of each basic event is equal, information entropy gets the maximum value. In other words, when the value of LB is the largest, the number of edges on each sink node is equal. The upper bound of LB is $\log n$, and the conversion process is as follows:

$$LB(x) = -\sum_{i=1}^{n} p(x_i) \log p(x_i) = \sum_{i=1}^{n} p(x_i) \log \frac{1}{p(x_i)} \leq \log \sum_{i=1}^{n} p(x_i) \frac{1}{p(x_i)} = \log n \tag{6.9}$$

Since $\log x$ is a concave function and the sum of p_i is 1, Eq. (6.9) can be scaled according to Jensen's inequality [15]. It can be seen that the above inequality obtains the "=" when $p_i = \frac{1}{n}$.

6.3.3 Fitness Function

For the three performance indicators mentioned above, the fitness function is designed as follows. Where LB is load balancing, E is the value of energy efficiency index FNDT, and R represents the value of robustness.

$$Fit(x) = \omega_1 * \frac{LB}{\log n} + \omega_2 * \frac{E}{E_{max}} + \omega_3 * \frac{R}{0.5} \tag{6.10}$$

In Eq. (6.10), $\log n$ and 0.5 represent the maximum value of LB and R respectively. E_{max} represents the maximum value of energy efficiency E, which is affected by the number of sink nodes and super nodes in the network, so it needs to be determined in the experiment. The order relation analysis method [16] is used to determine the value of three weight coefficients ω_1, ω_2 and ω_3. This method is mainly divided into two steps. First step is to determine the order relation. In this section, the priority of the three objectives is set as LB, E and R, so the order relation is $x_1(LB) \succ x_2(E) \succ x_3(R)$. Second step is to judge the relative importance between x_{k-1} and x_k, that is, the ratio of weight coefficient r_k. The weight coefficients can be determined according to the following equation.

$$\omega_m = (1 + \sum_{k=2}^{m} \prod_{i=k}^{m} r_i)^{-1}, \quad \omega_{k-1} = r_k \omega_k \quad (k = m, m-1, \cdots, 3, 2) \qquad (6.11)$$

In Eq. (6.11), m is the total number of objective functions. The value of each weight coefficient can be calculated by assigning a value to r_k. An example is taken to verify the above results. When $\frac{\omega_1}{\omega_2} = r_2 = 1.4$ and $\frac{\omega_2}{\omega_3} = r_3 = 1.2$, then the values of $r_2 r_3$ and $r_2 r_3 + r_3$ can be obtained. The above factors are put into Eq. (6.11), the values of weight coefficients are obtained, that is, $\omega_3 = 0.2577$, $\omega_2 = 0.3093$, and $\omega_1 = 0.4330$.

6.4 Details of Algorithm

The multi-objective cooperative optimization algorithm for multi-sink network topology is introduced in detail. The whole optimization process mainly includes topology encoding, crossover and mutation, Pareto layering and layered-cooperation. Through the optimization of the above operations, this algorithm can obtain a balanced topology in terms of energy, robustness and load balancing, and can avoid the multi-objective optimization process from falling into premature convergence.

6.4.1 Topology Encoding

For the initial network topology obtained by the initialization operation, the connection relationship between the nodes is encoded and converted into chromosomes. The most common method is to convert the nodes and connections in the topology into an adjacency matrix, and then select the upper triangular matrix to expand into a row vector. Compared with the adjacency matrix, this method can reduce the storage space by half. However, the disadvantage is that there are many useless spaces in the row vector. For example, two nodes that are not in the communication range cannot be connected, but they occupy a space in the row vector. According to the above

First row vector: ID of node

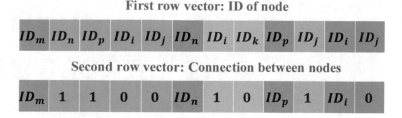

Second row vector: Connection between nodes

Fig. 6.2 Introduction to topology encoding and chromosome

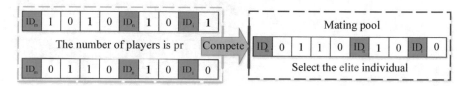

Fig. 6.3 Process of selecting parents

ideas, this section further compresses space on the basis of transforming adjacency matrix into row vector.

As shown in Fig. 6.2, the first row vector plays an auxiliary role, and it records the ID of the node corresponding to each space. The second row vector is the required chromosome, where the gray space records the ID of the node, and the following spaces record the connection relationship with the beginning node. "1" means that the two nodes are connected, and "0" means that they are not connected. It can be seen that the genes on the chromosome are segmented, and each segment begins with the ID of node. This section mainly uses two steps to shorten the length of the chromosome and reduce the complexity of calculation. First, this section selects the connection relationship of specific important nodes in the topology to expand into row vectors, which can shorten the length of chromosomes from the number of nodes. Second, the node positions in the row vector that are not in the communication range of other nodes are deleted to further compress the length of the chromosome. In addition, the existence of the first row vector facilitates the conversion between the adjacency matrix and the chromosome.

6.4.2   Crossover and Mutation

Next, the crossover and mutation operations are introduced to generate new individuals and maintain population diversity. First, a tournament selection method [17] is used to choose the parent individuals for crossover operation. The process is shown in Fig. 6.3, the number of players pr in each round is set to 2, and the size of the mating pool PL is $Pop/2$, where Pop refers to the number of all individuals in a population.

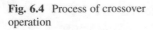

Fig. 6.4 Process of crossover operation

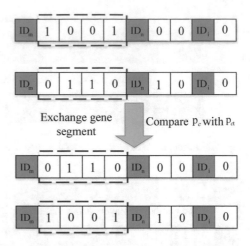

For a population with *Pop* individuals, *pr* players are randomly selected at each round, and These players are compared to select the best individual to enter the mating pool. The entire selection process is repeated until the pool is filled with selected individuals. For example, in a population of 20 individuals, two individuals are selected to compete at each round, and the winner enters the mating pool. The selection process is repeated for 10 times to obtain parent individuals that meet the size of mating pool. After the parent individuals are selected, the crossover operation is carried out.

The specific process of crossover operation is described in Fig. 6.4. First, two individuals are randomly selected from the *Pop*/2 parents for gene exchange on chromosomes. As can be seen from Fig. 6.2, genes on the corresponding chromosome of each individual appear in segments, and each segment starts with the *ID* of a super node. Crossover operation corresponds to gene segments, and a random number p_c is generated for each gene segment, and compared with the crossover probability p_{ct}. If $p_c < p_{ct}$, the corresponding gene segments of two individuals are exchanged. Otherwise, no operation is performed. Different crossover probabilities are set for different populations to ensure the diversity of evolution. When all the gene segments on the chromosome are traversed, two new individuals can be obtained. Repeat the crossover operation *Pop*/2 times, and the *Pop* offspring individuals are generated. The crossover operation generates new offspring by selecting different individuals as parents, which increases the genetic diversity of the population.

For the *Pop* offspring generated by crossover operation, mutation operation is performed to increase new genes. This section sets the different mutation probability p_{mt} for multiple populations. Crossover is performed on a gene segment of a chromosome, while mutation is performed on each gene locus of a chromosome. Figure 4.5 describes the entire mutation process. First, an individual is selected from the population. Since each gene segment starts with the *ID* of the super node, this gene locus is not mutated. Then, a random number p_m is generated for each gene

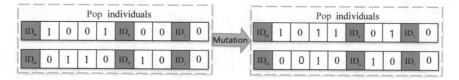

Fig. 6.5 Process of mutation operation

locus and compared with the mutation probability threshold p_{mt}. If $p_m < p_{mt}$, the value of this gene locus mutates to the opposite value. In Fig. 6.5, The position marked in red is where the mutation occurs. Repeat the process until the genes of all individuals in the population have been accessed.

Through the above selection, crossover and mutation, Pop parents can produce Pop offsprings. In order to ensure the consistency of the number of individuals during the next generation evolution, the new offsprings and the old parents are combined, and the Pop elite individuals are selected from the $2 * Pop$ individuals by fitness function to enter the next iteration evolution.

6.4.3 Pareto Layering

For the multiple indicators, the solution obtained by optimizing a problem is not one, but a set. This set is called the Pareto frontier, and the solution in this set is called the Pareto optimal solution. In the multi-objective cooperative optimization strategy, it is also necessary to find such a Pareto optimal solution set. Therefore, this section introduces the Pareto layering strategy to divide individuals into different Pareto layers, which mainly includes fast non-dominated sorting and crowded distance operations. The following describes the two operations separately.

The first is fast non-dominated sorting. The increase of edge between super nodes will improve the robustness and energy consumption of the network. In other words, when the robustness of network topology is improved, another performance indicator of the network, namely energy efficiency, will be reduced. Therefore, the final goal of this section is to obtain a non-dominated solution that can balance the above two indicators. In order to solve the above problems, a fast non-dominated sorting operation is added in optimization process to divide multiple individuals into different Pareto layers. The purpose is that the Pareto solution set can be quickly found. The specific flow is as follows.

For each individual p in the population, two variables need to be stored, that are n_p and S_p. The larger the load balancing (LB), energy efficiency (E) and robustness R are, the better the network performance is, which is a maximization optimization problem. When the values of q in the above objective functions are less than p, p is better than q, and q is put into S_p. In addition, n_p records the number of individuals that can dominate p, where the individuals with $n_p = 0$ constitute the first Pareto

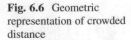

Fig. 6.6 Geometric representation of crowded distance

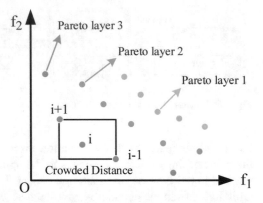

layer F_1. The remaining Pareto layer F_i ($i \geq 2$) needs to be determined according to the previous Pareto layer F_{i-1}. Taking F_2 as an example, for each individual p in F_1, each individual q needs to be selected from S_p to determine whether $n_q - 1$ is equal to 0. If true, it means that q is only dominated by individual p, and q belongs to Pareto layer F_2. Subsequent Pareto layers can be obtained through the above process.

The second is crowded distance. By calculating the crowded distance of individuals, it can deal with the situation of selecting some individuals in the same Pareto layer. Crowded distance is mainly to maintain the diversity of individuals in the population, and it reflects the density of individuals in a Pareto layer. Figure 6.6 shows the geometric representation of the crowded distance of individuals under two objective functions. Points with different colors represent individuals in different Pareto layers. In the same layer, individuals are arranged according to the objective function values. The crowded distance of node i is equal to half of the perimeter of the rectangle formed by the adjacent $i - 1$ and $i + 1$ nodes. When the number of objective functions is more than 2, the calculation process is the same. The calculation formula of crowded distance is expressed as follows.

$$I_d(i) = \sum_{j=1}^{m} \frac{f_j(i+1) - f_j(i-1)}{f_j^{max} - f_j^{min}} \tag{6.12}$$

In Eq. (6.12), $I_d(i)$ is the crowded distance of node i, and m is the number of objective functions. f_j^{max} and f_j^{min} represent the extreme values of all individuals in a Pareto layer on the j_{th} objective function. The initial crowded distance of each individual is set to 0, and the crowded distance of boundary individual in the j_{th} objective function is set to Inf. The reason is that the boundary individual has no two adjacent individuals.

6.4.4 Layered-Cooperation Mechanism

In order to avoid premature convergence in the process of multi-objective optimization, this section designs a layered-cooperation mechanism between populations based on Pareto layering, which can strengthen the communication of high-quality genes between adjacent populations after each iteration. The idea of this mechanism is to replace the worst individual in the same Pareto layer of the next population with the best individual in one population. The following is a specific example to explain. Suppose there are three populations, and the individuals in each population are divided into different Pareto layers. For example, in Fig. 6.7, MP_i represents the i_{th} population and F_j is the j_{th} Pareto layer. L_{ij} represents the best individual on the j_{th} Pareto layer in the i_{th} population, and S_{ij} corresponds to the worst individual on the j_{th} Pareto layer in the i_{th} population. The quality of individuals is judged by fitness function.

In the above figure, different colors are used to represent different Pareto layers, and the number of Pareto layers of the three populations is 3, 2, and 3 respectively. The order of population replacement is $MP_1 \rightarrow MP_2$, $MP_2 \rightarrow MP_3$, $MP_3 \rightarrow MP_1$. When layered-cooperation is implemented between adjacent populations, the Pareto layers with the least number in the two populations are selected as the benchmark. For example, the minimum number of Pareto layers in MP_2 and MP_3 is 2. Therefore, S_{31} is replaced by L_{21} in F_1 layer, and S_{32} is replaced by L_{22} in F_2 layer. F_3 layer in MP_2 population is not replaced because no matching layer is found in MP_3. The arrows between adjacent populations in Fig. 6.7 represent the remaining replacement operations. This layered-cooperation mechanism can accelerate the global convergence of the evolution.

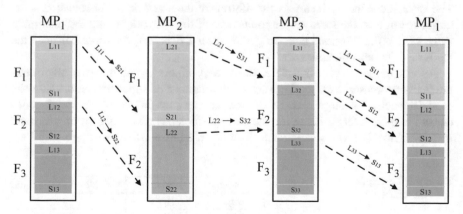

Fig. 6.7 Process of layered-cooperation mechanism

6.5 Performance Evaluation

This section analyzes the performance of the proposed multi-objective cooperative optimization algorithm. We set up an $800 * 800\text{m}^2$ simulation area, and 1000 nodes are randomly deployed. The communication radius of ordinary nodes and super nodes are 50 m and 150 m, respectively. The initial number of super nodes is set to 5% of the total number of nodes. According to the sensing range of nodes and the area of monitoring area, the number of sink nodes is determined as 10. Table 6.1 describes the values of several parameters in the energy model and in the process of multi-objective evolution.

The first two columns in Table 6.1 show the parameters in the energy consumption model. E_c and E_s represent the initial energy on the ordinary nodes and the super nodes respectively. In addition, pk indicates the size of the data packet, which is set as 1000 bits. The distance threshold d_0 is 87.7m, which is used to judge the type of channel. The energy E_{Ag} consumed by the super node to aggregate data is set to $5 * 10^{-9}\text{J}$. β shows the energy consumption generated by adding new connections, which can limit the number of added connections. The last two columns in Table 6.1 represent the values of each parameter in the evolution process, where Gen represents the number of iterations. p_λ and p_μ represent the baseline of crossover and mutation probabilities. M indicates the number of objective functions.

Next, the TOSG algorithm [18] is used to compare the performance of the algorithm proposed in this section. The optimization effect of the proposed algorithm is evaluated by changing the number of super nodes or total nodes in the topology respectively. The specific experimental results are shown in Table 6.2. The number of super nodes is expressed as a percentage of the total number of nodes, while the energy efficiency of the network is the number of rounds in which the first node fails. The larger the value is, the longer the lifetime of the network is. For robustness, the larger R value is, the stronger the robustness of the network is, and the maximum value of R is 0.5. For load balancing, the closer LB is to 1, the more balanced the loads on different sink nodes are.

As can be seen from the table, the energy efficiency of the two algorithms gradually decreases with the increase of the number of super nodes, because the establishment of a large number of new connections between the super nodes consumes more energy. However, the energy efficiency of the algorithm proposed in this section is always superior to TOSG. In addition, for robustness and load

Table 6.1 Description of different variables in algorithm

Variables	Description	Variables	Description
E_{elec}	$5 * 10^{-8}\text{J}$	MP	10
β	$5 * 10^{-3}\text{J}$	Pop	20
ξ_{fs}	$1 * 10^{-11}\text{J}$	Gen	150
ξ_{mp}	$1.3 * 10^{-15}\text{J}$	M	3
E_c	0.5J	p_λ	0.7
E_s	1.5J	p_μ	0.03

Table 6.2 Comparison under different numbers of super nodes

Sink nodes	Proposed algorithm			TOSG		
	Energy (E)	Robustness (R)	Load (LB)	Energy (E)	Robustness (R)	Load (LB)
5%	150	0.2714	0.9449	84	0.2677	0.9087
10%	138	0.2756	0.9743	78	0.2698	0.9430
15%	136	0.2984	0.9632	66	0.2731	0.9356
20%	132	0.3211	0.9476	56	0.2920	0.9216
25%	116	0.3484	0.9347	49	0.3276	0.9154
30%	114	0.3513	0.9231	46	0.3357	0.9055

Table 6.3 Comparison under different numbers of network nodes

Network nodes	Proposed algorithm			TOSG		
	Energy (E)	Robustness (R)	Load (LB)	Energy (E)	Robustness (R)	Load (LB)
1000	151	0.2814	0.9379	73	0.2796	0.8597
1100	139	0.3036	0.9409	62	0.2984	0.8957
1200	134	0.3161	0.9252	53	0.3124	0.8854
1300	123	0.3220	0.9182	51	0.3181	0.8721
1400	116	0.3263	0.9351	49	0.3237	0.8997
1500	109	0.3310	0.9571	41	0.3277	0.9202

balancing, the optimization effect of the proposed algorithm is better than TOSG algorithm.

Then, the scalability of the algorithms is evaluated, and the different number of nodes are deployed to observe the changes of three performance indicators in the network. The number of super nodes is fixed at 10% of the total number of nodes. The total number of nodes is set to $N = 1000, 1100, 1200, 1300, 1400, 1500$. As can be seen from Table 6.3, under the same conditions, the proposed algorithm outperforms TOSG on E, R and LB. In addition, Fig. 6.8 shows that the layered-cooperation mechanism can make multiple populations converge to the optimal solution, which avoids the population from falling into a local optimum due to the improper genetic probability.

In conclusion, multiple experimental results show that the algorithm proposed in this chapter can improve the robustness and energy efficiency of the network through multi-objective optimization, and avoid the problem of evolution falling into premature convergence.

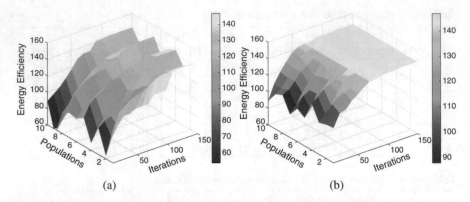

Fig. 6.8 Effect of layered-cooperation mechanism on multi-objective evolution. (**a**) No layered-cooperation. (**b**) Layered-cooperation

References

1. Navarro-Ortiz, J., Romero-Diaz, P., Sendra, S., Ameigeiras, P., Ramos-Munoz, J. J., & Lopez-Soler, J. M. (2020). A survey on 5g usage scenarios and traffic models. *IEEE Communications Surveys & Tutorials, 22*(2), 905–929.
2. Li, W., Wang, J., Yang, G., Zuo, Y., Shao, Q., & Li, S. (2018). Energy efficiency maximization oriented resource allocation in 5g ultra-dense network: Centralized and distributed algorithms. *Computer Communications, 130*, 10–19.
3. Mertikopoulos, P., & Belmega, E. V. (2016). Learning to be green: Robust energy efficiency maximization in dynamic mimo–ofdm systems. *IEEE Journal on Selected Areas in Communications, 34*(4), 743–757.
4. Pirayesh, H., Sangdeh, P. K., & Zeng, H. (2019). Ee-iot: An energy-efficient iot communication scheme for wlans. In *IEEE INFOCOM 2019-IEEE Conference on Computer Communications* (pp. 361–369). IEEE.
5. Guidoni, D. L., Mini, R. A. F., & Loureiro, A. A. F. (2012). Applying the small world concepts in the design of heterogeneous wireless sensor networks. *IEEE Communications Letters, 16*(7), 953–955.
6. Fathy, Y., & Barnaghi, P. (2019). Quality-based and energy-efficient data communication for the internet of things networks. *IEEE Internet of Things Journal, 6*(6), 10318–10331.
7. Schneider, C. M., Moreira, A. A., Andrade, J. S., Havlin, S., & Herrmann, H. J. (2011). Mitigation of malicious attacks on networks. *Proceedings of the National Academy of Sciences, 108*(10), 3838–3841.
8. Zhou, M., & Liu, J. (2016). A two-phase multiobjective evolutionary algorithm for enhancing the robustness of scale-free networks against multiple malicious attacks. *IEEE Transactions on Cybernetics, 47*(2), 539–552.
9. Peng, G.-S., & Wu, J. (2016). Optimal network topology for structural robustness based on natural connectivity. *Physica A: Statistical Mechanics and Its Applications, 443*, 212–220.
10. Deb, K., Pratap, A., Agarwal, S., & Meyarivan, T. A. M. T. (2002). A fast and elitist multiobjective genetic algorithm: Nsga-ii. *IEEE Transactions on Evolutionary Computation, 6*(2), 182–197.
11. Li, J., & Chen, M. (2016). Multiobjective topology optimization based on mapping matrix and nsga-ii for switched industrial internet of things. *IEEE Internet of Things Journal, 3*(6), 1235–1245.

12. Pandey, H. M., Chaudhary, A., & Mehrotra, D. (2014). A comparative review of approaches to prevent premature convergence in ga. *Applied Soft Computing, 24*, 1047–1077.
13. Ren, J., Zhang, Y., Zhang, K., Liu, A., Chen, J., & Shen, X. S. (2015). Lifetime and energy hole evolution analysis in data-gathering wireless sensor networks. *IEEE Transactions on Industrial Informatics, 12*(2), 788–800.
14. Zhao, N., Bao, J., & Chen, N. (2020). Ranking influential nodes in complex networks with information entropy method. *Complexity*, 2020.
15. Bradley, C. J. (2006). *Introduction to Inequalities*. UK: United Kingdom Mathematics Trust.
16. Zhiwei, L., Litong, D., Zhihong, G., Yinghua, C., Huiwen, Q., & Yanqin, G. (2020). Evaluation model of utilization efficiency of equipment assets in power distribution network based on order relation-improved entropy weight method. In *2020 3rd International Conference on Electron Device and Mechanical Engineering (ICEDME)* (pp. 72–77). IEEE.
17. Arabas, J., & Opara, K. (2019). Population diversity of nonelitist evolutionary algorithms in the exploration phase. *IEEE Transactions on Evolutionary Computation, 24*(6), 1050–1062.
18. Qiu, T., Li, B., Qu, W., Ahmed, E., & Wang, X. (2018). Tosg: A topology optimization scheme with global small world for industrial heterogeneous internet of things. *IEEE Transactions on Industrial Informatics, 15*(6), 3174–3184.

Chapter 7
Robustness Optimization Based on Self-Learning

This chapter explores the construction method of robust topology from the perspective of machine learning. Traditional optimization schemes based on genetic evolution or swarm intelligence have a long running time when the large-scale nodes are deployed in a scenario. In order to further reduce the time for topology construction, this chapter studies the application of artificial intelligence in topology to obtain a robust topology deployment model, which can guide the connection of subsequent nodes. The application of machine learning model in network topology is explored from three perspectives: malicious node identification, highly robust topology optimization and highly robust topology generation.

7.1 Malicious Node Identification Scheme Based on Gaussian Mixture Model

This section tries to reduce the probability of network attacks by identifying malicious nodes (spammer) that send spam in the IoT, which can improve the robustness of the topology. Different from other chapters on topology optimization, this section identifies attackers from the perspective of attack to ensure the stability of network topology. The existing identification methods based on machine learning have the following two limitations. One is the unbalanced data. The quantity of unlabeled data is much larger than labeled data, which hinders the direct construction of models. The other is multi-dimensional data. Excessive features lead to over-fitting of the model. In order to solve the above problem, this section combines user behavior data and semi-supervised training features to propose a malicious node identification model. This model can obtain an accurate classification result by training a small amount of labeled data. The following is a detailed introduction to this model.

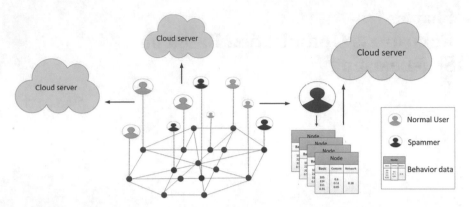

Fig. 7.1 Spammers hiding among users

7.1.1 Statement of Problem

As a large number of smart devices are connected in the IoT, mobile networks
have gradually become the main access method. Therefore, it has also become
the main target of spammers. Spam is one of the most common forms of attacks
on mobile networks. Spammers pretend to be ordinary users to send spam [1],
which is the malicious node to be detected. The spams contain links with viruses.
When these links are clicked, the user's personal information will be stolen, which
will affect the stability of the network. As shown in Fig. 7.1, these ordinary nodes
communicate with each other, and spammers are hidden among them. The network
structure with small icons on the left represents the network data extracted from
mobile cloud computing, and the right is the behavior data of each user. The red
icon represents spammer, and the green icon represents ordinary users. As more
users join the network, malicious nodes also organize spam dissemination in order
to seek greater benefits, which brings the loss to many ordinary users. The increase
in data dimensions makes it more and more difficult to identify these spammers.

As machine learning algorithms are applied in different fields, many scholars
consider using machine learning algorithms to identify spammers. The main goal
of supervised learning is to learn a model from labeled data to make predictions
on unknown data. This type of algorithm requires that the label of the data is
known. In the spam detection algorithm based on logistic regression [2], an online
network spam classifier is established by inputting the features of the user data.
When a spammer is detected, the output of algorithm is 1. This model is trained
on a large training set. However, due to the emphasis on user data confidentiality,
the collection of label data has become difficult. Unsupervised learning algorithms
do not need a known label to guide the training of the model. The identification
problem of spammer can be transformed into a clustering problem. In the reality
mining algorithm based on k-means (RMA) [3], a silhouette function with the
number of clusters as a parameter is proposed to judge the accuracy of clustering.

The best value of k can be determined by calculating the average silhouette value under different values. However, it takes extra time to determine the value of k, and the experimental results are unstable. When using the same k value for multiple experiments, the results are not the same. Hybrid fuzzy c-means clustering algorithm (HFCM) [4] minimizes the objective function and updates the membership function by repeating arithmetic operations, which is very time-consuming. The accuracy of the experiment depends on the volume of the data set.

In addition, a recursive least squares algorithm [5] based on the reinforcement learning is proposed to identify specific users. This algorithm searches a user by friendship relationships, which limits the scope of the search and reduces the detection efficiency. The above-mentioned methods mainly rely on the relationship between users to identify spammers. However, due to the development of the intelligent recommendation mechanism, the association relationship is not necessarily based on the user's true preferences or intentions. Therefore, under fuzzy user relationships, this section proposes a Spammer Identification scheme based on Gaussian Mixture Model (SIGMM). Malicious nodes are identified by analyzing the behavioral data of spammers and ordinary users in the mobile network.

7.1.2   Data Preprocessing Operations

The quality of the data and the number of features are the key factors to determine the learning effect of the model. Therefore, before the data set is input into the model, the data set needs to be preprocessed, which mainly includes feature scaling and feature grouping. The data set used includes the following content: ID of users, relationship between users, post records with time stamps, and activities in the last three months. Based on these content, this section can calculate the frequency of user postings, percentage of posts with URL or @ character, and the average similarity between user posts. There are two main constraints on the data set.

- The amount of labeled data is much smaller than unlabeled data, which seriously reduces the accuracy of training.
- There is a large amount of data noise. Data points that do not belong to any class are defined as data noise, which can be reduced by calculating the similarity between users.

First, feature scaling is introduced. The purpose is to reduce the number of features and prevent the model from over-fitting. The relevant distances are calculated to judge the similarity between users, which include Euclidean distance and cosine distance. Euclidean distance is the straight-line distance between two data objects in space, and cosine distance uses a vector angle to represent the distance between two users. Since the Euclidean distance is more sensitive to the change of the vector modulus, the cosine distance cannot perceive this change. Therefore, this section uses Euclidean distance to calculate the similarity between users. In addition, in order to accurately learn the model parameters, Pearson correlation coefficient and

Table 7.1 Pearson coefficients of different features

F1	Labels	Fans	Follow	Post	fre_follow	Accountage	Fans/follow
	Values	−0.72	0.57	0.37	0.58	0.11	0.14
F2	Labels	fre_post	Similarity	url_portion	@number	Forward_number	
	Values	0.68	0.91	0.88	0.15	0.08	
F3	Labels	friend_portion	ne_posts	ne_fans			
	Values	−0.84	0.20	0.11			

Principal Component Analysis (PCA) are used to express the features of the data. The Pearson correlation coefficient can calculate the linear correlation coefficient between two variables x and y, and the value range is $(−1, +1)$, where $−1$ means linear negative correlation, 0 means non-linear correlation, $+1$ is linear positive correlation. The calculation formula of Pearson correlation coefficient is as follows.

$$\rho_{X,Y} = \frac{Cov(X, Y)}{\sigma_X \sigma_Y} \tag{7.1}$$

$$r = \frac{\sum_{i=1}^{n}(x_i - \bar{x})(y_i - \bar{y})}{\sqrt{\sum_{i=1}^{n}(x_i - \bar{x})^2} * \sqrt{\sum_{i=1}^{n}(y_i - \bar{y})^2}} \tag{7.2}$$

In Eq. (7.1), $Cov(x, y)$ is the covariance of the variables x and y. σ_X and σ_Y are the standard deviations of x and y, respectively. The correlation coefficient r between two n-dimensional vectors can be calculated by Eq. (7.2). Table 7.1 shows the Pearson correlation coefficient values of different features. In order to perform feature scaling, this section excludes features with an absolute value of correlation coefficient less than 0.2. Therefore, *Accountage* and *Fans/follow* in $F1$, *@number* and *Forward_number* in $F2$, and *ne_fans* in $F3$ are deleted.

Next, the feature grouping is explained. This section divides the multi-dimensional features in user data into three groups, which include basic features, content features and network features.

- Basic features include the number of fans, following users, posts, and following frequency. Spammers tend to follow a large number of users, but their fans and followers are few. Spammers follow others more frequently than ordinary users.
- Content features mainly reflect the information sent by the user in the last three months, which can analyze the user's activities.
- Network features include the number and proportion of following each other. The proportion of spammers following each other is lower than ordinary users.

We use a data visualization view to evaluate the basic features of users. PCA is used to compress data and find the direction of maximum variance in high-dimensional data, which is projected onto a low-dimensional subspace. As shown in Fig. 7.2, $x1$ and $x2$ are the original feature axes, and $PC1$ and $PC2$ are the principal components. By constructing a four-dimensional transformation matrix W, PCA

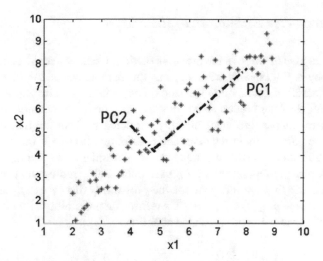

Fig. 7.2 Results of dimensionality reduction using PCA

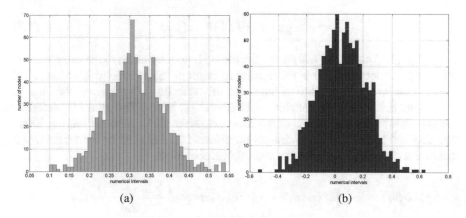

(a)   (b)

Fig. 7.3 The basic features of different users after dimensionality reduction. (**a**) Ordinary users.
(**b**) Spammers

can map a sample with the four-dimensional features into one-dimensional features.
Figure 7.3a and b show the training data sets of ordinary users and spammers after
dimensionality reduction. The distribution of the two types of data approximately
obeys the Gaussian distribution with different parameters. Similarly, the results of
content features and network features after dimensionality reduction also show the
similar structure. Therefore, after observing the data, a Gaussian mixture model is
used to separate the two types of users.

7.1.3   Parameter Estimation of the Model

From the data visualization in the previous section, it can be seen that the two types of users obey a Gaussian distribution, but the parameters of the distribution are unknown. Therefore, this section is based on expectation maximization to estimate the parameter θ of the model. According to the probability density $p(x|\theta)$, some ordinary users samples are independently extracted to form the training set X. θ represents the parameters in the Gaussian distribution $N(\mu, \sigma)$, i.e., $\theta = [\mu, \sigma]^T$, which can be estimated by the sample set X. Consider $X = \{x_1, x_2, \cdots, x_n\}$ as a set of samples, x_i represents the i_{th} user data, and n represents the number of samples. Because they are independent, the probability that x_i and x_j are extracted at the same time is $p(x_i|\theta) * p(x_j|\theta)$. Therefore, the probability of n samples being extracted at the same time is calculated as follows.

$$L(\theta) = L(x_1, x_2, \cdots, x_n; \theta) = \prod_{i=1}^{n} p(x_i; \theta) \tag{7.3}$$

$$\hat{\theta} = \arg\max L(\theta), \quad \theta = [\mu, \sigma]^T \tag{7.4}$$

In Eqs. (7.3) and (7.4), $L(\theta)$ is the likelihood function related to the sample set X and the parameter θ, and $\hat{\theta}$ is the maximum result of the likelihood function $L(\theta)$. When $\theta = \hat{\theta}$, the probability of independently selecting n samples is the largest. Therefore, $\hat{\theta}$ is called the maximum likelihood estimator. The goal of parameter estimation is to determine a parameter that maximizes the likelihood function. Since the likelihood function is a continuous multiplication, $L(\theta)$ can be converted into a continuous addition form through logarithmic operations.

$$\ln L(\theta_1) = \ln \prod P(x_i; \theta_1) = -[k \ln(\sqrt{2\pi}\sigma_1) + \frac{\sum(x_i - \mu_1)^2}{2\sigma_1^2}] \tag{7.5}$$

$$\frac{\partial \ln L(\theta_1)}{\partial \mu_1} = 0, \frac{\partial \ln L(\theta_1)}{\partial \sigma_1} = 0 \Rightarrow \mu_1 = \frac{1}{k} \sum_{i=1}^{k} x_i, \sigma_1 = \sqrt{\frac{\sum_{i=1}^{k}(x_i - \mu_1)^2}{2k}}$$

$$\tag{7.6}$$

In order to obtain the maximum value of $L(\theta)$, the partial derivatives of Eq. (7.5) in the μ_1 and σ_1 directions are respectively obtained. In Eq. (7.6), when the partial derivative is equal to 0, the corresponding values of μ_1 and σ_1 can be obtained.

After the above process, the parameter value θ of the Gaussian distribution that the ordinary user obeys can be estimated. Similarly, for the Gaussian distribution of spammer, the same method can be used to obtain the parameter. But this kind of sample extraction is unfair and has extreme trends. The trained models are highly biased. The sample needs to be extracted from the entire data set, which does not consider the label of the sample. Therefore, this sample is a mixture of two distributions, and two questions need to be considered. One is from which distribution the sample comes from, and the other is what is the parameter of this distribution.

$$\ln \prod p(x_i; \theta) = \sum \ln p(x_i; z_i; \theta) \tag{7.7}$$

To solve this problem, each sample is described by a triple $y_i = (x_i, z_{i1}, z_{i2})$. Where x_i represents the i_{th} data, z_{i1} represents the data x_i generated by the Gaussian distribution of ordinary users, and z_{i2} represents the data x_i generated by the Gaussian distribution of spammers. For example, if a triple is $(1.8, 1, 0)$, it indicates that this data sample belongs to the Gaussian distribution of ordinary users. z_{i1} and z_{i2} are hidden variables, Eq. (7.7) shows the expression form of the likelihood function after adding hidden variables. The process for solving the probabilistic model parameter θ using maximum likelihood estimation is as follows.

- The Gaussian distribution parameter θ is initialized.
- The posterior probability of variable z is calculated according to the parameter θ, and $Q_i(z^i)$ represents the expectation of the z. $Q_i(z^i) := P(z^i | x^i; \theta)$.
- The parameter θ is updated. $\theta := \arg\max_\theta \sum_i \sum_{z^i} Q_i \log \frac{p(x^i, z^i; \theta)}{Q_i(z^i)}$.

The above process is repeated, and the parameter θ continues to iterate by maximizing the likelihood function until the model converges.

7.1.4   Training and Prediction Process of the Model

This section trains the model according to the parameter estimated in the previous section. Since the proportion of labeled data in the data set is very small, this section uses the principle of semi-supervised learning to obtain the initial form of the model based on a small amount of labeled data. Then we update and optimize the model by continuously predicting unlabeled data and adding unlabeled data to the training set. Finally, the model reaches a stable state. This section mainly considers two methods of predicting unlabeled data, namely probability method and distance method. The first method calculates the probability $r(i, k)$ of the data x_i generated by the k_{th} distribution through the expectation maximization.

$$r(i, k) = \frac{\pi_k N(x_i | \mu_k, \Sigma_k)}{\sum_{j=1}^k \pi_j N(x_i | \mu_j, \Sigma_j)} \tag{7.8}$$

The estimated values of μ and σ have been obtained by Chap. 7.1.3. The ratio of ordinary users to spammers is taken as prior knowledge. However, due to the large amount of unlabeled data, the ratio of the two users cannot be estimated. In

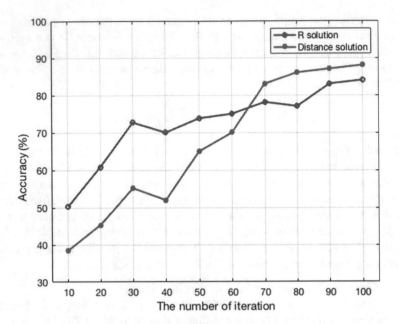

Fig. 7.4 Accuracy comparison of two labeling methods

Eq. (7.8), π_k is an uncertain variable. By roughly estimating the value of π_k, the probability that a sample belongs to the k_{th} distribution can be calculated. Then the sample belongs to the distribution with the highest probability.

The second method is implemented through data visualization. It can be seen that the unlabeled data are distributed on the inside and outside of the two ellipsoids, and each ellipsoid represents a distribution. The class to which a data belongs depends on the distance from the data point to the ellipsoid. Compared with the first method, the second method is more convenient to calculate.

Figure 7.4 shows the accuracy of the two methods when 1000 labeled data are randomly selected. The x-axis represents the number of iterations, and the y-axis represents the accuracy of the two methods. The pink line represents the distance method, and the blue line represents the probability method. It can be seen from the figure that the distance method fluctuates due to unstable features at the beginning of the iteration, and the probability method is slightly higher than the distance method. However, the probability method does not change much in subsequent iterations, and the accuracy of the probability method is lower than the distance method at the end of the iteration. The reason is that due to the large amount of unlabeled data, the rough estimation of π_k cannot represent the proportion of each distribution in the entire data set.

If a sample has been classified into one of two classes, this sample will be deleted from the unlabeled data set and added to the training set. Recently added samples may cause the model to adjust parameters. In the whole iterative process,

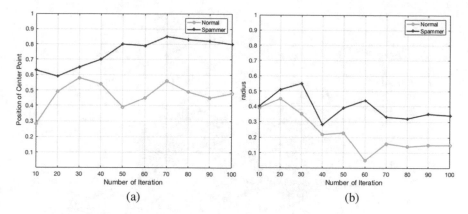

Fig. 7.5 Changes in the center position and radius of the ellipsoid. (**a**) Center position. (**b**) Radius

the parameters of the model are gradually adjusted to the optimal results. The entire training and prediction process is described as follows.

First, the labeled data set is randomly divided into two parts, one is the training set with initial parameter, and the other is the test set. The remaining unlabeled data is labeled by the predictive method, which is added to the training set. The maximum likelihood function is used to build and update the model. Through multiple iterations, the model parameters gradually converge. Figure 7.5 shows the change trend of the two model parameters with the number of iterations. At the beginning of iteration, the fluctuation of center coordinate and radius is relatively large. After several iterations, the curves of these two parameters gradually flatten and finally reach the convergence state.

The Gaussian mixture model [6] is a probability model of statistical learning, and each Gaussian model represents a class. The probability can be obtained by matching the sample with multiple Gaussian models, and the class with the highest probability is selected as the classification result. Figure 7.6 shows the ellipsoid during the iteration and the ellipsoid after reaching a stable state. As can be seen from the figure, the data in the two classes are clearly separated. Because the behavior data among a large number of ordinary users are not similar, the data samples deviate from the center of the ellipsoid, so the green ellipsoid has a larger radius. However, spammers have similar behaviors when attacking others, so the radius of the red ellipsoid is smaller. In addition, by comparing the ellipsoids under the two states, it is found that the radius and position of the two ellipsoids do not change much, which shows that the model is convergent.

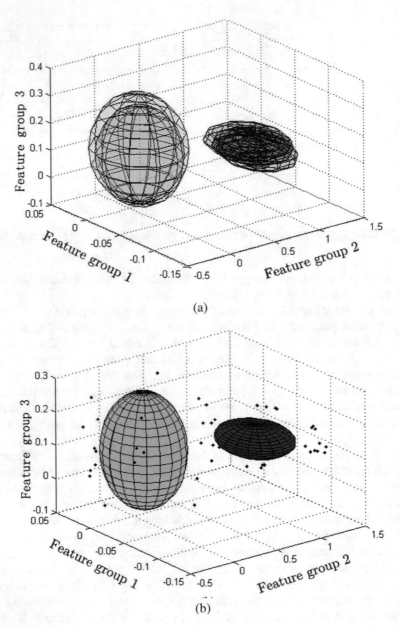

(a)

(b)

Fig. 7.6 Comparison of ellipsoid shapes in different iteration stages. (**a**) Iteration state. (**b**) Stable state

7.1.5 Performance Evaluation

This section verifies the performance of the SIGMM algorithm. Taking accuracy, recall and precision as metrics, SIGMM is compared with the other two algorithms, namely RMA [3] and HFCM [4]. The number of iterations is set to 100, and all data is preprocessed by the same way. The labeled data is divided into two parts, one part is to generate the initial value, and the other part is used as the test set. The accuracy represents the proportion of spammers that the model correctly predicted. The recall represents the proportion of spammers who are correctly identified, and accuracy is the proportion of all users who are correctly classified.

Figure 7.7 shows the performance of the three algorithms on different metrics. The larger the value of the metrics, the better the performance of the algorithm. Because spammers have similar behaviors and data dispersion is low, the recall metrics of the three algorithms are higher than other indicators. For the same metrics, it can be seen that the SIGMM algorithm is better than the other two comparison algorithms.

In addition to the above three indicators, the time complexity of the algorithm is also an important factor for judging the performance of the algorithm. Therefore, Fig. 7.8 compares the three algorithms in terms of running time. The x-axis represents the number of samples, and the y-axis represents the running time. As the number of samples increases, the difference in running time of the three

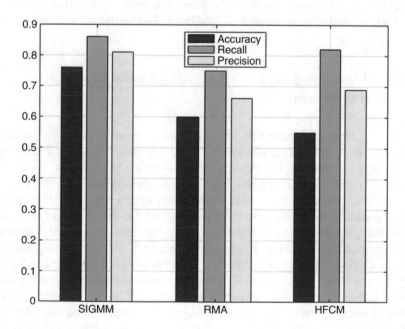

Fig. 7.7 Comparison of the three models on different metrics

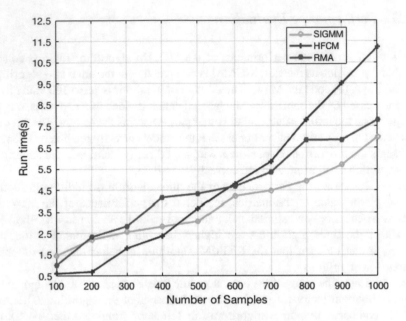

Fig. 7.8 Comparison of running time among the three algorithms

algorithms gradually increases. When the data set is large, the SIGMM algorithm is significantly better than the other two algorithms in terms of running time.

7.2   Highly Robust Topology Learning Model Based on Neural Network

IoT data will increase dramatically with the applications of large-scale devices [7], which has unique application advantages. How to utilize the topology data to guide the topology optimization has become a hot research topic. Iterative updating of machine learning technology makes it possible to process and analyze rough IoT data and obtain valuable results to direct topology optimization [8]. However, IoT data is limited by the storage space and computing capacity of nodes that can not support complex computational calculation [9]. Therefore, how to use lightweight intelligent machine learning to compute and deal with IoT topology optimization became a challenging problem. In this section, we first explore the Back Propagation (BP) neural network model of WSNs topology evolution method, propose a robust optimization model based on evolution learning (ROEL), achieving the goal of extracting learning characteristics and reducing the computational overhead from traditional optimal topology of scale-free network. A highly robust topology learning evolution model is constructed to support intelligent IoT technology.

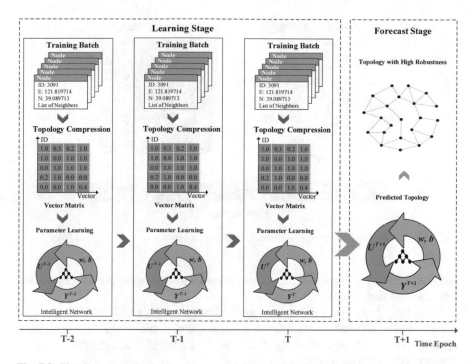

Fig. 7.9 The diagrammatic sketch of our model for topology forecast, where the parameters are learned from the data set and used for forecasting the future IoT topology

7.2.1 Learning Framework based on Neural Network

As shown in Fig. 7.9, we illustrate the evolution process of IoT topology to improve the robustness based on the topology data set, which is discussed below.

Different from previous research works [10–14], in this section, we first propose a novel network topology optimization based on neural network. By constructing intelligent network to train the topology data and learn the matrix parameters, the proposed model can provide high QoS for low latency applications and highly reliable through the rapid optimization model and realize the self-optimizing goal on the edge of network topology and devices. In forecast state, the optimized model can provide high robustness topology for the initial IoT.

7.2.2 Preliminary Details

The proposed algorithm is designed to promote the robustness of IoT topologies. By supervising the training of a large number of data sets, the proposed algorithm recombines the low-robustness topology into a high robustness topology and

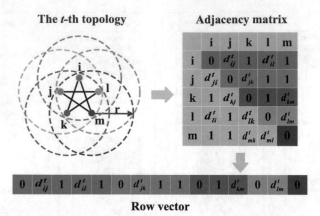

Fig. 7.10 The topology's preprocessing and conversion operations

preserves scale-free properties. To better illustrate the proposed algorithm, we first introduce the basic idea in this section.

Generally, similar with abstraction method mentioned above [10], the algorithm design several adjustments that improve convergence speed and approach local optimum. Furthermore, a row vector is designed from the adjacency matrix to reduce computational overhead as shown in Fig. 7.10.

The details of data set is described below. We design topology samples $\{x, y\}$, where x represents the initial topology and y represents the optimized topology. Then, the data set is divided into training subset and testing subset. As shown in Fig. 7.10, firstly, the practical topology is abstracted into an adjacency matrix. In order to improve the convergence speed and learn more evolution features, non-neighbor information is added in the matrix [15].

We apply supervised learning framework to extract the evolution learning behavior for IoT topology. For problem model, H is the hypothetical solution space and F is a series of decision functions.

$$H = \{F \mid Y = F(X)\} \tag{7.9}$$

X and Y are the input space and output space, respectively, obtained from the training set. We assemble initial topology into input space, and optimized predicted topology is output space. According to machine learning rules, the F is determined by model parameter vector and can describe the evolutionary behavior for IoT topologies.

$$F = \{f \mid Y = f_\theta(X), \ \theta \in \mathbf{R}^n\} \tag{7.10}$$

The parameter vector θ is determined by a n-dimensional Euclidean space $\mathbf{R}^n$, which is called the parameter space that divided into weight and bias. f corresponds to the topology sample. Then, in order to optimize the ROEL, F is modified based on the error between the training results and the target values, which is defined as Eq. (7.11).

$$L(U, \ F(X)) = (U - F(X))^2 \qquad (7.11)$$

Where $L(U, F(X))$ is the loss function about the error, which applies the Mean-Square Error (MSE) method.

In order to evaluate the performance of data set, we introduce the average loss of $L(U, F(X))$ is defined as the empirical loss and recorded as $E(X, U)$ which is defined as Eq. (7.12). In other words, the empirical loss E is the optimizing goal for the learning model in ROEL.

$$E(X, U) = \frac{1}{N} \sum_{i=1}^{N} L(\boldsymbol{u}_i, F(\boldsymbol{x}_i)) \qquad (7.12)$$

The proposed ROEL is positive related to the empirical loss $E(X, Y)$, whose goal is to minimize E. Furthermore, through supervised training by topology data set, ROEL can prospect the evolution direction of initial IoT topology and improve the robustness against malicious attacks with low computational overhead.

7.2.3   Performance Evaluation

In this section, the simulation and experimental results are introduced to validate the effectiveness of our evolution learning model ROEL.

The important parameter setting in Table 7.2 are determined by many experiment results. Due to the topology data set and preprocessing operation, we set the number of neural units 5050 that matches the topology vector. As shown in Fig. 7.11, we illustrate the robustness value distribution of 10,1000 topology samples from ROCKS [10]. In order to improve the convergence speed, we remove topology samples with low robustness.

For optimization speed and computational overhead, ROEL has better performance than other existing algorithms in Table 7.3. The bold values of the ROEL present the best performance in terms of running time than other algorithms. The proposed optimized learning model can provide high robust network topology with less computation cost.

Table 7.2 Simulation parameter setting

Parameters	Values
The number of neural units	5050
The number of layers	5
Learning rate	0.1
Momentum factor	0.5

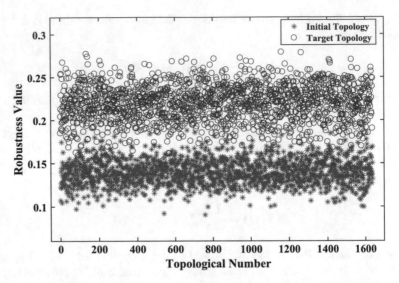

Fig. 7.11 The Statistics about Robustness of Data set. The robustness values of target and initial topologies have clear boundary which represents the data set has optimization space for initial topology

Table 7.3 The comparison of running time (s) of algorithms

Algorithm	Data set	Single sample
The learning process of ROEL	**543.0011**	–
The forecasting process of ROEL	**0.2351**	–
Hill climbing	42,248.7592	268.2302
Simulated annealing	11,0852.0746	848.525

For training and testing simulation, ROEL has the optimal result around 350 iterations as shown in Fig. 7.12. The two lines describe the prediction rate of topology robustness from the data set. Through the trend of lines, we can conclude that a optimal topology can output from the ROEL and the important network features are learned by ROEL. Considering the limitation of data set, the training simulation is 96.82%, and the test simulation is 96.68%, which is a less error. The trained ROEL can dynamic optimize IoT topology with less running time, and not loss robustness ability. The robustness error with the optimized network topology is less than 4%.

In robustness optimization for random attacks, we compare ROEL with other existing optimization algorithms. As shown in Fig. 7.13, we use the number of nodes in the maximum connected component as the index to present the network performance for the current IoT topology. The IoT topology has 100 nodes. From the Fig. 7.13, all lines are slowly declining and are less difference. The IoT topology of data set is generated by scale-free model that is more robust against random attacks. Therefore, all algorithms have similar capability to resist the random attacks. Furthermore, our ROEL model does not change the scale-free features of

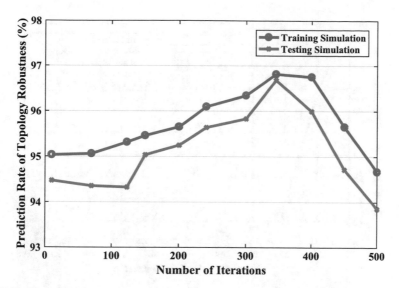

Fig. 7.12 The prediction rate between the predicted results and optimized value in robustness of network topology

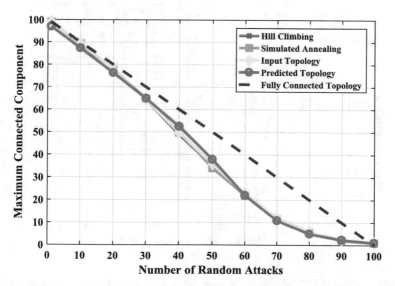

Fig. 7.13 Comparison of the capacity of the different topologies against random attack

initial topology, and the degree distribution of optimized topology confirms power-law rules.

For robustness optimization for malicious attacks, there are two different attacks strategies as shown in Fig. 7.14, i.e., with or without recalculating the degrees of the remaining network. The fully connected network has the most edges so it has the most ability to resist malicious attacks, which is mentioned in previous chapters [10]. ROEL is close to the performance of fully connected network, which

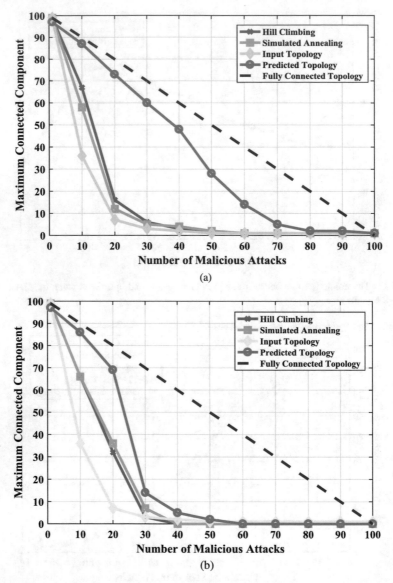

Fig. 7.14 Comparison the capacity of different network topologies to resist different malicious attacks. (**a**) The malicious attack without recalculating the degrees of the remaining network. (**b**) The malicious attack with recalculating the degrees of remaining network

illustrates that the predicted topology is better than initial topology against malicious attacks.

In addition, ROEL has significant advantages without recalculating the remaining network degrees as shown in Fig. 7.14a. Compared to other existing algorithms, ROEL is still robust after 8 node failures. Besides, from Fig. 7.14b, ROEL also has better performance when 40 node failures than other algorithms. ROEL learns the evolution processing and directions from the data set and improves the robustness of IoT topology.

7.3 Highly Robust Topology Generation Strategy Based on Temporal Convolutional Network

In this section, the generation problem of a highly robust topology is transformed into a sequence prediction task, which can improve optimization efficiency without losing the optimization effect. Based on the machine learning algorithm and the convolutional neural network model, an efficient robust networking strategy for scale-free IoT (EROS) is designed to generate the topology. This strategy mainly includes three stages: data set generation and processing, model training and prediction topology generation. Firstly, the network connection relationship is transformed into a sequence model suitable for feature extraction in data set preprocessing. In order to extract the mapping between initial topologies and highly robust topologies, convolutional neural networks are used to learn the structural features of robust topologies in data sets. In addition, the empirical loss function and optimization effect measure index are combined to train and screen the network model. Finally, taking full account of the degree and communication capability constraints of nodes in the IoT, the predictive topology generation algorithm is designed to restore the obtained predictive topology sequence to the connection relation. This topology generation strategy not only ensures topology robustness but also does not change the scale-free distribution characteristics of topology.

7.3.1 Statement of Problem

Breakthroughs in key technologies such as big data and cloud computing have made the IoT widely deployed in smart cities. However, the damage of some key nodes in the transmission path will seriously affect the transmission efficiency and communication capacity of the entire network. For example, in smart agriculture, a large number of sensors are deployed to monitor the growth status of crops and prevent pests and diseases. With the extension of the network running time, some key nodes carrying higher data traffic may be the first to run out of energy, and the Internet of Things will lose the ability to monitor the growth of crops. Wrong operation of irrigation and ventilation systems can cause unavoidable economic losses. Therefore, it is necessary to construct a highly robust IoT topology. In addition, the large-scale deployment of IoT applications and the rapid development of technology have put forward higher requirements for the response speed and optimization efficiency of robust optimization strategies. The traditional heuristic algorithm optimizes the robustness of the IoT through iterative edge-changing operations, which has high computational cost and long running time. It is difficult to meet the actual needs of robustness optimization. Therefore, designing an efficient and robust networking strategy for the IoT with fast response speed has become a research hotspot.

In recent years, neural network models have provided strong support for the application of IoT with its good feature extraction ability and model reusability. The research work in Chap. 7.2 shows that the neural network model has the ability to learn the evolution rules of the IoT topology, and optimize the robustness of the IoT against malicious attacks. Kaminski et al. [16] mapped intelligent devices in the IoT to input layer and output layer in neural network, and minimized communication cost and transmission delay to ensure communication quality. Chen et al. [17] showed that artificial neural network has the ability to learn infrastructure failures and attack events in wireless networks, so as to improve the communication system's resistance to these attacks. Timothy et al. [18] introduced a method to construct a communication system as an auto-encoder by using convolutional neural network, which greatly improved the reliability of the network and reduced the delay of the network. Neural network model has good learning ability for feature mapping from input space to output space and is suitable for mass processing of large samples. Considering the model reusability of neural networks, it is feasible to design an efficient IoT robustness optimization strategy and provide real-time robustness optimization services in data centers. Therefore, this section implements an efficient robust networking strategy for the IoT based on the neural network model.

7.3.2   Feasibility Analysis of Sequence Prediction

This section analyzes the feasibility of sequence prediction in topology generation. Firstly, the limitation of edge-swapping strategy is analyzed. Hill-Climbing algorithm [12], Simulated-Annealing algorithm [13] and ROCKS algorithm [10] all optimize the robustness of topology through iterative edge-swapping operations. After each iteration, the proportion of the largest connected component in the network under malicious attack strategy is used to guide network optimization. Because the search space is multi-modal, the whole search process is very long and easy to fall into the local optimal solution. Although ROCKS and other algorithms can achieve better optimization results by introducing global search in the optimization process, the co-evolution of multiple populations will consume more computational resources, and the iteration time is unstable for different initial topologies. Through the analysis of the above heuristic algorithms, it is found that they introduce a large amount of computational overhead in the process of robustness optimization, resulting in low optimization efficiency, which is difficult to meet the real-time response requirements of the IoT applications. Therefore, improving the mechanism of the robust optimization algorithm and reducing the computational cost is of great significance for the robust optimization of the IoT topology.

Machine learning algorithms have advantages in processing high-dimensional data mapping, especially neural networks have strong feature extraction ability for mapping from input space to output space. The larger the amount of data, the better the feature extraction effect. Machine learning algorithm can not only give application intelligence, but also greatly improve the optimization efficiency. The neural network model trained successfully has the repeatability, and can give constant time complexity optimization ability to new samples. By matching the connection relation between the neurons in the neural network and the nodes in the IoT, the decision function is constantly optimized to learn the feature mapping between the initial topology sequence with low robustness and the optimized topology sequence with high robustness. This mechanism can avoid complex iterative edge-swapping operations. The trained neural network model can quickly optimize the new initial topology with low robustness and greatly improve the optimization efficiency.

The multi-population co-evolution algorithm ROCKS introduced in Chap. 4 has excellent robustness optimization effect, and the optimization topology has an obvious onion-like structure. Therefore, the ROCKS algorithm can be used to generate the data set required for neural network model training. After the preprocessing of the data set, topology information can be transformed into a sequence form suitable for supervised learning tasks, and all the network connection information needed in the optimization process can be kept. Therefore, it can satisfy the input and output requirements of neural network model. In addition, the loss function is designed based on the connection relation between nodes in the IoT, which can measure the structural difference between the prediction topology and the target topology, and guide the training of neural network model. Robust topologies can be learned by gradient descent in machine learning. The optimized topology structure of IoT generated by ROCKS algorithm has onion-like structure characteristics. In the optimized topology, nodes with similar degrees remain connected, and such nodes pairs do not pass through nodes with higher degrees as much as possible for data routing. In the data set preprocessing, the network connection information is transformed into topological sequence, and the structural characteristics of the optimized topology are transformed into the dependency between elements in the sequence model. The feature extraction capability of neural network model promises to learn these features.

However, neural network models with different structures have different performance abilities in different tasks. For the fully connected neural network in Chap. 7.2, the learning effect of robustness is poor in this task, and the model convergence rate is slow. The model converges only after about 300 to 400 iterations. Therefore, it is necessary to explore other models with better feature extraction ability. Recurrent Neural Network model (RNN), Long and Short-Term Memory network (LSTM) and Gated Recurrent Unit model (GRU) have good performance in the sequence prediction problem [19], but the network model is difficult to train due to the large number of parameters and is prone to the problem of gradient disappearance. In practical application, RNN models can solve some long-term dependency problems, but they do not have the infinite memory ability [20]. In recent years, the temporal convolutional neural network model (TCN) proposed by Bai et al. [20] has surpassed the performance of RNN, LSTM and GRU models in many benchmark tasks. This model has the characteristics of fast convergence speed and strong ability to extract features of temporal and spatial sequences, so it is suitable for learning robust structural features of topological sequences. Combined with the sequential convolutional neural network model, the sequence structure features of the ROCKS optimization topology are extracted to ensure the robustness optimization effect and reduce the running time of the algorithm.

7.3.3 Construction of Topological Sample Sequence Model

To learn the structural features of robust topology using neural network models, topology connections need to be processed to be suitable for neural network inputs. The adjacency matrix of the network is usually used to represent the connection relation between nodes. This section designs a data filling method for the adjacency matrix and transforms it into a sequence form suitable for neural network inputs. The data generation and processing methods are introduced to prepare for the following neural network model and optimization strategy designs.

The data set of supervised learning task consists of a large number of topology samples, each topology sample contains an initial topology and the corresponding optimization topology. The initial topology has a scale-free distribution with low robustness. The optimized topology has an onion-like structure that can resist malicious and random attacks. First, the generation of the initial topology and the optimization topology in the data set is introduced. Nodes in the initial topology are randomly deployed in the region, and the connection relationship is established by setting the topology edge density and calculating the connection probability between nodes and neighbors. It needs to ensure that a node can connect to only nodes within the communication range and the node degree does not exceed the maximum. For each initial topology, ROCKS algorithm is used to obtain the corresponding optimization topology. Through the above methods, a large number of topology samples can be generated as data sets.

In the past research, the adjacency matrix of the topology is used to represent the connection relationship of the network nodes. Since the communication range of the node is limited, the effective data in the adjacency matrix is sparse, which seriously affects the learning rate and convergence speed of the algorithm. This section converts the adjacency matrix into a sequence model as shown in Fig. 7.15, which can save storage space and enrich the diversity of data. The five nodes in

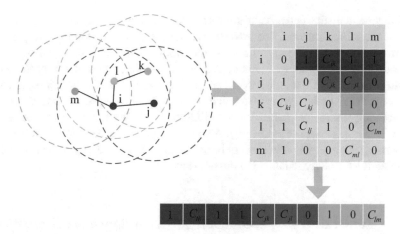

Fig. 7.15 Construction of topological vector model

Fig. 7.15 join the network in the order of i, j, k, l, m. This operation ensures that the topological sequence has a certain sequential relationship, that is, the connection relationship of the nodes that newly join the network is placed in front of the sequence. The connection relationship of the nodes newly joined to the network depends on the existing connections in the network. The sequence model constructed in this way conforms to the generation process of the network.

In the adjacency matrix, 0 represents that there is no connection between two nodes or the two nodes are out of communication range, 1 indicates that a connection is established between two nodes. In order to reduce the sparsity of data in adjacency matrix, a data filling method is designed. This method adds a logical message C_{ik} between two unconnected neighbor nodes i and k. It is calculated as follows.

$$C_{ik} = \frac{max\{\Delta d_i\} + max\{\Delta d_k\} - 2\Delta d_{ik}}{max\{\Delta d_i\} + max\{\Delta d_k\} + 1} \tag{7.13}$$

In Eq. (7.13), $max\{\Delta d_i\}$ represents the maximum degree difference between node i and its neighbor. Δd_{ik} represents the degree difference between node i and node k. Adding a normalization factor to the denominator ensures that the value range of C_{ik} is (0, 1), so that nodes with different connection relationships can be compared. The closer C_{ik} value is to 1, the higher the probability of establishing a connection between nodes i and k, which conforms to the logical connection relation of onion-like structure. Since the IoT topology of the data set is an undirected network, $C_{ik} = C_{ki}$. After the above operation, the topological matrix is a symmetric matrix. The sequence model of the network can be obtained by connecting the row vectors of the upper triangular matrix which do not contain the main diagonal. The sequence model contains abundant topological structure information, such as the connection, the degree and the number of neighbors. Moreover, the order of elements in the sequence indicates the order of edge establishment in the network. Therefore, the topological sequence model has a certain sequential relation. Meanwhile, the length r of the topology sequence is determined by the number n of nodes in the topology, that is, $r = n * (n - 1)/2$.

According to the above method, the initial topology x_t and the optimization topology y_t of the same network are respectively transformed into a topology sequence model, which together constitute a topology sample (x_t, y_t). All topology samples generated by ROCKS constitute the data set $D = (x_1, y_1), \cdots, (x_t, y_t), \cdots, (x_N, y_N)$. A sequence prediction problem is constructed by learning the mapping relationship between the initial topology sequence and the optimization topology sequence in the data set.

7.3.4 Model Learning and Topology Reconfiguration Strategies

In order to learn the construction method of robust IoT topology, this section defines a sequential to sequential supervised learning problem based on data set D. The feature extraction capability of neural network is used to learn the mapping rules between sequences. All initial topologies constitute the input space of supervised learning task $X = (x_1, \cdots, x_t, \cdots, x_N)^T$. Similarly, all optimization topologies are constructed as output space $Y = (y_1, \cdots, y_t, \cdots, y_N)^T$. Therefore, it is necessary to learn the mapping between input space X and output space Y to guide topology optimization. Different mapping rules jointly constitute the hypothesis space H of the supervised training problem, whose definition is shown in Eq. (7.14).

$$H = f|Y = f_\theta(X), \theta \in R^n \tag{7.14}$$

Each mapping rule is determined by a decision function f, which is represented by the parameter vector of the n-dimensional feature space R^n. Therefore, it is necessary to find the most suitable decision function f in the hypothesis space H to guide the optimization of the IoT topology.

In order to learn the mapping between the initial topology sequence and the optimized topology sequence, this section adopts the TCN network model to extract the features of the topology. The connection of robust topology is actually a kind of spatial feature. The structural feature of topology is transformed the dependency relation between elements in the sequence, which is an approximate sequential relation. It reflects that nodes with similar degree in the network establish connections. The TCN model [20] adopted in this section has been verified by a large number of benchmark tasks and has better feature extraction capability and convergence speed than RNN and LSTM, which is very suitable for feature extraction of spatial and time series. TCN combines the structural characteristics of residual network [21] and dilated convolution [22] to access historical experience with high bandwidth. In addition, the application of causal convolution [23] ensures that the future information in the sequence model will not interfere with the past. The following details the structure and design motivations of the network.

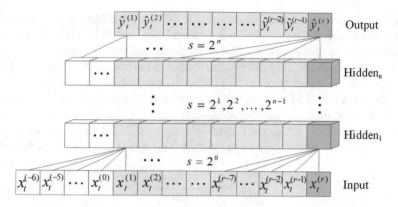

Fig. 7.16 Architecture of TCN network

The structure of the network is shown in Fig. 7.16, and its input layer corresponds to the initial topological sequence model $x_t = (x_t^{(1)}, x_t^{(2)}, \cdots, x_t^{(r)})^T$, the output layer represents the predictive topological sequence derived from the neural network model $f(x_t) = (f(x_t^{(1)}), f(x_t^{(2)}), \cdots, f(x_t^{(r)}))^T$. To ensure that the connection information of the network topology is not lost, it is necessary to maintain the same length of the input and output layers of the neural network, that is, $x_t = f(x_t)$. Therefore, the model adopts the form of zero padding [53] to keep each feature map obtained from the network with the same length. In Fig. 7.16, white cells are used to indicate some zero padding elements. The entire neural network model does not include a fully connected network, that is, the full convolutional network is used to learn the connection relationships in the topology sequence. In addition, the length of the input layer and output layer is determined by the length of the topological sequence. During network construction, the next connection can be inferred from the current network connection state.

The model in Fig. 7.16 uses causal convolution to extract the construction criteria for onion-like structures. The element at any position in each layer of the model can only be convolved with the element at the corresponding position in the previous layer and before it. The application of causal convolution is beneficial to feature extraction of onion-like structures. Dilated convolution is used to connect different layers of neural network model, which can reduce the number of layers required by the whole network model and provide long-term historical experience access. The parameter s of dilated convolution represents the number of intervals of convolution slots in the convolution kernel. We adopt the suggestion of Bai et al. [20] to make parameter s grow exponentially with the increase of network layers. For example, the parameter value $s = 2^0$ between the input layer and the first hidden layer is a normal convolution operation. The parameter s between the n_{th} hidden layer and the output layer is set as 2^n. In addition, when the size of the convolution kernel is k, the size of the perception domain of the element in each layer compared to the previous layer is $(k - 1) * s$, which also represents the size of the zero padding in each layer. In the neural network model, the number of hidden layers ensures that the receptive field of each element in the output layer is sufficient to cover the length of the input layer. These parameters need to be selected through repeated simulation experiments, which not only ensures the feature extraction ability of the model, but also reduce the complexity of the model and the computational overhead.

In the design of hidden layer, residual connection is introduced. The input and output of each hidden layer are added and activated by the hyperbolic tangent function as the input of the next layer. The hyperbolic tangent function is better than the other activation functions in the experiment, and it is defined as follows.

$$\tanh x = \frac{e^x - e^{-x}}{e^x + e^{-x}} \tag{7.15}$$

Residual connection can effectively avoid the problem of gradient disappearance in the neural network training process, and ensure that each hidden layer learns at least one identity mapping. The feature extraction ability of the whole network is not affected. The hidden layer contains regularization and dropout operations [24] to ensure model learning. Similar to the classical TCN network, the hidden layer in this model contains two dilated convolution and nonlinear transformation, which ensures the stability of the model in training. The application of the whole residual block prevents information back-flow from being blocked in the process of gradient descent, and improves the applicability of the model. This approach reduces the training difficulty and makes the model have better convergence.

In order to measure the optimization capability of decision function f, this model defines the square loss of prediction topological sequence $f(x_t)$ and optimization topological sequence y_t as the loss function. It is shown in Eq. (7.16), where r represents the length of the topological sequence.

$$L(y_t, f(x_t)) = \frac{1}{r} \sum_{i=1}^{r} (y_t^{(i)} - f(x_t^{(i)}))^2 \tag{7.16}$$

$$R_{emp}(f) = \frac{1}{N} \sum_{t=1}^{N} L(y_t, f(x_t)) \tag{7.17}$$

The smaller the loss function $L(y_t, f(x_t))$ is, the smaller the difference between the prediction topology sequence $f(x_t)$ and the optimization topology sequence y_t is. The loss function measures the performance of the neural network model under one prediction. In order to measure the effect of model average prediction, the average loss of decision function on data set is defined as empirical loss, namely R_{emp}. In Eq. (7.17), N indicates the total number of topologies. The smaller the value of R_{emp} is, the better the learning effect of neural network model is. Therefore, this model adopts the minimization strategy of empirical loss function to learn the appropriate decision function, which can accurately reflect the topological characteristics of onion-like structure. In the neural network model, the weights and biases between layers together form parameter sets, which are learned by updating network parameters iteratively with gradient descent algorithm. R_{emp} is also used to measure the convergence of the model. When R_{emp} reaches a very small value and tends to a stable state, it can be determined that the neural network model has converged.

In addition, this section also defines R_{rate} to measure the optimization effect and scalability of the model on topology robustness. For a topology sample (x_t, y_t), the robustness of the optimization topology is denoted as R_{opt}, and the robustness of the prediction topology is denoted as R_{pred}. R_{rate} is defined as the ratio of R_{pred} to R_{opt}. Therefore, the value range of R_{rate} is $(0, 1)$. The closer the R_{rate} value is to 1, the closer the network structure of the prediction topology $f(x_t)$ is to the optimization topology y_t. By calculating the mean value of R_{rate} of all topology samples, the prediction effect of neural network model is measured. Note that R_{rate} is only used for model evaluation and selection, and it does not participate in the model training process. Therefore, there is no need to calculate a large number of R values iteratively during the training process, which greatly reduces the calculation overhead.

After the trained model is obtained, a topology reconstruction method needs to be designed to restore the prediction sequence to the form of topology connection. For element x_t^r in topological sequence x_t, its value range is $[0, 1]$. The closer the value of element x_t^r is to 1, the easier it is to establish connection relation between corresponding nodes. When the element x_t^r is weighted and activated by the neural network, its value range in the prediction topology $f(x_t)$ will change. However, the relative size and semantics of the elements do not change. Therefore, the node connection of the topology can be reconstructed according to the size of elements in the predicted topological sequence $f(x_t)$. The reconstructed predictive topology must satisfy the following constraints.

- The degree of each node in the predicted topology is no greater than the degree of the nodes in the corresponding initial topology. The total degree of the predicted topology is not greater than the total degree of the corresponding initial topology.
- The degree distribution of nodes in the predicted topology still conforms to the scale-free distribution.
- The larger the value of the element in the predicted topology is, the more likely the corresponding node pair is to establish the connection.

The first constraint ensures that no more connections than the initial degree are added to the nodes in the network. Furthermore, the total degree of the entire predicted topology is no higher than the total degree of the initial topology. This shows that no excess energy consumption is introduced while optimizing the robustness of the topology. The second constraint restricts the degree distribution of the prediction topology to maintain the scale-free distribution and does not reduce its robustness against random attacks. The third constraint makes the meaning of the elements in the prediction topology conform to the specification in data processing. Since the network topology only undergoes weighting and activation operations during the evolution, the semantics of the elements in the sequence do not change.

The elements in the prediction topology sequence are arranged in descending order. If the node pairs corresponding to the elements are judged to be neighbors that meet the degree limit, then a connection relationship is established between them. Experimental results show that the reconstructed prediction topology still satisfies the scale-free distribution.

7.3.5 Performance Evaluation

In this section, simulation experiments are conducted to verify the robustness optimization effect and optimization efficiency of the EROS. The onion-like structure of the predicted topology is analyzed, and the connectivity of the predicted topology is compared with the other two heuristic algorithms. In order to simulate the actual environment of IoT application, the initial topology is deployed in a circular area with a diameter of 500 m, and a total of 100 nodes are randomly deployed in this area. In order to form dense connections between nodes in the network, the communication range of nodes is set to 200 m, the maximum degree of nodes is set to 40, and two new connections are created after new nodes are added. In addition, ROCKS is used to optimize the initial topology to construct the data set required by the experiment. In the data set, 2000 topology samples are used for model training and prediction. 1440 topology samples, i.e. about 70% of the data set, are selected as the training set D_{train}, and the remaining samples are used for cross-validation as the test set D_{test}.

All topology samples are converted into sequence models, and the length of each sequence model is 4950 elements, which is also the length of the input layer and output layer of the neural network. Parameter Settings of the neural network model are shown in Table 7.4. Adam operator [25] is adopted in this section to learn the model. The maximum number of iterations is set to 30, and the size of each batch data is 32. When the empirical loss function R_{emp} is less than 0.01 and tends to be stable, it indicates that the neural network model tends to converge. To prevent over-fitting of the model, the dropout operation is used to randomly empty 20% of the channels in each layer during training. The other parameters are determined by grid search through a large number of experiments.

Table 7.4 Description of different variables in EROS

Variables	Description
L	Number of hidden layers is 8
C_l	Number of channels per hidden layer is 10
K_l	The size of the convolution kernel is 8
λ	Learning rate is 0.0005
ω_0	The initial weight conforms to normal distribution $N(0, 0.01)$
p_{dr}	The ratio of dropout is 20%

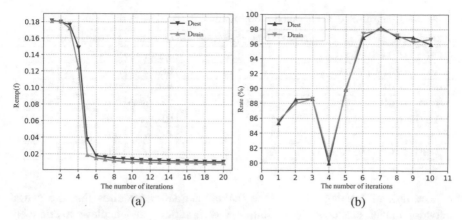

Fig. 7.17 Convergence and prediction rate analysis of neural network model. (**a**) Empirical loss. (**b**) Prediction rate

First, the convergence of the network model is measured by empirical loss function R_{emp}. As shown in Fig. 7.17 (a), the x-axis represents the number of iterations of model training, and the y-axis represents the empirical loss of each iteration. The empirical loss of training set D_{train} and test set D_{test} is plotted respectively, which is shown in blue curve and red curve. The empirical loss is minimum when the prediction topology is close to the optimization topology. It can be observed from the figure that the model gradually converges from the 6_{th} iteration, and no over-fitting phenomenon occurs. Considering the particularity of data set and optimization problem, the value of empirical loss function cannot reach 0. Therefore, the empirical loss of the model reaches a reasonable accuracy.

After the model converges, the robustness of the prediction topology needs to be studied to verify the optimization effect of EROS on the initial topology. The R_{rate} defined in the previous section is used to measure the robustness prediction rate of the prediction topology. It represents the ratio of robustness between the prediction topology and the optimization topology. The closer its value is to 1, the better the robustness effect of the prediction topology is. In Fig. 7.17 (b), the y-axis represents the robustness prediction rate of each iteration. With the increase of the number of iterations, the R_{rate} of the training set D_{train} and the test set D_{test} has been improved. In the 7_{th} iteration, R_{rate} reaches the maximum value. At this time, the average value of the D_{test} and the D_{train} reaches 98.11%. And in the 7_{th} iteration, the model is already in a state of convergence. Therefore, it can be shown that the EROS has an excellent robustness prediction effect on the initial topology, and the robustness of predicted topology is only less than 2% different from the optimized topology. As the number of iterations continues to increase, the neural network model continues to adjust its parameters to find the better robust optimization rules. The R_{rate} of the data set has a slight jitter, but the overall trend is within an acceptable range.

Table 7.5 Comparison of optimization effects of different neural network models

Model	R_{emp}	R_{rate}	Iterations	Hidden	Dimensions	Operator	Learning rate	Dropout
TCN	0.0095	98.11%	7	8	10	Adam	0.0005	0.2
RNN	0.0137	77.63%	15	3	10	SGD	0.1	None
BiRNN	0.0279	76.65%	25	3	5	SGD	0.1	0.2
LSTM	0.0172	94.49%	54	3	10	RMSprop	0.1	None
BiLSTM	0.0101	89.13%	87	3	5	RMSprop	0.05	None
GRU	0.0099	96.24%	95	2	5	Adam	0.1	None
BiGRU	0.0167	92.98%	66	2	5	Adam	0.1	0.1

The task of topological sequence feature extraction requires that the neural network model can converge within a few iterations and achieve a relatively high robustness prediction rate. Therefore, this section analyzes and compares the performance of neural network models commonly used in sequence modeling tasks, which includes RNN, bidirectional recurrent neural network (BiRNN), LSTM, bidirectional long and short-term memory network (BiLSTM), GRU, bidirectional gated recurrent unit network (BiGRU) and TCN [50]. This section uses the same dataset to train these models and statistics the performance of different models in the D_{test}. Table 7.5 shows the R_{emp}, R_{rate}, the number of iterations, the size of model structure and relevant training parameters.

As shown in above table, the R_{rate} of RNN and BiRNN is less than 80%, and their ability to extract robust topological features is poor. LSTM and GRU can theoretically solve the problem of long-term memory, and the R_{rate} is greatly improved compared with RNN, but they need more model parameters and deeper network structure, which is difficult for the model to converge due to complex parameter. In addition, BiRNN does not significantly improve the R_{rate} compared with RNN. Therefore, the feature of robust topological structure can be extracted only by using the unidirectional temporal relation between elements in the sequence. TCN has absolute advantages in terms of convergence and R_{rate}. Moreover, TCN has the parameter sharing feature of convolutional network and can carry out parallel training. Therefore, the topology sequence robustness optimization task is suitable for feature extraction using TCN model.

Next, it is verified whether the predicted topology has learned the onion-like structure of the optimized topology obtained by the ROCKS algorithm. As shown in Fig. 7.18, the x-axis represents the degree d of nodes, and the y-axis represents the value of S_d/N_d, where N_d is all nodes with degree d, and S_d is the number of nodes with degree d that do not need to route through nodes with higher degree. When the value of S_d/N_d is closer to 1, the set of nodes with degree d is closer to the onion-like structure. 20 topologies in the test set are selected for statistical analysis. In Fig. 7.18, the curves of the initial topology, the optimized topology and the predicted topology gradually increase with the degree of the node, which indicates that nodes with higher degree are more connected to each other. Compared with the initial topology, the curves of the optimized topology and the predicted topology have

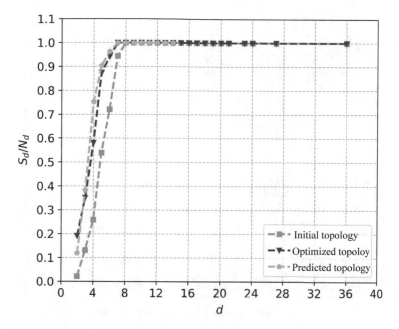

Fig. 7.18 Analysis of onion-like structure

reached the maximum value first. In addition, the curves of predicted topology and the optimized topology basically maintain the same trend, which shows that the predicted topology structure is very close to the optimized topology.

Finally, this section analyzes the ability of topologies derived from different algorithms to resist malicious attacks. The experimental results are shown in Fig. 7.19. The y-axis is the number of nodes in the largest connected component in the network, which can represent the connectivity of the network. The x-axis is the number of attacks, which is consistent with the total number of nodes in the network. The comparison topologies include the initial topology, the topology derived from Hill-Climbing, the topology derived from Simulated-Annealing, and the fully connected topology. The malicious attack adopts HDA, an attack method aimed at degree centrality under an adaptive strategy, that is, the node with the largest degree is reselected after each round of attack. It can be seen that as the attack progresses, the curves of the initial topology and the topologies obtained by the three algorithms drop sharply. After about 30% of the nodes are attacked, the initial topology collapses. When the percentage of attacked nodes reaches 40%, the topologies obtained by the Simulated-Annealing and the Hill-Climbing algorithms become a completely isolated node set. When 50% of the nodes fail, the topology obtained by the EROS algorithm collapses. Therefore, the topology obtained by the EROS algorithm shows better performance.

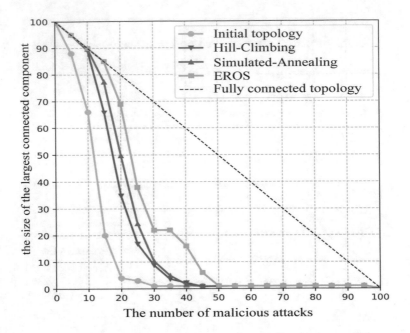

Fig. 7.19 Comparison of different algorithms in malicious attacks

References

1. Tan, E., Guo, L., Chen, S., Zhang, X., & Zhao, Y. (2012). Spammer behavior analysis and detection in user generated content on social networks. In *2012 IEEE 32nd International Conference on Distributed Computing Systems* (pp. 305–314). IEEE.
2. Zhu, X., Nie, Y., Jin, S., Li, A., & Jia, Y. (2015). Spammer detection on online social networks based on logistic regression. In *International Conference on Web-Age Information Management* (pp. 29–40). Springer.
3. Yang, X., Wang, Y., Wu, D., & Ma, A. (2010). K-means based clustering on mobile usage for social network analysis purpose. In *2010 6th International Conference on Advanced Information Management and Service (IMS)* (pp. 223–228). IEEE.
4. Yang, S., Kim, J., & Chung, M. (2014). A prediction model based on big data analysis using hybrid fcm clustering. In *The 9th International Conference for Internet Technology and Secured Transactions (ICITST-2014)* (pp. 337–339). IEEE.
5. Peyravi, F., Derhami, V., & Latif, A. (2015). Reinforcement learning based search (rls) algorithm in social networks. In *2015 The International Symposium on Artificial Intelligence and Signal Processing (AISP)* (pp. 206–210). IEEE.
6. Roberts, S. J., Husmeier, D., Rezek, I., & Penny, W. (1998). Bayesian approaches to gaussian mixture modeling. *IEEE Transactions on Pattern Analysis and Machine Intelligence, 20*(11), 1133–1142.
7. Sangaiah, A. K., Medhane, D. V., Han, T., Hossain, M. S., & Muhammad, G. (2019). Enforcing position-based confidentiality with machine learning paradigm through mobile edge computing in real-time industrial informatics. *IEEE Transactions on Industrial Informatics, 15*(7), 4189–4196.
8. Park, J., Samarakoon, S., Bennis, M., & Debbah, M. (2019). Wireless network intelligence at the edge. *Proceedings of the IEEE, 107*(11), 2204–2239.

9. Antonio, L. M., & Coello, C. A. C. (2017). Coevolutionary multiobjective evolutionary algorithms: Survey of the state-of-the-art. *IEEE Transactions on Evolutionary Computation, 22*(6), 851–865.
10. Qiu, T., Liu, J., Si, W., & Wu, D. O. (2019). Robustness optimization scheme with multi-population co-evolution for scale-free wireless sensor networks. *IEEE/ACM Transactions on Networking.*
11. Zhou, M., & Liu, J. (2014). A memetic algorithm for enhancing the robustness of scale-free networks against malicious attacks. *Physica A: Statistical Mechanics and Its Applications, 410*, 131–143.
12. Herrmann, H. J., Schneider, C. M., Moreira, A. A., Andrade Jr., J. S., & Havlin, S. (2011). Onion-like network topology enhances robustness against malicious attacks. *Journal of Statistical Mechanics: Theory and Experiment, 2011*(01), P01027.
13. Buesser, P., Daolio, F., & Tomassini, M. (2011). Optimizing the robustness of scale-free networks with simulated annealing. In *International Conference on Adaptive and Natural Computing Algorithms* (pp. 167–176). Springer.
14. Louzada, V. H. P., Daolio, F., Herrmann, H. J., & Tomassini, M. (2013). Smart rewiring for network robustness. *Journal of Complex networks, 1*(2), 150–159.
15. Chen, N., Qiu, T., Daneshmand, M., & Wu, D. O. (2021). Robust networking: Dynamic topology evolution learning for internet of things. *ACM Transactions on Sensor Networks (TOSN), 17*(3), 1–23.
16. Kaminski, N., Macaluso, I., Di Pascale, E., Nag, A., Brady, J., Kelly, M., Nolan, K., Guibene, W., & Doyle, L. (2017). A neural-network-based realization of in-network computation for the internet of things. In *2017 IEEE International Conference on Communications (ICC)* (pp. 1–6). IEEE.
17. Chen, M., Challita, U., Saad, W., Yin, C., & Debbah, M. (2019). Artificial neural networks-based machine learning for wireless networks: A tutorial. *IEEE Communications Surveys & Tutorials, 21*(4), 3039–3071.
18. Oshea, T., & Hoydis, J. (2017). An introduction to deep learning for the physical layer. *IEEE Transactions on Cognitive Communications and Networking, 3*(4), 563–575.
19. Arjovsky, M., Shah, A., & Bengio, Y. (2016). Unitary evolution recurrent neural networks. In *International Conference on Machine Learning* (pp. 1120–1128). PMLR.
20. Bai, S., Kolter, J. Z., & Koltun, V. (2018). An empirical evaluation of generic convolutional and recurrent networks for sequence modeling. Preprint. *arXiv:1803.01271.*
21. He, K., Zhang, X., Ren, S., & Sun, J. (2016). Deep residual learning for image recognition. In *Proceedings of the IEEE Conference on Computer Vision and Pattern Recognition* (pp. 770–778).
22. Yu, F., & Koltun, V. (2015). Multi-scale context aggregation by dilated convolutions. Preprint. *arXiv:1511.07122.*
23. Long, J., Shelhamer, E., & Darrell, T. (2015). Fully convolutional networks for semantic segmentation. In *Proceedings of the IEEE Conference on Computer Vision and Pattern Recognition* (pp. 3431–3440).
24. Srivastava, N., Hinton, G., Krizhevsky, A., Sutskever, I., & Salakhutdinov, R. (2014). Dropout: a simple way to prevent neural networks from overfitting. *The Journal of Machine Learning Research, 15*(1), 1929–1958.
25. Kingma, D. P., & Ba, J. (2014). Adam: A method for stochastic optimization. Preprint. *arXiv:1412.6980.*

Chapter 8
Robustness Optimization Based on Node Self-Learning

We outline the global optimization of network topology with several methods in previous chapters, including edge switching, genetic algorithm, multi-objective optimization, machine learning, etc. In this chapter, we focus on exploring the self-learning ability of topological nodes to improve the dynamic optimization ability of network topology. Furthermore, we adopt a deep deterministic reinforcement learning policy model [1] (DDLP) to improve the dynamic optimization ability of network topology, which regards the network topology as learning environment to train nodes' learning behaviors. Experimental results show that DDLP has better optimization performance in robustness optimization when compared to other existing algorithms.

8.1 Problem Model

As shown in Fig. 8.1, the proposed framework is introduced. We set a replay buffer (RB) to store necessary topology parameters [2] including current and next topology states, online reward, and current action. In online network phase, actor network is input the topology vector that is converted by previous methods [3]. Then, in order to improve the selecting probability of actions, we apply OU noise [4] in exploration phase with the continue action. Besides, robustness optimization in IoT topology contains numerous discrete actions. Thus, we propose an action mapping operator using the wolpertinger architecture [5]. Furthermore, the best action is selected based on the analysis of reward value of discrete action in critic network. Then, an immediate reward will be obtained from DDLP, and action network will be updated according to the policy gradient that is calculated from the critic selecting the best action.

© The Author(s), under exclusive license to Springer Nature Singapore Pte Ltd. 2022   191
T. Qiu et al., *Robustness Optimization for IoT Topology*,
https://doi.org/10.1007/978-981-16-9609-1_8

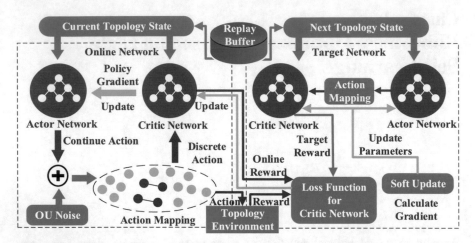

Fig. 8.1 Overview of DDLP

In the target network phase, the parameters are the same with the online network. We obtain target reward from the critic network that is depended on the next topology state and the actor network. Then, the loss of critic network is calculated to provide update guideline for the online critic network. For the target network, we updates its parameters by using soft update behaviors, and the details of these operators are described below.

$$L(\theta) = \mathbb{E}(\mathbf{r}_1 + \gamma \mathbf{r}_2 + \gamma^2 \mathbf{r}_3 + ... | \pi(, \theta)) \qquad (8.1)$$

We define the problem model as Eq. (8.1). The $\mathbf{r}_1$ denotes the reward value of the 1st action and γ denotes the discount factor in the reinforcement learning rules [6]. We set the policy function $\pi(\theta)$, expected function $\mathbb{E}()$, the object function $L(\theta)$. The goal of DDLP is to search the optimum policy function and maximize the expected function. The details of the DDLP are introduced below.

8.1.1 Topology State

For the formalization of IoT topology, we adopt the previous methods [7], such as $G = (V, E)$. In DDLP, we keep the position and degree of each node unchanged between both the initial topology and optimized topology that is constructed based on scale-free model rules [7].

As shown in Fig. 8.2, we set the initial IoT topology as the environment state in the proposed algorithm which converts the topology to a corresponding fixed-length environment vector. In order to reduce the storage space for IoT topology, the upper

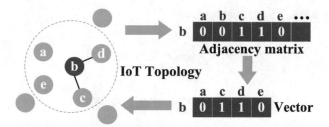

Fig. 8.2 The conversion of IoT topology to vector state

triangle of the adjacency matrix of the network is applied commonly to represent the structure of IoT topology. Besides, through analyzing the topology and the edge-swap action operators, we find that only the nodes within the communication range connect with others. Therefore, only necessary node information is reserved and saved. All nodes' converted information of the topology is linked to a vector that denotes the environment state. For example, node b only stores its neighbors' connection information.

8.1.2 Actor—Critic Model

The proposed algorithm is based on the deep deterministic policy gradient (DDPG) [8]. In order to fully explore the learning ability of topological nodes, we design actor and critic models which separately have two different deep learning neural networks.

$$\mathbf{a}_t = \pi_\theta(\mathbf{s}_t|\theta^\pi) \tag{8.2}$$

We define the actor network as Eq. (8.2). $\mathbf{a}_t$ and $\mathbf{s}_t$ are separately the deterministic action and environment state in time t. $\pi_\theta()$ is the optimum actor policy.

$$Q^\pi(\mathbf{s}_t, \mathbf{a}_t) = \mathbb{E}[\mathbf{r}(\mathbf{s}_t, \mathbf{a}_t) + \gamma Q^\pi(\mathbf{s}_{t+1}, \pi(\mathbf{s}_{t+1}))] \tag{8.3}$$

For critic network, the definition is Eq. (8.3) which fits the reward value $(\mathbf{s}, \mathbf{a})$. θ^Q is the parameter of the critic network. Based on the Eq. (8.2), $Q^\pi(\mathbf{s}_t, \mathbf{a}_t) = Q^\pi(\mathbf{s}, \pi(\mathbf{s}))$ presents the reward expected value when the environment selects the action $\mathbf{a}_t$ under the state $\mathbf{s}_t$ by using the π policy. The critic network calculates the immediate reward according to the action generated from the actor network and the environment state.

Based on the rules of reinforcement learning, the immediate reward and future reward are grouped to the real reward value. The parameters of Q' and π' are the same with critic and actor networks.

$$L = \frac{1}{n} \sum_{i=0}^{n} (T_i - Q(\mathbf{s}_i, \mathbf{a}_i | \theta^Q))^2 \tag{8.4}$$

$$T_i = \mathbf{r}_i + \gamma Q'(\mathbf{s}_i, \pi'(\mathbf{s}_{i+1} | \theta^{\pi'}) | \theta^{Q'}) \tag{8.5}$$

According to Eq. (8.4), the critic is updated based on the loss calculated by the critic network. Real reward value T_i is calculated by the Eq. (8.5). The parameters of critic network θ^Q is modified according to loss value.

$$\nabla_{\theta^\pi} \pi \approx \mathbb{E}_{\pi'}[\nabla_{\mathbf{a}} Q(\mathbf{s}, \mathbf{a} | \theta^Q)|_{\mathbf{s}=\mathbf{s}_i, \mathbf{a}=\pi(\mathbf{s}_i)} \nabla_{\theta^\pi} \pi(\mathbf{s} | \theta^\pi)|_{\mathbf{s}_i}] \tag{8.6}$$

Actor network is correspondingly modified to produce better actions after updating the critic network, which improves the performance in optimizing the robustness of IoT topology in the Eq. (8.6). The parameters θ^π are updated based on the sampled policy gradient. Finally, the target actor and critic network are modified based on the θ^π and θ^Q by using the soft update method.

8.1.3   Action Mapping

For robustness optimization in IoT topology, the important edge-swap operator involves large numbers of discrete actions, while the deep deterministic policy is only suitable for continuous actions. Therefore, an action mapping operator is proposed to generalize over the set of discrete actions. In this part, the action mapping operator how to convert the discrete actions to continuous actions is introduced below.

$$\mathbf{d}_t = MAP(\mathbf{a}_t) \tag{8.7}$$

Figure 8.3 and Eq. (8.7) show an action mapping operator that converts discrete actions into continuous action that can input the DDLP. $\mathbf{d}_t$ is the discrete action space in time t. For example, the selected action ((p, h), (g, k)) represents the connections between the nodes p, h, g, and k. According to the optimization rules, the edges (p, h) and (g, k) will break down and the new edges (p, g) and (k, h) will be added to the topology. Through the swapping operator, the topology state will be updated.

Nevertheless, in order to improve the convergence speed, we store all the possible valid actions in the $\mathbf{d}$. For these valid actions, they can exchange their connections to keep the degree unchanged [9]. For the update of action index, to reduce the store cost and accelerate the searching ability, we reset the action index in period.

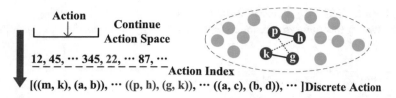

Fig. 8.3 Action mapping operator

8.1.4 Exploration and Exploitation

In order to improve the optimizing efficiency of DDLP, exploration and exploitation operators are introduced. We apply a noise sampled from a noise process $\mathcal{N}$ [8] into the actor network, which is based on Ornstein-Uhlenbeck process [4]. The $\mathbf{a}_t$ is modified by the Eq. (8.8).

$$\mathbf{a}_t = \pi_\theta(\mathbf{s}_t) = \pi_\theta(\mathbf{s}_t|\theta^\pi) + \mathcal{N} \tag{8.8}$$

$$(\mathbf{s}_t, \mathbf{a}_t, \mathbf{r}_t, \mathbf{s}_{t+1}) \rightarrow RB \tag{8.9}$$

For the exploitation, a replay buffer RB is proposed which is defined in the Eq. (8.9) to store previous learning experience. According to the RB, a best selection is chose to update the critic network, which ensures a good optimization direction when the exploratory reward is bad. Besides, for the training process of DDLP, the RB is a memory agent that can provide vital actions and environment state.

In DDLP, the exploration and exploitation can improve the convergence speed for robustness optimization. Furthermore, more optimal solutions are searched, explored, and saved to provide an exploratory direction for the robustness optimization in DDLP.

8.1.5 Algorithm Design

In this section, we outline the main process of DDLP in Algorithm 2. The details of the settings are presented in the simulation [1]. The abbreviation of variables used in DDLP is as follows.

- R: The robustness value of the topology.
- RB: The replay buffer which stores the previous learning experience.
- $EPISODES$: The number of training generations.
- $STEPS$: The number of training operators in each $EPISODES$
- $\mathbf{r}_t$: The reward value about the $\mathbf{a}_t$ for the topology state.

- $EXPECT$: The expected improved robustness value for the topology.
- M: We set the value to guarantee that the topology achieves the best optimum.

Algorithm 2 Main process of DDLP

Require: The initial real IoT network topology
Ensure: The optimized IoT network topology
 1: Generate a IoT topology based on scale-free model
 2: Calculate the initial robustness value R of the topology
 3: Convert the IoT topology to the state vector $\mathbf{s}$
 4: Initialize the possible valid action space AS and valid action VA for existing edges of the
    topology
 5: Initialize the parameters of actor network, critic network, factors, and settings
 6: Initialize a relay buffer RB
 7: **for** EPISODES **do**
 8:     Reset the environment state $\mathbf{s}_1$
 9:     **for** STEPS **do**
10:         Select discrete action $\mathbf{d}$
11:         Execute the actor and critic network
12:         Convert the state $\mathbf{s}_t$ to the topology structure
13:         Calculate the robustness value R_t of the current topology based on robustness metric
14:         Store transition $(\mathbf{s}_t, \mathbf{a}_t, \mathbf{r}_t = R_t, \mathbf{s}_{t+1})$ in RB
15:         **if** $R_t - R > EXPECT$ and R_t is not changed in M times **then**
16:             Store the parameters of the learning network
17:             **return**
18:         **end if**
19:     **end for**
20: **end for**

We present the details of the algorithm. Firstly, we generated the initial IoT topology based on scale-free model and set the initial parameters of DDLP. Secondly, for each iteration, the topology will reset as an environment state to input the DDLP and extend the exploration space. Besides, according to the action mapping operator and actor-critic model, the topology with high robustness will be saved in the replay buffer memory. Finally, the critic network will output the optimum topology. The training model is updated and executes a series of performance simulations for IoT topology. Furthermore, we use different scale network topologies to verify the scalability of the training model.

8.2   Performance Evaluation

In this part, extensive simulations about the performance of the DDLP algorithm are illustrated. Existing algorithms are compared with the algorithm.

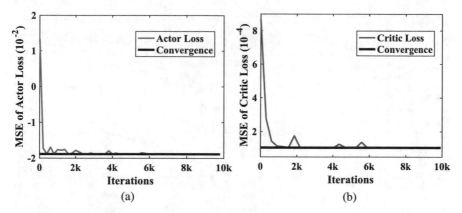

Fig. 8.4 The convergence of the DDLP. (**a**) Actor network loss. (**b**) Critic network loss

8.2.1 Convergence of DDLP

As shown in Fig. 8.4, the two neural networks of actor and critic are converged with the increasing iterations. The immediate reward **r** is utilized to minimize the loss of actor network. The loss is negative to the **r**. As shown in Fig. 8.4a, we simulate the performance of actor loss which guide the actor network to choose the optimum action. For loss in critic network as shown in Fig. 8.4b, Q and **r** are calculated to provide the updates of critic network. When the cumulative reward achieves the maximum, the DDLP converges to the minimum. The error of squared loss value is also converged within a range of fluctuations.

8.2.2 Robustness Optimization of IoT Topology

A robustness metric R [10] is introduced to measure the robustness of the IoT topology. In this part of experiments, we obtain the optimal network optimization model by ensuring the invariance of scale-free network characteristics and independent repeated simulations. The robustness value of the environment topology is calculated at end of each iteration. The best network model parameters are stored for the testing experiment as shown in Fig. 8.5a. The training and testing experiments achieve the optimum performance than the initial network topology. The optimization rate of the robustness for training and testing are separately 75.25% and 73.55%.

In DDLP model, the testing results may outperform the training results. Because the testing experiments have the previous optimum model parameters from training experiments. According to the deep deterministic learning policy, the testing model can choose better action with less overhead. Besides, RB stores the previous

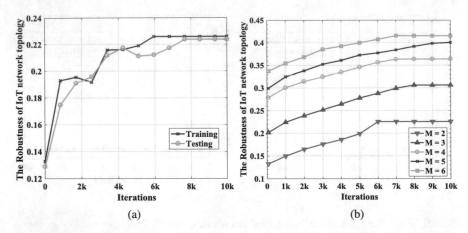

Fig. 8.5 Performance of DDLP algorithm on topology robustness. (**a**) Training and testing results. (**b**) Different link density

optimum learning experience, which improves the optimization efficiency for the testing experiments in robustness optimization for IoT topology.

To further validate the effectiveness of DDLP, we simulate the topology with different density. As shown in Fig. 8.5b, DDLP can optimize the topologies and acquire the optimum robustness value. For DDLP, the robustness of IoT with higher link density is more larger, and the optimized topology outperforms initial topology in resisting cyber-attacks. Through DDLP model, we can obtain a optimum topology with different link density in a limited time.

8.2.3 Comparison Between Initial and Optimized Topologies

We execute comparison between initial topology and optimized topology. As mentioned before, all nodes of IoT topology have fixed positions and the degree distribution is not changed. As shown in Fig. 8.6, the robustness of initial topology is 0.1289, while the robustness of optimized topology is 0.2259. In DDLP, we only modify the connections among nodes to improve the robustness for IoT topology and keep the scale-free features unchanged.

8.2.4 Comparison Between the Algorithm and Other Algorithms in Different Link Density

Furthermore, we also compare DDLP with other existing algorithms as shown in Fig. 8.7. All the algorithms have better performance against cyber-attacks than

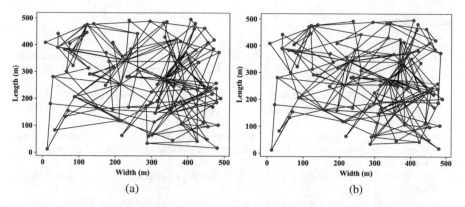

Fig. 8.6 Comparison of initial and optimized topologies. (**a**) R $= 0.1289, N = 100, M = 2.$ (**b**) R $= 0.2259, N = 100, M = 2$

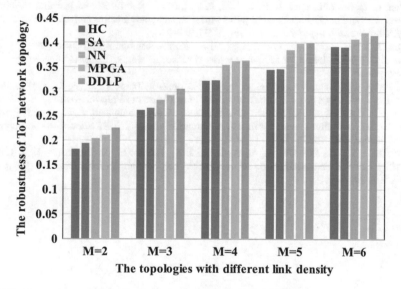

Fig. 8.7 Comparison of the optimized robustness with other algorithm

initial topology, and have similar increasing trends. DDLP has better performance than other algorithms when the link density is less than 5, while MPGA outperforms DDLP when the density is 5 and 6. Therefore, the proposed algorithm has better optimization results compared with other algorithms under sparse network topologies.

The DDLP can optimize IoT topology without data set, and make the topology self-learning improve its robustness against cyber-attacks. A novel representation of topology is introduced to reduce storage and computational overhead. Furthermore, to improve the scalability of DDLP, we design an action mapping operator. DDLP is an off-policy algorithm to improve the robustness of IoT which accumulates the previous experience instructing future learning behavior.

References

1. Chen, N., Qiu, T., Mu, C., Han, M., & Zhou, P. (2020). Deep actor–critic learning-based robustness enhancement of internet of things. *IEEE Internet of Things Journal, 7*(7), 6191–6200.
2. Liu, I.-J., Jain, U., Yeh, R. A., & Schwing, A. (2021). Cooperative exploration for multi-agent deep reinforcement learning. In *International Conference on Machine Learning* (pp. 6826–6836). PMLR.
3. Chen, N., Qiu, T., Zhou, X., Li, K., & Atiquzzaman, M. (2019). An intelligent robust networking mechanism for the internet of things. *IEEE Communications Magazine, 57*(11), 91–95.
4. Uhlenbeck, G. E., & Ornstein, L. S. (1930). On the theory of the brownian motion. *Physical Review, 36*(5), 823.
5. Dulac-Arnold, G., Evans, R., van Hasselt, H., Sunehag, P., Lillicrap, T., Hunt, J., Mann, T., Weber, T., Degris, T., & Coppin, B. (2015). Deep reinforcement learning in large discrete action spaces. Preprint. *arXiv:1512.07679*.
6. Yau, K. L. A., Komisarczuk, P., & Teal, P. D. (2012). Reinforcement learning for context awareness and intelligence in wireless networks: Review, new features and open issues. *Journal of Network and Computer Applications, 35*(1), 253–267.
7. Qiu, T., Liu, J., Si, W., & Wu, D. O. (2019). Robustness optimization scheme with multi-population co-evolution for scale-free wireless sensor networks. *IEEE/ACM Transactions on Networking*.
8. Lillicrap, T. P., Hunt, J. J., Pritzel, A., Heess, N., Erez, T., Tassa, Y., Silver, D., & Wierstra, D. (2015). Continuous control with deep reinforcement learning. Preprint. *arXiv:1509.02971*.
9. Qiu, T., Zhang, Y., Qiao, D., Zhang, X., Wymore, M. L., & Sangaiah, A. K. (2017). A robust time synchronization scheme for industrial internet of things. *IEEE Transactions on Industrial Informatics, 14*(8), 3570–3580.
10. Schneider, C. M., Moreira, A. A., Andrade, J. S., Havlin, S., & Herrmann, H. J. (2011). Mitigation of malicious attacks on networks. *Proceedings of the National Academy of Sciences, 108*(10), 3838–3841.

Chapter 9
Future Research Directions

In this chapter, we outline future research directions, point out important issues, and introduce several industrial applications about robustness optimization for future networks. For the future network, ultra-dense network connected devices put forward higher requirements for topology optimization, such as real-time, optimization speed, processing data volume, etc. In the future research direction, we can use machine learning technology to improve the real-time performance of network topology optimization, use network motif structure to explore the basic essential law of network topology optimization, and use quantum theory and parallel optimization mechanism to improve the optimization speed and increase the scale of topological data that can be processed. Furthermore, in industrial applications, we mainly focus on Industrial Internet of Things (IIoT), smart city, and Underwater Internet of Things (UIoT), which play vital roles in supporting communication services based on robust network topology.

9.1 Theory Exploration for Future Networks

In the future network [1], including fifth generation (5G) [2], sixth generation (6G) [3], topology optimization is an important technical foundation to support ultra-dense communication. Exploring the future network topology optimization theory is an important foundation for constructing high robust topology. As shown in Fig. 9.1, we summary three research layers containing critical theories and technologies for future network.

(i) *Theory and Modeling*: Future robustness optimization for IoT topology will be a large-scale and complex computing task, which includes various network models and controlling algorithms. Therefore, we need to improve traditional theories and models to meet strong robustness topology, such as graph

T. Qiu et al., *Robustness Optimization for IoT Topology*,
https://doi.org/10.1007/978-981-16-9609-1_9

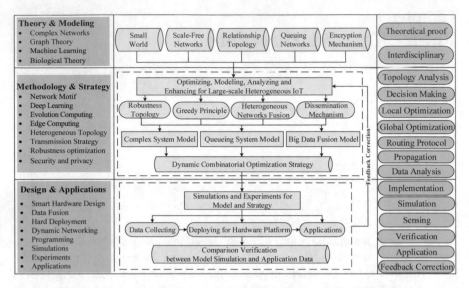

Fig. 9.1 Theories and technologies of future network topology robustness optimization

theory, biological theory, and machine learning. According to interdisciplinary analysis, theoretical proofs should be provided.

(ii) *Methodology and Strategy*: Based on above-mentioned theories, we may use network motif, deep learning, evolution computing, heterogeneous topology, transmission strategy, multi-objective optimization, edge computing, security and privacy mechanisms to improve, model, analyze, and optimize robustness of large-scale and complex network topologies.

(iii) *Design and Applications*: For the network topology with high robustness, key technologies including smart hardware design, data fusion, hard deployment, dynamic networking, programming, and simulations are more important to provide support for IoT infrastructures. Through simulations and experiments, we can get the difference between simulated results and application data. Based on the feedback correction between methodology and applications, we can meet the high requirements for IoT applications.

Based on the above key technologies and theories, several novel optimization theories are introduced for future network topology, which provide further research directions of IoT applications for readers and designers. With the increase of the number of smart devices connected together, how to guarantee the QoS of ultra-dense networks [4] when part of devices failed. Therefore, we need to explore new dynamic optimization theory to improve the robustness of ultra-dense network. Furthermore, network motif [5] has been proved a significant local structure in some network applications. Failure and joining of local nodes make the global network highly dynamic and uncontrollable. Thus, the discussion on the influence mechanism of network motif on global network topology will uncover the basic law of dynamic changes for IoT. Besides, IoT topology is a multi-dimensional, high-dynamic, and complex architecture. How to measure its robustness that the ability against cyber-attacks is a challenge to comprehensively sensitively represent the dynamic changes of ultra-dense network topology. Finally, how to improve the parallel optimization speed of topology optimization is a challenge for ultra-dense network. Quantum computing has great advantages in parallel computing. Therefore, we can explore the performance of quantum computing in robustness optimization for ultra-dense network.

9.1.1 Real-Time Topology Robustness Optimization for Ultra-Dense Networks

Machine learning technology has significant advantages in processing large scale data, which is feasible to be applied to optimize the ultra-dense network topology and reduce the computational overhead. However, machine learning technique based on central server may bring several challenges including poor data security privacy protection, large computing resources demand, bad ability of data transmission. Therefore, how to explore edge machine learning method to make full advantage of the computing resources of smart devices, reduce data leakage risk and pressure, has important research significance. In this section, we highlight several machine learning methods that can be used to optimize super-large scale network topology.

Edge machine learning is an emerging research technology that does not rely on cloud computing and big training data, which only requires a small fraction of data and communicates with widely distributed devices at the same time to train and improve its own learning network model that provides important supports for IoT applications. In the future ultra-dense IoT, mobile device nodes are dispersed over a wide monitoring area and have strong dynamic, increasing the threat of data leakage and communication interruption. Therefore, there are research directions that how to apply edge machine learning technology with enhanced mobile broadband, ultra-low latency communication technology to ensure data security and overall network service quality in the process of topology dynamic adjustment.

For ultra-dense IoT topology, scattered nodes store private training data, which is important to ensure the security of these data used by the whole network. Besides, heterogeneous network units are widely existed in IoT applications, which face the lack of effective communication mechanisms and privacy of training data. Therefore, for distributed learning method, such as federated learning, part of data or training learning model parameters will be exchanged of each device, which can protect the sensitivity of data. However, when the central server of the federated learning network is at risk of being compromised, the security of the data is threatened. For topology optimization, the cooperation exchanging data of each device is important to provide communication.

9.1.2   The Influence of Network Dynamic Local Motif on Global Network

9.1.2.1   Dynamic Evolution of Ultra-Dense Network Topology

The topology of ultra-dense scale network changes greatly due to node failure and mobility, which makes topology optimization difficult. Therefore, it is of great important to discover the dynamic evolution of network topology to guide the robust optimization of IoT applications. The behavior characteristics of local topological motifs are worth analyzing, and a self-adaptive topology optimization methods are designed. Besides, the rules of cascading failures from topology are analyzed for finding loopholes in robustness optimization and extending the network lifetime. Finally, by analyzing and comparing dynamic optimization methods, a reasonable topology generation strategy is constructed to improve the resistance of network topology against cyber attacks in real time.

For the ultra-dense IoT topology, each node has its own behavior characteristics, such as energy change, transmission data change, communication interaction frequency, failure probability, etc. These behavior data describe the dynamic changes of the topology. Using relevant technical methods combining with the behavior data of each node, optimum topology optimization strategy is designed to meet the requirements of different IoT applications.

Cascading failures occur on the network topology caused by the failures of individual nodes, which is an important factor to reduce network quality of service. The failure of a single node increases the data transmission pressure of its surrounding nodes, sharply increases the computing overhead, easily leads to data congestion, chain-collapse, and decline of the overall network service. Therefore, it is worth researchers to analyze the law of cascading failure in network topology, study its propagation process, and design effective methods to delay and avoid the occurrence of such disasters and improve the topology robustness.

The traditional robust topology optimization methods process and optimize topology data centrally based on central servers. As a result, the speed of topology optimization cannot keep up with the dynamic changes of network. Therefore, how to take full advantage of the dynamic rule of topology structure, design a reasonable topology robust dynamic optimization method, and meet the real-time requirements for topology applications, is worth exploring by the IoT designers.

9.1.2.2   Which Type of Network Local Motif Has the Greatest Importance in Global Network Topology

Nowadays, network topology optimization methods focus on describing network features from the global perspective, which lack sensitivity to sense local failure. Tiny local structure, network motif, affects the whole network performance to the greatest extent, and how the local specific topology affects the global topology performance, these research questions are worthy of researchers to explore.

The traditional topology optimization method represents the performance of the whole network by comparing the maximum connected subgraph, which is a coarse-grained measurement method. However, the maximum connected subgraph cannot fully describe the influence of local failures on the whole network. Recent studies have shown that motif is an important structure in the regulatory gene network of Escherichia coli [5, 6]. In the super-scale IoT, exploring what type of local structure can affect the global network has important guiding significance for designing network topology optimization methods.

Except from studying the influence of different types of local structures on global networks, the mechanism of how local structures affect global networks is also worth exploring. Whether the number, concentration, and density of local topology of particular structures affect the performance of the global network? How can specific local structure be distributed in IoT to improve QoS? How can multiple specific local structure be combined to effectively avoid cascading failures? These problems are important research directions for further improving network topology optimization ability in the future.

9.1.3   A Dynamic and Comprehensive Measure of Network Robustness

The key of topology robustness optimization is how to design a metric of network robustness. A reasonable metric can effectively guide the direction of topology robustness optimization, comprehensively describe the law of dynamic change of network, and fully reflect the basic rule of topology. Most topology optimization methods [7, 8] represent the performance of network topology based on the correlation of the maximum connected subgraph. Besides, the centrality, betweenness and closeness of network nodes are also measured to present the robustness of network. However, these statistical metrics have good optimization performance ability in their own research fields, but how to comprehensively measure the ability of network topology and design a general metric to represent the robustness of IoT is worth exploring for researchers and designers.

9.1.4   Quantum Computing to Improve the Robustness Optimization Speed for Ultra-Dense Networks

The continuous addition of IoT devices makes the topology of the ultra-dense network more complex. For a billion-level device networking, traditional computers cannot handle such a large-scale topology optimization problem due to the design limits of transistors. However, The emergence of quantum computing [9] provides an idea to solve the above problem.

Quantum computing is a new computing model based on the principles of quantum mechanics, and its smallest computing unit is called the qubit [10]. Assuming there is a memory of N physical bits, traditional bits can only store any one of 2^N possible data, but qubit can store 2^N data simultaneously due to the law of quantum superposition [11]. The effect is equivalent to that a classical computer repeatedly performs 2^N operations, or uses 2^N different processors to achieve parallel operations. This is the reason that quantum computing has strong parallel computing capability [12]. By setting different quantum measurement methods [13], we can make quantum system collapse into different states.

It can be seen that when one bit of quantum is added, the advantage of quantum computing will increase exponentially. In order to improve the robustness optimization speed of the ultra-dense network topology, we need to design a suitable quantum algorithm [14]. Therefore, in the future research on the robust optimization of large-scale network topology, we will explore how to use the idea of quantum computing to achieve the distributed processing of the topology and improve the optimization speed of topology robustness.

9.2   Industrial Applications

Topology optimization technology is widely applied in industrial applications, which guarantee the high communication QoS. With the increasing of connected smart devices, there are several challenges to ensure long-term stable lifetime and robustness of these industrial applications. How to solve these problems is an important research direction in the future. The following is a detailed introduction to the challenges faced by the Industrial IoT, smart city and smart underwater IoT.

9.2.1   Industrial Internet of Things

For industrial Internet of Things (IIoT) [15], we discuss some challenges and opportunities, including 5G-based edge communication, edge intelligence and data sharing security.

(1) 5G-Based Edge Communication
Nowadays, IIoT networks are constructed by wired and wireless modes [16]. The wired mode is stable, while the wireless mode is developing slowly, owing to a low transmission rate and poor stability [17, 18]. For IIoT, edge devices and edge servers require frequent scheduling and data exchange, whose goals are high transmission rate and low delay. The development and application of 5G and extended communication technology play a vital role in network optimizing and

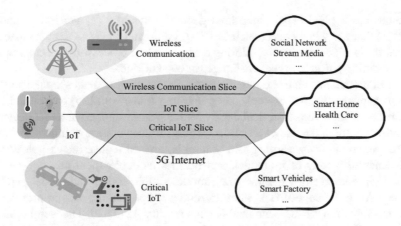

Fig. 9.2 5G network slicing

data exchanging in IIoT system [19]. Despite the promising industrial prospects, the integration of 5G into edge-based IIoT still faces many potential problems. For example, system QoS, edge node management, and network slicing. In system QoS, the 5G network will support the high quality and low delay services for IIoT [20, 21]. 5G core networks can optimize the node management strategy whose edges nodes are fixed. The application of 5G can make these fixed edge nodes avoid the shackles of cables and become movable edge nodes [22]. Meanwhile, The edge node management issues will be easy to handle in a 5G network [23]. As shown in Fig. 9.2, 5G network can be sliced. The characteristics of 5G network including low latency communication (URLLC), massive machine-type communication (mMTC), and enhanced mobile broad-band(eMBB) are based on indispensable network slicing. Therefore, the network slicing can make specific optimization and user-defined configuration for edge application scenarios.

The fusion of 5G and IIoT based on edge computing can lead to development momentum for typical IIoT application scenarios, such as VANET, digital twin, remote control, and maintenance. However, long-term integration still has many of the above potential technical challenges to overcome.

(2) Edge Intelligence

For current IIoT systems based on edge computing, smart edge devices only provide lightweight computing services. To enable edge devices and edge servers to support complex computing services, edge intelligence (EI) is utilized on the edge of IIoT. While an Ai model can perform better with high accuracy, it need large amounts of training data. However, the computing and storage resources are limited in edge devices. Therefore, there are two basic approaches to resolve the conflict between limited resources and high computing services, enhancing the computing power of edge devices; simplifying or partitioning the AI model deployed on edge devices.

For EI devices [24], adding intelligent processing modules or designing intelligent chips can make edge devices more powerful. The hardware design of edge devices applied in AI algorithms generally includes (1) general computing modules that are widely used, such as CPU, GPU, and FPGA; (2) customized AI processors, such as AI chips. Exploring customized AI processors that can improve the computing power is urgent challenge for edge devices.

For EI model, machine learning is a emerging theory that makes breakthrough in various applications. For example, deep learning framework [25] can fit and learn features from numerous historical data, which is widely applied in target detection, image recognition, etc. However, deep learning framework are complex to deploy. Therefore, taking deep learning as as example, how to reduce the complexity and deployment difficulty of its model, and discuss its deployment on edge devices. Therefore, there are two methods. i.e., model simplification and model partition, to adapt AI to the edge IIoT system. In model simplification, weight pruning and data quantification are the main methods to simplify AI model. The weight pruning method firstly sorts the neurons of model according to the contribution of neurons, and neurons with small contributions are removed to reduce the size of the model [26]. Another commonly used method of model simplification is data quantization, which uses a data format with fewer bits to represent the layers of neural network to reduce the operation law and improve the operation speed [27].

(3) Data Sharing Security

Massive amount of real-time data from multiple devices need to be processed in IIoT system. Analyzing data values and making accurate decisions are significant to improve industrial production efficiency [28]. However, data islands always occur in the traditional IIoT system due to vertical, closed applications that focus on maintaining the proper functioning of a single machine or site. Adding edge computing to IIoT subdivides the data and enhances its flexibility. The complexity of data security sharing problem is increased to some extent. There are two problems in edge data sharing: the inevitable increase of data interfaces may lead to more serious consequences, such as intrusion and destruction; and the performance of edge devices is limited, and powerful security algorithms are often difficult to run directly on edge devices. The introduction of blockchain in edge computing in IIoT brings new challenges and opportunities for the secure sharing of data [29].

The important premise of data sharing is to ensure data security. Therefore, how to rationally open and utilize data access control is the research challenge of IIoT system [30]. Blockchain that a new technology provides the security of data combines with edge computing to solve the data sharing security in IIoT system that every node/device can access the data. Combining the attribute-based access control model and the blockchain may achieve an ideal access control effect, which is worth studying and optimizing.

The good performance of data sharing based on blockchain relays the distributed data storage. According to the blockchain policies, data generated by edge devices become tamper-proof after being stored applying blockchain technology. Moreover, as shown in Fig. 9.3, blockchain has a broad application prospect in ensuring the security of edge data sharing and storage. However, nowadays, few studies have discussed the details of systematically incorporating blockchain into edge computing, which is worth exploring the industrial application of blockchain.

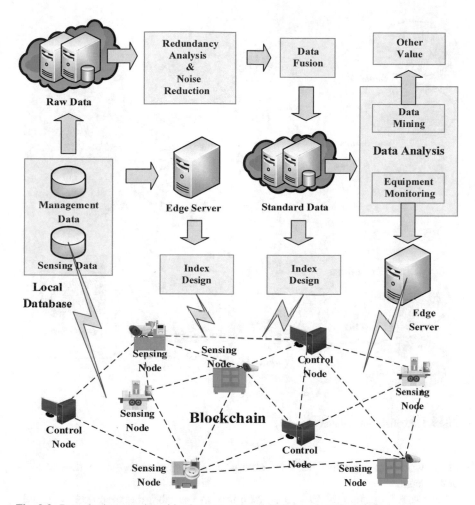

Fig. 9.3 Data sharing security with edge computing in IIoT based on blockchain

9.2.2 Smart City

Based on domestic and international data since 1999 [31], IoT has been widely applying in many industry sectors as shown in Fig. 9.4, including agriculture, transportation, smart home, industry, healthcare, etc. For different application fields, there are corresponding network topology, such as social mobile network based on cellular network, wireless fidelity networks depending on long-distance transmission devices, etc. Numerous devices are connected by intelligent IoT, and data collected are transferred to sink node by queuing priority. The remote monitor center can utilize cloud services to analyze data and adopt the corresponding strategy to improve the QoS of applications. Therefore, robustness optimization

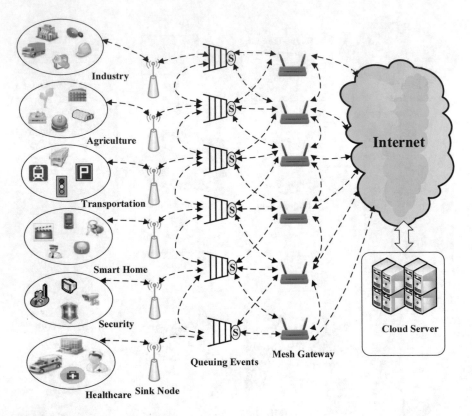

Fig. 9.4 Applications of smart city

of network topology has been an emerging challenge to improve the network performance.

For smart agricultural IoT, as an example to describe, the specified devices in real-time automatically turn on or off according to sensed environmental parameters. Most of current agricultural system are battery without power supply [32], which will cause network collapse due to part of node failures. Therefore, how to construct wireless network topology to improve the robustness against cyberattacks by applying novel communication technology (5G/6G/B6G). Besides, data transmission scheduling is another research direction that improves the network performance when encounter large scale of sensing data from numerous sensors. Furthermore, in other applications, such as smart home, vehicular network, and healthcare, robustness optimization and data processing is worthy exploring especially in large scale of network.

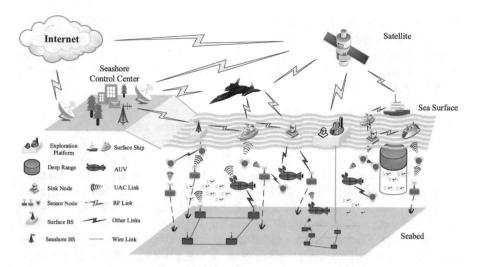

Fig. 9.5   Smart underwater Internet of Things

9.2.3   Smart Underwater Internet of Things

Apart from above mentioned industrial applications, robustness optimization technology can be widely used in smart underwater IoT (UIoT). As shown in Fig. 9.5, a large amount of smart devices are consisted of the complex UIoT system, including underwater sensors, transmission modules (surface nodes), autonomous underwater vehicles (AUVs), surface base station, etc. [33]. The UIoT is also the same as the frameworks mentioned above, with data collection, data fusion, processing, system decision-making, sever service, edge computing, etc, which apply a variety of underwater communication technologies. Besides, the seashore control centers can make best decisions based on the sensing data from underwater devices. Therefore, in order to improve the robustness and QoS of UIoT, the robustness optimization is an urgent research challenge [34, 35].

(1) Underwater Wireless Communication Technology
The underwater environment is very complex and communication signals and acoustic signals are attenuated and occluded in different degrees. Therefore, how to ensure the communication quality of underwater networking is a research focus. Furthermore, an important issue related to acoustic signals is their irregularity. Network topology and connectivity are directly or indirectly affected by this signal irregularity. To address this problem, a reliable wireless communication technology should be designed to meet the requirements for UIoT, such as data reliability, data accuracy transmission, etc. For future UIoT, oceans consist of ultra-dense monitoring networks. In order to realize smart ocean, there are three aspects that we summary for the main research interests in underwater communication. (1) It is necessary to design an underwater multi-model communication intelligent

framework to dynamic switch different technology based on different transmission tasks. (2) High speed remote underwater wireless communication technology is urgently needed in UIoT. (3) Intelligent medium access control protocol based on machine learning is worth exploring to promote the transmission stability under the complex environment.

(2) Underwater Networking Strategy
The devices of UIoT have high mobility and dynamic, which is an unavoidable problem [36] that is drawn much attention for researchers. The reliability of network topology is seriously challenged. For future ultra-dense UIoT, robustness and reliability are the main optimizing goals. We introduce three open issues for underwater networking strategy. (1) How to combine machine leaning to design routing protocols for UIoT and dynamic path planing for AUVs. (2) Research on self-learning underwater topology control, topology reconstruction and smart detection for malicious node is critical to the future UIoT. (3) The generation and deployment of UIoT require an efficient underwater node location strategy due to irregular dynamic movement of ocean currents.

References

1. Darwish, T., Kurt, G. K., Yanikomeroglu, H., Senarath, G., & Zhu, P. (2021). A vision of self-evolving network management for future intelligent vertical hetnet. *IEEE Wireless Communications, 28*(4), 96–105.
2. Narayanan, A., Zhang, X., Zhu, R., Hassan, A., Jin, S., Zhu, X., Zhang, X., Rybkin, D., Yang, Z., Mao, Z. M., et al. (2021). A variegated look at 5g in the wild: performance, power, and qoe implications. In *Proceedings of the 2021 ACM SIGCOMM 2021 Conference* (pp. 610–625).
3. Tataria, H., Shafi, M., Molisch, A. F., Dohler, M., Sjöland, H. & Tufvesson, F. (2021). 6g wireless systems: Vision, requirements, challenges, insights, and opportunities. *Proceedings of the IEEE, 109*(7), 1166–1199.
4. Sharma, S. K., & Wang, X. (2019). Toward massive machine type communications in ultra-dense cellular iot networks: Current issues and machine learning-assisted solutions. *IEEE Communications Surveys & Tutorials, 22*(1), 426–471.
5. Milo, R., Shen-Orr, S., Itzkovitz, S., Kashtan, N., Chklovskii, D., & Alon, U. (2002). Network motifs: simple building blocks of complex networks. *Science, 298*(5594), 824–827.
6. Dey, A. K., Gel, Y. R., & Poor, H. V. (2019). What network motifs tell us about resilience and reliability of complex networks. *Proceedings of the National Academy of Sciences, 116*(39), 19368–19373.
7. Chen, N., Qiu, T., Zhou, X., Li, K., & Atiquzzaman, M. (2019). An intelligent robust networking mechanism for the internet of things. *IEEE Communications Magazine, 57*(11), 91–95.
8. Qiu, T., Lu, Z., Li, K., Xue, G., & Wu, D. O. (2020). An adaptive robustness evolution algorithm with self-competition for scale-free internet of things. In *IEEE INFOCOM 2020-IEEE Conference on Computer Communications* (pp. 2106–2115). IEEE.
9. MacQuarrie, E. R., Simon, C., Simmons, S., & Maine, E. (2020). The emerging commercial landscape of quantum computing. *Nature Reviews Physics, 2*(11), 596–598.
10. Clarke, J., & Wilhelm, F. K. (2008). Superconducting quantum bits. *Nature, 453*(7198), 1031–1042.

11. Friedman, J. R., Patel, V., Chen, W., Tolpygo, S. K., & Lukens, J. E. (2000). Quantum superposition of distinct macroscopic states. *Nature, 406*(6791), 43–46.
12. Harrow, A. W., & Montanaro, A. (2017). Quantum computational supremacy. *Nature, 549*(7671), 203–209.
13. Clarke, M. L. (2013). Emerging interpretations of quantum mechanics and recent progress in quantum measurement. *European Journal of Physics, 35*(1), 015021.
14. Giri, P. R., & Korepin, V. E. (2017). A review on quantum search algorithms. *Quantum Information Processing, 16*(12), 315.
15. Qiu, T., Chi, J., Zhou, X., Ning, Z., Atiquzzaman, M., & Wu, D. O. (2020). Edge computing in industrial internet of things: Architecture, advances and challenges. *IEEE Communications Surveys & Tutorials, 22*(4), 2462–2488.
16. Chen, N., Qiu, T., Zhou, X., Li, K., & Atiquzzaman, M. (2019). An intelligent robust networking mechanism for the internet of things. *IEEE Communications Magazine, 57*(11), 91–95.
17. Vitturi, S., Zunino, C., & Sauter, T. (June 2019). Industrial communication systems and their future challenges: Next-generation ethernet, iiot, and 5g. *Proceedings of the IEEE, 107*(6), 944–961.
18. Qiu, T., Li, B., Qu, W., Ahmed, E., & Wang, X. (2019). Tosg: A topology optimization scheme with global small world for industrial heterogeneous internet of things. *IEEE Transactions on Industrial Informatics, 15*(6), 3174–3184.
19. Agiwal, M., Roy, A., & Saxena, N. (2016). Next generation 5g wireless networks: A comprehensive survey. *IEEE Communications Surveys & Tutorials, 18*(3), 1617–1655.
20. Olwal, T. O., Djouani, K., & Kurien, A. M. (2016). A survey of resource management toward 5g radio access networks. *IEEE Communications Surveys Tutorials, 18*(3), 1656–1686.
21. Chettri, L., & Bera, R. (Jan 2020). A comprehensive survey on internet of things (iot) toward 5g wireless systems. *IEEE Internet of Things Journal, 7*(1), 16–32.
22. Santoyo Gonzlez, A., & Cervell Pastor, C. (June 2019). Edge computing node placement in 5g networks: A latency and reliability constrained framework. In *2019 6th IEEE International Conference on Cyber Security and Cloud Computing (CSCloud)/ 2019 5th IEEE International Conference on Edge Computing and Scalable Cloud (EdgeCom)* (pp. 183–189).
23. Kumareshan, N., & Poongodi, P. (Jan 2016). Dynamic mobility management architecture to improve quality of experience (qoe) in wireless networks. In *2016 10th International Conference on Intelligent Systems and Control (ISCO)* (pp. 1–4).
24. Zhou, Z., Chen, X., Li, E., Zeng, L., Luo, K., & Zhang, J. (2019). Edge intelligence: Paving the last mile of artificial intelligence with edge computing. *Proceedings of the IEEE, 107*(8), 1738–1762.
25. Svozil, D., Kvasnicka, V., & Pospichal, J. (1997). Introduction to multi-layer feed-forward neural networks. In *Chemometrics IV Conference* (vol. 39, pp. 43–62).
26. Han, S., Pool, J., Tran, J., & Dally, W. J. (2015). Learning both weights and connections for efficient neural networks. In *29th Annual Conference on Neural Information Processing Systems* (vol. 2015, pp. 1135–1143).
27. H. Yan, E. C. Ahn, and L. Duan. (Oct 2017). Work-in-progress: enabling nvm-based deep learning acceleration using nonuniform data quantization. In *2017 International Conference on Compilers, Architectures and Synthesis For Embedded Systems (CASES)* (pp. 1–2).
28. Jbair, M., Ahmad, B., Ahmad, M. H., & Harrison, R. (2018). Industrial cyber physical systems: A survey for control-engineering tools. In *2018 IEEE Industrial Cyber-Physical Systems (ICPS)* (pp. 270–276).
29. Frey, M., Gundogan, C., Kietzmann, P., Lenders, M., Petersen, H., Schmidt, T. C., Juraschek, F., & Wahlisch, M. (2019). Security for the industrial iot: The case for information-centric networking. In *2019 IEEE 5th World Forum on Internet of Things (WF-IoT)* (pp. 424–429).
30. Zhang, Q., Zhang, Q., Shi, W., & Zhong, H. (2018). Firework: Data processing and sharing for hybrid cloud-edge analytics. *IEEE Transactions on Parallel and Distributed Systems, 29*(9), 2004–2017.

31. Qiu, T., Chen, N., Li, K., Atiquzzaman, M., & Zhao, W. (2018).   How can heterogeneous internet of things build our future: A survey. *IEEE Communications Surveys and Tutorials, 20*(3), 2011–2027.
32. Patota, F., Chiaraviglio, L., Bella, F., Deriu, V., Fortunato, S., & Cuomo, F. (2016).   Dafnes: A distributed algorithm for network energy saving based on stress-centrality. *Computer Networks, 94*, 263–284.
33. Qiu, T., Zhao, Z., Zhang, T., Chen, C., & Chen, C. L. P. (2019).   Underwater internet of things in smart ocean: System architecture and open issues. *IEEE Transactions on Industrial Informatics, 16*(7), 4297–4307.
34. Berlian, M. H., Esa Rindang Sahputra, T., Jofi Wahana Ardi, B., Dzatmika, L. W., Rachmat Anom Besari, A., Sudibyo, R. W., & Sukaridhoto, S. (2016).   Design and implementation of smart environment monitoring and analytics in real-time system framework based on internet of underwater things and big data. In *2016 International Electronics Symposium (IES)* (pp. 403–408). IEEE.
35. Zhao, Z., Liu, C. F., Li, Z. H., Wu, B., Ma, M. D., Zhao, Z. H., & Liu, L. F. (2018).   Ebtcor: an energy-balanced 3d topology control algorithm based on optimally rigid graph in uwsns. *Adhoc & Sensor Wireless Networks*, 42.
36. Akyildiz, I. F., Pompili, D., & Melodia, T. (2005).   Underwater acoustic sensor networks: research challenges. *Ad Hoc Networks, 3*(3), 257–279.

Printed in the United States
by Baker & Taylor Publisher Services